Postsecondary
Education in British Columbia

UBCPress

GRATIS COPY
NOT FOR RESALE
ubcpress.ca

Postsecondary Education in British Columbia

Public Policy and Structural Development, 1960–2015

ROBERT COWIN

UBCPress · Vancouver · Toronto

© UBC Press 2018

All rights reserved. No part of this publication may be reproduced, stored in a retrieval system, or transmitted, in any form or by any means, without prior written permission of the publisher, or, in Canada, in the case of photocopying or other reprographic copying, a licence from Access Copyright, www.accesscopyright.ca.

27 26 25 24 23 22 21 20 19 18   5 4 3 2 1

Printed in Canada on FSC-certified ancient-forest-free paper (100% post-consumer recycled) that is processed chlorine- and acid-free.

Library and Archives Canada Cataloguing in Publication

Cowin, Robert, author
Postsecondary education in British Columbia :
public policy and structural development, 1960-2015 / Robert Cowin.

Includes bibliographical references and index.
Issued in print and electronic formats.

ISBN 978-0-7748-3833-7 (hardcover). – ISBN 978-0-7748-3834-4 (pbk.). –
ISBN 978-0-7748-3835-1 (PDF). – ISBN 978-0-7748-3836-8 (EPUB). –
ISBN 978-0-7748-3837-5 (Kindle)

1. Postsecondary education – British Columbia – History – 20th century.
2. Postsecondary education – British Columbia – History – 21st century.
3. Higher education – British Columbia – History – 20th century. 4. Higher education – British Columbia – History – 21st century. 5. Education and state – British Columbia – History – 20th century. 6. Education and state – British Columbia – History – 21st century. I. Title.

LC1039.8.C22B753 2018	378.711	C2018-902647-2
		C2018-902648-0

UBC Press gratefully acknowledges the financial support for our publishing program of the Government of Canada (through the Canada Book Fund), the Canada Council for the Arts, and the British Columbia Arts Council.

This book has been published with the help of a grant from the Canadian Federation for the Humanities and Social Sciences, through the Awards to Scholarly Publications Program, using funds provided by the Social Sciences and Humanities Research Council of Canada, and with the help of the University of British Columbia through the K.D. Srivastava Fund.

Printed and bound in Canada by Friesens
Set in Zurich, Univers, and Minion by Artegraphica Design Co. Ltd.
Copy editor: Deborah Kerr
Proofreader: Lauren Cross
Cover designer: Jazmin Welch

UBC Press
The University of British Columbia
2029 West Mall
Vancouver, BC V6T 1Z2
www.ubcpress.ca

FOR THE TWO BUGS

Contents

List of Tables and Figures / viii

Preface / ix

Introduction / 3

1 Setting the Stage / 18

2 Policy Rationales / 33

3 Clear Intentions (1960–79) / 64

4 Assumptions Challenged (1980–99) / 91

5 Cynicism (2000–15) / 124

Conclusion / 162

Notes / 187

References / 193

Index / 223

Tables and Figures

Tables

1 BC public postsecondary institutions, 2015 / 31
2 Public administration principles / 58
3 BC postsecondary system, 1960 and 1979 / 71
4 BC postsecondary system, 2012–13 / 127
5 Relevance of policy rationales in each historical moment / 167

Figures

1 Student mobility in the BC public postsecondary system, 2012–13 / 11
2 Population distribution in British Columbia / 19
3 University of British Columbia enrolment, 1940–41 to 1970–71 / 73
4 Registered apprentices and pre-apprenticeship enrolment, 1945–75 / 80

Preface

Around 2010, I realized that the conversations I was hearing about potential new programs at my British Columbia college had changed since I started working there two decades earlier. The original tone had been, "Some adults in our surrounding community have particular educational needs. Do we have the resources to respond to them?" A subtle shift had occurred since then, and though the actual words were seldom as blatant as appear here, the new sentiment was more, "If we were to meet those needs, how might the college benefit?" We were still attending to the community, but the focus was now on using the community rather than on serving it.

In fact, now that the college had gained limited authority to grant four-year baccalaureate degrees, it no longer even described itself as a community college. In seeking to shed the connotations of the junior, university-transfer component of our mandate (though transfer was still an important reason why students enrolled), we were also losing the egalitarian, progressive philosophy that had differentiated us from both universities and technical schools. Our emphasis on pedagogy and honest appraisals of our strengths and weaknesses were being superseded by image cultivation and self-promotion. Despite being a publicly funded institution of higher learning in a freedom of information era, we were increasingly reluctant to disclose data that might portray us in a poor light.

Of course, new winds were also blowing on neighbouring postsecondary institutions. Not only had the BC public postsecondary system become more complex, the sectors and subsectors were fragmenting. Research universities distanced themselves from teaching-intensive ones.

Urban colleges bickered with rural colleges about the priorities to present to government. New advocacy groups sprang up and others folded. Clearly, the ethos of postsecondary education was changing in British Columbia.

I knew that change and adaptation to shifting environments are essential for the survival of both biological and social entities, but I wondered how aware the busy decision makers were of the long-term, cumulative implications of their day-to-day choices. The original architects and pioneers of BC postsecondary education had long since retired, and many of their replacements, coming from elsewhere, had little idea of its distinctive strengths and peculiarities. I did not mind the new guard making changes, but I thought it should at least know what it was changing and not blindly imitate other jurisdictions.

In 2007, I had decided to use some of my professional development time – I was an administrator on the non-instructional, services side of the college – to assemble a short and accessible history of BC postsecondary education that could be part of the orientation of new administrators in institutions and government. As I turned to colleagues around the province for help in filling the inevitable gaps, I was taken back by how little some of them knew about the history of their own institution and by how difficult it was for some to uncover it. I decided to add an appendix to my report with a few paragraphs of history about each individual public institution – a fateful precedent for the disappearance of far too many of my evenings and weekends in subsequent years.

Some months after I completed my history, the BC Council of Post Secondary Library Directors surprised me by asking me to present my work during the hour-long professional development session with which the council began its business meetings. A week after the presentation, one of the directors sent me a couple of books that piqued my curiosity, prompting me to write a second history, this time about the neglected faith-based sector in British Columbia. In the process, I became hooked on writing local, postsecondary history – nothing grand, just a first step in describing what had happened.

Six subsequent histories emerged, the last written in 2013. Issues arising in my regular work prompted many of the topics. Why, for example, was continuing education bedevilling efforts to report enrolments comparably across institutions? How could we be respectful of Aboriginal perspectives when I had not even heard of the Indigenous Adult and Higher Learning Association? Some historical background seemed essential, but if I wanted it, I would need to gather it myself.

As I prepared those histories, I was struck with how the character of the times had changed: some university arts professors had originally argued against having to conduct research in favour of protecting their teaching function, college personnel had been described as imbued with a missionary zeal, a vocational school had viewed itself as an elite institution, and so on. I could describe some of the changes, but I could not explain how they had come about, even though I was curious about their origins.

I suspected I could assemble some sort of descriptive historical overview on my own, but I was haunted by the unexplained qualitative changes that I was observing. It was at this point that my ongoing conversations with such people as Lesley Andres, Jason Ellis, and Alison Taylor made a vital contribution to what eventually became the policy rationales that I present in this book – not to mention Jason's gentle yet persistent nudging that I would probably find it rewarding to prepare a full-length manuscript. Then, when I approached UBC Press, I was delighted not only that it accepted the manuscript but also with the supportive and constructive way in which the editors and reviewers helped to refine it.

The choice of what events are historically significant, and what theories are the most powerful in interpreting those events, inevitably involves some subjective decisions. This study is therefore just one contribution to the ongoing historical discussion through which a consensus gradually emerges about the plausible present meaning, and the current relevance, of past events.

Postsecondary Education in British Columbia

Introduction

Prior to 1960, British Columbians who wished to remain in their home province for their postsecondary education had limited options. This stemmed partly from a small population of less than 2 million that had the capacity to support only a modest number of specialized educational institutions. As in larger jurisdictions, though, the small postsecondary system also reflected low rates of high school completion: dropping out between Grades 8 and 12 remained common throughout the 1950s. Low graduation rates and a labour market that required few highly skilled workers combined to suppress the demand for more advanced levels of education. But the first waves of baby boom children were reaching college age, and their educational aspirations were rising. The province teetered on the threshold of change.

This book traces the development of the *entire* contemporary postsecondary system in British Columbia (BC):

- the research and teaching universities, community colleges, and provincial institutes that constitute the public sector
- the less known for-profit and not-for-profit career colleges, faith-based institutions, Aboriginal-governed institutions, and private universities that make up the private sector
- and the boundary-spanning apprenticeship system, as well as the continuing education quasi-sector.

In referring to the postsecondary system, I conceive of it not in terms of legal authorities and formal governance, but rather in terms of interactions and relationships among institutions.

Although the focus is on British Columbia, my methodology is broadly applicable to other jurisdictions. The distinctive contribution of this study is to provide an integrative and dynamic analysis that concentrates on the interactions among postsecondary sectors. It sets the stage for future work by others.

The type of development I examine is structural,[1] concerning the establishment and modification of postsecondary institutions, both private and public. In calling for a revival of the attention in the 1960s to the mix of institutions, Skolnik (2005) defines postsecondary structure as the distribution of institutions by size, mission and type, and geographic location. I concur with his rationale for examining structures: "No matter how well each institution does its job, the net result will be less than optimal if the whole configuration of institutions is inappropriate ... Thus it is sometimes important to stand back from the trenches and look at the big picture" (p. 54).

On the surface, the structure of the postsecondary system addresses the questions of what types and how much enrolment capacity exist in a jurisdiction. At a deeper level, seemingly "hard" organizational structures provide clues, as do budgets, about what decision makers value and see as important – clues, in other words, about worldviews. Many other types of development, such as pedagogical or curricular trends, are of course worthy of investigation for understanding value orientations and worldviews, but they fall beyond the scope of the present study.

In 1960, when my historical narrative begins, Sputnik and the American space race with the Soviet Union had sensationalized a societal goal of raising the population's level of education, especially in science and technology. Another important, if less spectacular, driver propelling the expansion of postsecondary education was the embrace by governments across North America of economic theory about human capital formation. Expenditure on education came to be viewed as an investment that would eventually benefit not only the individual student but also society at large. Furthermore, education was increasingly seen in British Columbia as a means to a better quality of life in a society that was evolving beyond its frontier roots. The economy was sufficiently buoyant to fund education that previous decades might have viewed as too expensive to be made available to the masses, especially during the Great Depression of the 1930s and the war years of the 1940s.

With increasing popular demand across Canada and the United States for education, the new decade unleashed a series of developments that changed the face of postsecondary education. The changes began in British Columbia when the federal Technical and Vocational Training Assistance Act of 1960 led to the establishment of eight postsecondary vocational school campuses throughout the province. Then the University of Victoria opened in 1963, followed by Simon Fraser University in 1965, tripling the number of universities in the province. The British Columbia Institute of Technology started accepting students in 1964. The following year saw the opening of the first of fourteen community colleges (later fifteen colleges when Kwantlen College split from Douglas College) that would serve every region of the province. By the end of the 1960s, British Columbians had far more postsecondary options than at the beginning of the decade, and there were more to come.

Changes in private postsecondary education followed a different trajectory and later timeline than those in the public sector. Although enrolments in the BC private sector have been smaller than in the public sector, they have nevertheless been significant – and all too often downplayed or even overlooked. This study acknowledges the tens of thousands of students who attend private institutions every year, most frequently in vocational and applied programs. It traces the evolution of their institutions not as independent threads but as integral components of the fabric of the postsecondary system.

Audience

This book may be conceptualized as a three-layer pyramid. The bottom layer is a descriptive summary that traces the evolution of the BC postsecondary system. It answers such questions as why some universities offer welding and carpentry, whereas some comprehensive, public colleges provide no trades training at all. Readers who are largely interested in this historical narrative, in contrast to the theoretical and analytical components, may focus on Chapters 3 through 5.

The significance of the descriptive layer arises from the wide disparity in the types and amounts of historical writing about the various postsecondary sectors. For example, there are hardly any histories of British Columbia's private career colleges, the former public postsecondary vocational schools, and the faith-based sector. It seems that the less prestigious the institutional type, the less scholarly attention has been devoted to it. I illustrate how scrutinizing public policy affecting students and programs in *all* sectors leads to a better understanding not only of the system as a whole but also of *each* particular sector – even of the universities and public colleges that are currently its most thoroughly studied components.

The middle layer considers how three general goals, or policy rationales, for education have fluctuated and endured in British Columbia since 1960. The rationales, which are social justice, human capital formation, and marketization, exist to varying degrees throughout the Western world. I use them to interpret the cumulative impact of decisions made to address immediate needs. I also see them as some of the evaluative criteria that should be used in assessing future public policy options. This methodology of assessing events through multiple theoretical lenses is not new, having famously been employed by Alison (1971) in his analysis of the Cuban missile crisis, but it is rarely seen in the postsecondary literature.

The top layer uses the other two layers to illustrate a systems approach to the study of postsecondary education. This systems approach is discussed below.

My envisaged audience became my basis for determining where to position this study on the spectrum between simplicity and memorability versus a more nuanced but less accessible discussion. Because I have written for readers who are knowledgeable about the field of higher education but who may be largely unfamiliar with many aspects of the BC postsecondary system and its history, I have chosen to focus on predominant forces and developments. Without some sort of an easily remembered framework, the details and untidiness of real life can quickly become overwhelming for readers who are new to the subject.

I have therefore chosen a rather tidy analytical approach, which provides an introductory framework that can lead to more in-depth study.

Readers who are already expert will undoubtedly also use their own frameworks for interpreting the historical narrative; I have chosen an ordered and easily comprehended approach that I trust will be appropriate for most readers.

My preference for clarity and memorability influenced my decision not to be granular in defining historical periods. I chose to demarcate only three periods of similar duration, partly because analyzing one or two historical moments in each period from three policy perspectives across disparate postsecondary sectors generated as much complexity as I wanted my readers to sustain.

To help bound the analytical aspect of this study, I focused on the initial intent and rationale for policy decisions, steering away from the subsequent complexities of implementation and ultimate impacts. Furthermore, I concentrated on the structural implications of the rationales, asking how the aspirations influenced the types and locations of postsecondary institutions rather than posing the broader question of all the ways in which these decisions mattered. The result was more analogous to a map than to a satellite photo, but for some purposes and users the simplicity of a map can be the more useful tool.

Book Organization

This book consists of three sections. In the first, the Introduction and Chapters 1 and 2 set the stage for the historical narrative that appears in the second. This introductory chapter explains what I set out to do in terms of a holistic systems approach and how my readership influenced my methodology. Chapter 1 provides background about postsecondary education in British Columbia: the particular ways that certain terminology is understood in the province and the state of postsecondary education as of 1960, when my account begins. Chapter 2 is theoretical, presenting three enduring public policy rationales that affected the structures of both public and private postsecondary sectors. It brings together a number of concepts from a variety of literatures.

The second section is historical, tracing the structural development of the contemporary BC postsecondary system. It divides the years since 1960 into three periods and devotes a chapter to each one. After providing an overview of the period, the chapters examine one or two historical moments in greater detail. Each moment is then analyzed from the perspectives of the three enduring policy rationales. Five historical moments considered from three perspectives yields fifteen discrete analyses.

Finally, the Conclusion steps back from the analytical details to identify broad fluctuations over time in the importance of the various policy rationales. This interpretive step of moving from the trees toward identifying the forest makes some trends or patterns evident, but it is, of course, just one contribution to the historiography of BC postsecondary education.

Systems Perspective

My goal is less to present new information about education in British Columbia than to assemble existing knowledge in new and revealing ways. My approach draws upon systems thinking (Mella, 2012) and falls firmly within Boyer's (1990) formulation of the scholarship of integration: that is, the giving of meaning to isolated facts, of putting them in perspective, and of interpreting past research within larger intellectual patterns. It is compatible with the notion of horizontal history, taking account of interlocking circles of influence and fluid networks rather than only of isolated postsecondary institutions or groups of institutions (Thelin, 2010).

I chose this all-encompassing approach because I wished to understand postsecondary education in the ways that students actually experience it throughout their life, often crossing boundaries to take courses in differing types of institutions,[2] and in the ways that governments view it when setting multi-sectorial policies such as student financial aid. The utility of looking at systems, and not simply components, can be illustrated by two examples of boundary-spanning interactions.

The public colleges of British Columbia have been studied as a distinct sector (e.g., Dennison and Gallagher, 1986; Gaber, 2002), but with their extensive university transfer component and more recent limited authority to grant baccalaureate degrees, they also maintain strong relationships with universities. Contradictory curricular changes in similar programs at differing universities can send college faculty into a tizzy as they struggle to maintain course transferability to as many universities as possible. Vacillations in university admission thresholds (high one year to admit the "brightest and the best," low another year to serve "all qualified applicants") can significantly affect college enrolment demand.

Public colleges provide some, but not all, of the classroom components of apprenticeship training, a quite separate sector in British Columbia. They partner regularly with Aboriginal-governed institutions, sometimes to award credentials but also to deliver programs and even to channel government funding to Aboriginal clienteles. At times, responding to government funding incentives, public colleges have co-operated with private career colleges in some program areas while competing with them for students in other areas; a federal funding change in the mid-1980s was simultaneously bad news for public colleges and good news for private career colleges.

The development of the college sector has thus been affected by characteristics and trends in other sectors. Studies of individual sectors can miss these important interdependencies and interactions, as well as such nuances as how student dropouts from one institution may simply be mobile, eventually graduating somewhere else.

A second example of the usefulness of a systems approach is how it helps us to understand the failure of private and out-of-province universities to thrive when new legislation in 2002 made it much easier for them to operate in British Columbia. The minimal impact of this policy initiative is best interpreted against the backdrop of the BC government's concurrent expansion of student spaces in all the public institutions and its introduction of bachelor's and master's degrees in applied subjects in selected public institutions other than universities. Private universities suddenly faced much more competition for students from public institutions that could charge lower tuition fees.

The connections and interactions between private and public institutions in British Columbia, as in many jurisdictions, are stronger than might be suggested by the distinct policy environments in which they operate. Private degree-granting institutions frequently serve mature students who began their studies at public institutions but later found that the course scheduling or availability of seats in such institutions were incompatible with their life situation. Aboriginal-governed institutions routinely partner with public ones. Some courses and programs from faith-based institutions and private career colleges are granted transfer credit by public institutions, and half a dozen faith-based institutions are affiliated with the University of British Columbia. Apprenticeship straddles the public-private divide. A number of private English as a second language schools are designed to prepare students for further education in both public and private systems.

Systems thinking helps not only with anticipating how policy changes in one sector will affect other sectors but also in choosing among potential policies in the first place. Sometimes one policy goal must be compromised to achieve other goals; making tradeoffs and finding the appropriate balance among conflicting goals is a value-laden exercise that is an inherent part of politics and economics. The fostering of competition among institutions in recruiting students, for example, could potentially undermine the achievement of some social justice goals. A government's interventions to increase the number of apprentices in anticipation of future labour shortages might not be compatible with its other views regarding the desirability of free markets.

As well as aiding in the choice between value-laden alternatives, systems thinking helps in the technical domain. The Student Transitions Project (2015a), for example, found that numerous BC students who initially appeared to be dropouts from the point of view of a single institution subsequently graduated elsewhere in the BC system: 45 percent of individuals who completed their bachelor's degrees in 2013–14 had attended two or more institutions. Such analyses at the system level had previously led to the reconceptualization of the administration of transfer credit in the province, from one in which some institutions (colleges) were seen as senders of students to other receiving institutions (universities). The new model perceived all institutions as both senders and receivers (British Columbia Council on Admissions and Transfer, 2006).

Although BC legislation prevented the Student Transitions Project from collecting data about students in private institutions – a situation that is changing – its results illustrate the utility of systems thinking in postsecondary education. Figure 1 was created by the project's staff to show the magnitude of multi-directional student flows in credit courses across public sectors, including mobility within sectors (moves between institutions of the same type), across sectors (moves to a different type of institution), stopouts (students who spent time away from their studies), entrants, and leavers. The diagram is complex and the details about its

FIGURE 1
Student mobility among sectors in the BC public postsecondary system, 2012–13

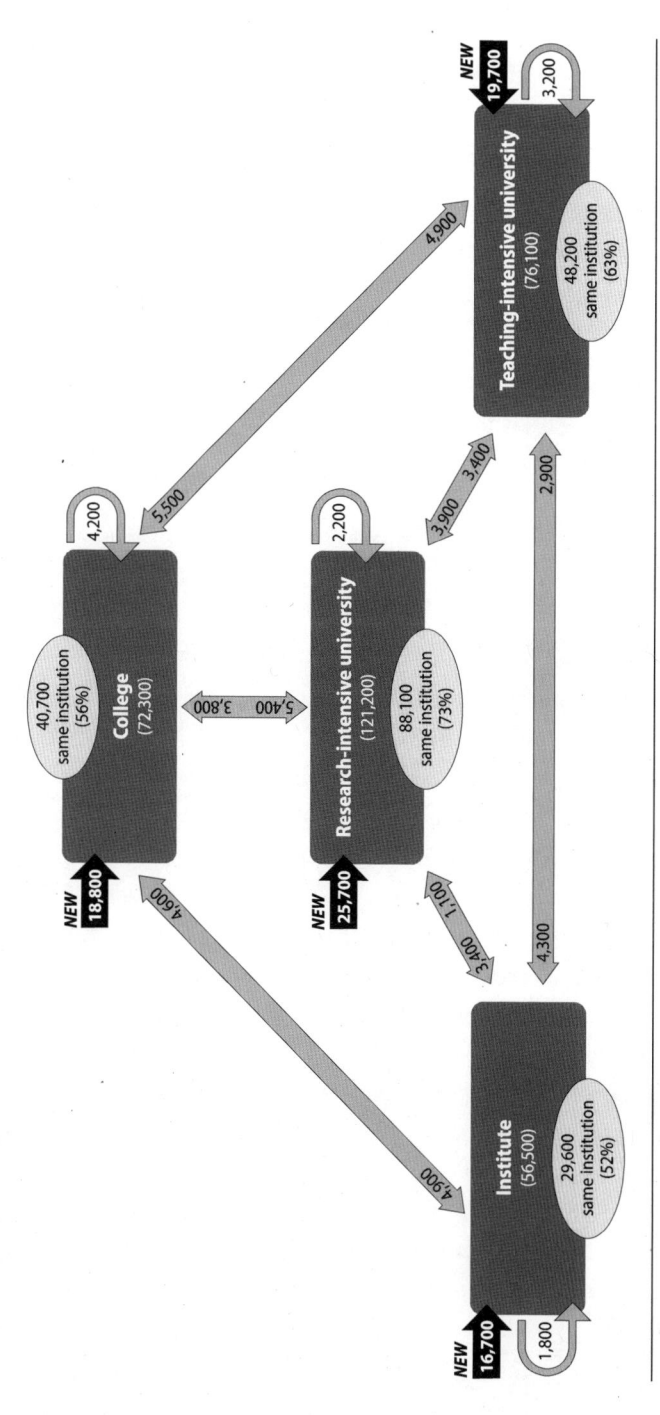

Notes: Mobile pathways include students moving to a new institution (↔) and returning to a previously attended institution (↺). Data includes direct mobility from the previous year (2011–12) and re-entering stopouts from earlier years.

Students may take multiple pathways between one or more institutions in a single year. The sum of pathways will therefore result in double-counting of unique students. 52,500 unique headcount students (17% of 314,000 unique academic credit course registrants) followed a mobile pathway to their institution of registration in 2012–13: ↔ 32,800 moved to a new institution; ↺ 20,600 returned to an institution they previously left.

Source: Adapted from a model and diagram developed by Joanne Heslop for the Student Transitions Project (2015b).

interpretation are not essential for my purposes. It suffices to note that it reveals that one in ten students switched institutions, and one in fifteen returned to his or her institution after stopping out for a year or more.

The high degree of mobility portrayed in Figure 1 is partly a reflection of the transience of students' lives, but it is also partly the result of a public system that was designed to facilitate transfer, reverse transfer, concurrent enrolment in two or more institutions, and what has generally become known as "student swirl" and a "seamless system."

Although not centrally co-ordinated or governed – potentially both a strength and a weakness – the constellation of postsecondary institutions in British Columbia does in fact partially function as a system from the viewpoint of students. I am not arguing for policy to force more system interaction but simply for policy to be developed with the recognition that there may be effects for students and institutions beyond those to which the policy directly applies.

Systems Approaches in the Study of Postsecondary Education

Calls for a systems perspective in the study of Canadian postsecondary education are not new (Jones, 1997; Sheffield, Campbell, Holmes, Kymlicka, and Whitelaw, 1982), but progress has been slow. Jones (2014) is typical of the continuing scholarly focus on university and public education, with only passing reference to private institutions and vocational programming. Some studies take a partial systems approach; Diallo, Trottier, and Doray (2009), for example, present a synthetic review but focus on public education. They attend to student transitions from colleges to universities but not to other student flows within postsecondary education.

Given this, the unevenness of the literature regarding the development of the BC postsecondary system should not be surprising: some sectors in some periods have received good coverage, whereas others have garnered only a brief mention. The literature is mainly descriptive, not apt to employ theoretical lenses, and is richest with respect to beginnings – namely, the establishment of institutions or points of significant transformation. Less attention has been devoted to detecting trends and patterns in subsequent institutional and sectorial development or to interactions within and across sectors.

Some of Dennison's work (1979a, 1979b, 1992) provides a more comprehensive overview of development, but his gaze falls mainly on the BC public sectors. Fisher et al. (2014) come closest to the approach I am advocating. However, they organize their analyses of public policy changes according to governing political parties, whereas I use three policy themes that have endured across governments.

In contrast to these integrative efforts in British Columbia, and despite a robust historiography of many aspects of American postsecondary education, some standard historical works on the United States (e.g., Altbach, Gumport, and Berdahl, 2011; Cohen and Kisker, 2009; Thelin, 2011) reinforce the distinction between higher (academic) education and other forms of postsecondary education (a divide that also characterizes much of the European literature). Nevertheless, some helpful integrative analyses of current American enrolment patterns across a range of postsecondary sectors are becoming available. Pusser and Turner (2004) articulate the need for integrative approaches in noting how changing patterns of student mobility were challenging policymakers.

The National Student Clearinghouse, a non-profit organization founded in 1993 by the US higher education community, is building on the work of Adelman (1999) to map student flows among postsecondary institutions. As of 2016, it had records for 97 percent of currently enrolled students. A series of longitudinal enrolment reports is emerging that includes data about persistence and attainment across state boundaries and about student flows from high school into public, private, for-profit, international, career, and technical institutions, and even from educational institutions into the workforce.

The Clearinghouse found that in 2013–14, 46 percent of all students who completed a degree at a four-year institution had enrolled in a two-year institution at some point in the previous ten years (National Student Clearinghouse Research Center, 2015, Spring). A more extensive report subsequently provided a national view of student movement in postsecondary institutions (Shapiro, Dunbar, Wakhungu, Yuan, and Harrell, 2015, July).

Historians of American postsecondary education have been slower than enrolment analysts to embrace a comprehensive systems perspective.

Part of the reason is that robust histories of individual sectors are needed before relationships among sectors can be assessed. These are not always available. Beach (2011), for example, notes that even in the extensively studied community college sector, very little historical work has been done.

Histories of vocational (career and technical) education in the United States are more apt to bridge the divide between K-12 and the postsecondary realm, tracing developments in secondary schools along with those in community colleges (e.g., O'Lawrence, 2013). In chronicling several centuries of career and technical education, H. Gordon (2014) also briefly considers tribal colleges, apprenticeship, and the impact of land grant universities.

The California Master Plan (California State Department of Education, 1960) has fostered systems thinking about relationships among sectors, albeit only among public sectors. Smelser (1993), for example, describes California as a multisegment system. Terms such as the "ecology" of higher education (Kirst and Stevens, 2015) sometimes appear in the literature. All too frequently, though, authors such as Bok (2013) mention four-year colleges, community colleges, and for-profit institutions in their opening descriptions of the American system but make little more than passing reference to them in subsequent pages that focus on universities.

In the literature from overseas, Australia, along with New Zealand, where tertiary education is defined in the same comprehensive way that I have conceptualized postsecondary education, is fertile ground for systems thinking. The elimination of the binary system of colleges and universities in favour of a Unified National System following the Dawkins Report (Dawkins and Australia, 1988) prompted Australian analysts to take a comprehensive view of the postsecondary system. Thus, for example, a recent Department of Education and Training review of postsecondary educational reviews (Australia, Department of Education and Training, 2015) was organized chronologically over a twenty-six-year period and encompassed both universities and non-university providers (offering programs of at least two years' duration) across public and private sectors. This policy analysis encompassed both academic and vocational institutions.

A decade after the Dawkins Report, Marginson (1997a) examined the historical roots of thirty years of educational policy, using citizenship as the central motif. Although he did not assess the proportion of academic versus vocational programming or their interactions, he did stress the relationship between public and private sectors. It is not surprising that Marginson, an Australian, should have used the California Master Plan (California State Department of Education, 1960) as the touchstone for his analysis of global trends in access and social stratification in postsecondary education (Marginson, 2016a).

Tight (2009) notes that a full twenty years had passed since the previous comprehensive account of post–Second World War higher education in the United Kingdom (W. Stewart, 1989). He examines the shifting binary divide as non-university institutions of technical and further education were redesignated as universities, a profound form of interaction between postsecondary sectors. However, his focus is on academic education, and thus vocational and continuing education do not feature in his analysis.

Two developments may be creating a European audience that is looking to North America and Australia for examples of integrative analyses and systems thinking in the study of postsecondary education. The Bologna Process, intended to significantly enhance student mobility across nations, has already resulted in a number of major reforms and has seen some countries restructure their university systems more along the lines of the Anglo-American tradition (Adelman, 2008). The second development is the growth of dual-sector or comprehensive postsecondary institutions that span the divide between European notions of higher and further education, with academic and vocational functions coming to exist within universities themselves and not only across differing types of postsecondary institutions (Garrod and Macfarlane, 2009). The emergence of hybrid qualifications that blur the distinction between academic and vocational programs accentuates the integrative significance of dual institutions (Deissinger, Aff, Fuller, and Jorgensen, 2013).

Other Types of Synthesis

I have also incorporated two other forms of synthesis into this study. One is to blend the knowledge developed by practitioners in the professional world with that from the scholarly literature. The other involves using differing theories concurrently to interpret the historical record.

Government officials, institutional administrators, and university scholars all view postsecondary education from different vantage points and employ different frameworks for interpreting what they see. Collectively, these multiple sets of knowledge enable fuller understandings to emerge and stimulate the rise of new interpretations.

Supplementing the scholarly literature on the history of the BC postsecondary system are eight historical reports that I completed for professional audiences (Cowin, 2007, 2009, 2010, 2011, 2012a, 2012b, 2013a, 2013b). Several of these were prompted by gaps in the scholarly literature.

I drew extensively upon practitioner and participant observation methodologies in preparing these reports. The interviews I conducted while employed full-time in a BC college, for example, certainly did not correspond to the academic model taught in research methodology classes: at province-wide meetings with my postsecondary colleagues, I regularly inquired at coffee breaks and lunch as to what they knew about a particular topic, or if they could consult within their institution to determine who might know something about it. I eventually amassed a rich pool of information, but it was difficult to reference according to traditional academic conventions because it was gathered in such bits and pieces. Nevertheless, peer reviews of my draft reports and the positive reception of the final versions by those working in government and institutions attested to their rigour.

After studying in the BC system, I worked for over three decades in postsecondary positions that gave me a ringside seat to some of the events I describe here, as well as access to people who were involved in other events. I was fortunate to have held positions that required me to pay attention to what was happening across the province, and I draw heavily upon those experiences.

Most of us who lived through the evolution of the contemporary system, and who therefore have a sense of its overall gestalt, are now retired. Some are dead. The fact that the eyewitnesses are vanishing from the scene was partly responsible for my decision to write this book. I find it hard to imagine that a newcomer would have much success in piecing together a history in as comprehensive a fashion as I have offered here.

As well as synthesizing across all postsecondary sectors and combining sources from academic and professional literatures, the third way I sought a more holistic gaze was by drawing upon more than one theoretical perspective for the analytical portions of this study. My process involved examining the various rationales adopted by policy actors to interpret the persistent background forces that have propelled developments in the BC postsecondary system over the past half century – policy rationales that resonate across the English-speaking world.

∼

This study encompasses the entire system of postsecondary education in British Columbia, presenting a comprehensive overview of how the structure has changed since 1960. It is especially relevant to those working in the system or studying it, but its methodology can inform others. My methodological contributions lie in considering the entire system by describing all its components and exploring how they interact, integrating information drawn from professional sources with academic sources, and going beyond proximate causes to assess some enduring policy rationales (drawing upon a variety of literatures and theories to explicate the rationales).

As more nuanced understandings emerge of student mobility across institutions, more dual institutions and hybrid credentials are established, the ramifications of the Bologna Process become better understood, and notions of organizational fields (W.R. Scott, 2014) and the ecology of postsecondary education are elaborated, British Columbia offers a glimpse of what the future might hold for the study of postsecondary education. Not that the province is necessarily a model for other jurisdictions to emulate – its postsecondary system has as many quirks and weaknesses as any other – but a number of forces have converged for it to serve as a good case study.

For example, the distinctive geographical challenges of the province became a key driver in the creation of an outstanding system of university transfer from community colleges. Although the BC approach to transfer is not very transportable even to some other provinces in Canada, much less abroad, the lessons learned from the BC experience have enabled the province to provide leadership in the Pan-Canadian Consortium on Admissions and Transfer. In the same manner, the historical narrative and analysis that follow are intended to serve as a catalyst for related studies in other jurisdictions.

1

Setting the Stage

BC Postsecondary Education in 1960

British Columbia had a small population of 1.6 million in 1960 – roughly equivalent to the current population of metropolitan Marseille, France – distributed across an area the size of France and Italy combined. Half of its residents lived in its southwest corner on less than 5 percent of its landmass, with the remaining half widely dispersed in clusters fragmented by mountains and vast forested plateaus (Figure 2). Today, the population approaches 5 million but is still concentrated in the southwest. The challenge of providing geographical access to postsecondary education for a small and scattered population in the hinterland is a theme in the history of the province.

The academic component of the BC postsecondary system, as represented by baccalaureate and higher levels of instruction, consisted of a single university in 1960, the University of British Columbia (UBC) in Vancouver, and an affiliated college in another city, Victoria College, that was aspiring to become a degree-granting body in its own right. A handful of tiny theological institutions, some affiliated with UBC, conferred bachelor's and graduate degrees in religion.

Half a century old, UBC had just transitioned from a teaching institution to a full-fledged research university, awarding its first PhDs in science in 1950 and its first PhD in arts in 1960 (Damer and Rosengarten, 2009). Federal funding for research was instrumental in fostering this development (D. Cameron, 1991). The role of federal grants and subsidies in shaping

FIGURE 2
Population distribution in British Columbia

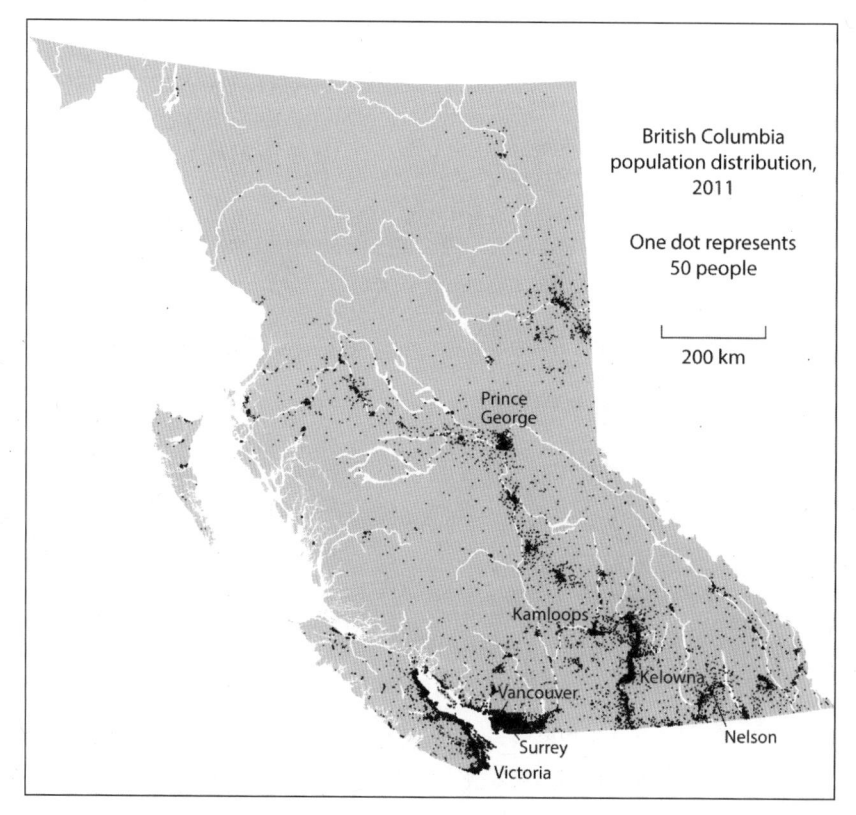

British Columbia population distribution, 2011

One dot represents 50 people

200 km

Prince George
Kamloops
Kelowna
Vancouver
Surrey
Victoria
Nelson

Cartography by Eric Leinberger

the BC postsecondary system, a field in which Ottawa lacks constitutional jurisdiction to govern directly, is another historical theme.

Finally, some secondary schools offered an additional year of study, known as Grade 13 or senior matriculation, for university-bound students. The Royal Commission on Education (Chant, 1960) recommended expanding Grade 13 throughout the province to give all students the option of receiving advanced standing when they entered university, but the opposite occurred in the mid-1960s, when the BC government decided to offer university transfer programs in the new community college system.

Other academic institutions in the private and not-for-profit sector, such as Notre Dame University College in Nelson, were very small. The growth of private education is yet another theme, but much of it did not occur until the 1980s, first in non-academic fields and two decades later in degree-level education.

In sub-baccalaureate education, the control of apprenticeship and the regulation of about a hundred small, private trade schools (which also encompassed correspondence education and business schools) came under the jurisdiction of the BC Department of Labour. Even though apprenticeship and pre-apprenticeship instruction has often been delivered by public institutions, its oversight has rarely been by the same government department responsible for the rest of postsecondary education (Cowin, 2012b). The government perceived the apprenticeship component of vocational education as primarily serving to meet the needs of employers rather than those of students.

Federal funding to secondary schools for vocational education – that is, for non-apprenticeship forms of vocational instruction that Ottawa viewed as falling under its constitutional authority for economic and labour market affairs – ended with the passage of the Technical and Vocational Training Assistance Act in 1960. The new act provided a means for federal capital funding to be directed to the provinces. It spurred the construction throughout the 1960s of a network of postsecondary vocational schools across British Columbia, as well as the opening of the diploma-level British Columbia Institute of Technology (BCIT) in 1964. Only three publicly funded vocational schools had previously operated in the province: Nanaimo (established in 1936), Vancouver (1949), and, as of 1958, the BC Vocational School in Burnaby (which held its first classes in buildings on the Pacific National Exhibition fairgrounds until its own campus adjacent to the future BCIT was completed a few years later).

The Vancouver School Board was an important supporter and midwife for several postsecondary institutions over the decades. It was this organization that affiliated with McGill University in Montreal around 1905 to establish a precursor to the University of British Columbia. Along with its Vancouver Vocational Institute, the school board launched what are now the Emily Carr University of Art and Design, Langara College, and Vancouver Community College. As described below, school districts were initially the vehicle by which the BC community college sector was created (Dennison, 1997). Since the late 1970s, however, the strong interest and involvement of school districts in adult education has declined precipitously.

In 1960, continuing education programs in school districts still provided vocational and other training in the evening for adults. The extension program of the University of British Columbia was at its zenith, with a national reputation (G.R. Selman, 1975).

Despite a temporary surge in university enrolment following the Second World War and plenty of indications in the late 1950s that more educational opportunities for adults in both academic and technical fields were needed, British Columbia's postsecondary system remained modest in size and scope in 1960. The province's heritage as a resource-based, frontier society – one that relied heavily on other jurisdictions to provide postsecondary education for its citizens and workers – was very evident. Significant changes were about to occur.

Comprehensive Histories of BC Postsecondary Education

Until 2000, Dennison was the principal author of studies on the evolution of BC postsecondary sectors. Thereafter, Fisher and his colleagues became the leading researchers, paying particular attention to government policy. A few key works of these authors are described here to situate my work in the historical scholarship.

A discussion paper written by Dennison (1979b) emphasizes public universities and colleges but touches upon some private academic institutions and the intermediary body for government, the Universities Council of British Columbia. Dennison (1997) surveys developments from 1945 through 1995, mentioning not only the establishment of institutions, but also discussing associated organizations and agencies. He considers government intentions and policy, insofar as they could be deduced from actions, because in his opinion, expressed policy was sometimes incoherent.

Fisher and his collaborators extended Dennison's approach for two more decades and attended to the means by which policy priorities originate, become modified as they are implemented, and sometimes have unintended consequences. Their 2006 book was national, not provincial, in scope, but it provided valuable background about federal government forces that affected the development of postsecondary education in British Columbia (Fisher et al., 2006). Fisher, Rubenson, Jones, and Shanahan (2009) consider British Columbia in the context of two other provinces, focusing on the priorities of government as articulated in policy documents. They conclude that the main theme since the mid-1980s has been a desire to create more access for students.

Fisher et al.'s (2014) long chapter is a key source for BC developments since 1990, contextualizing changes in terms of the overall orientation of the provincial government and not simply the government's point of view about education. Modifying the conclusion in Fisher et al. (2009) about the importance of access goals, the 2014 chapter observes that education as a wealth creator has dominated government policy discussion.

My study amplifies Fisher et al. (2014), especially regarding the private sector. It concentrates on interactions among postsecondary sectors rather than simply presenting parallel streams of development or considering only relationships between government and individual sectors. If Fisher et al. were viewed as extending Dennison on a vertical axis, my contribution could be seen more on a horizontal axis.

If these vertical and horizontal trajectories were to be pursued further – and I have just scratched the surface of relationships among sectors – some useful future research would be to use neoinstitutional theory as a tool for examining and interpreting the network of relationships more extensively, to expand my focus on just three policy rationales to include research and other policy goals, and to move beyond general policy intent and rationales to a more complete policy analysis that also encompasses the specifics of policy development, implementation, and outcome.

Definitions

Postsecondary Education

I use "postsecondary education" in the most wide-ranging manner possible, referring to all types of formal post-compulsory instruction for adults that are offered by organizations whose primary purpose is educational. (Training branches of other types of organizations and informal learning are thus beyond its scope.) Other terms, such as "tertiary education," may exclude some types of vocational and secondary school equivalent education for adults – the exception being in New Zealand, where tertiary education has the same comprehensive meaning as my usage of postsecondary education (Goedegebuure, Santiago, Fitznor, Stensaker, and van der Steen, 2008). The International Standard Classification of Education's notion of "post-secondary non-tertiary education" reflects a binary conception of education that is at odds with the comprehensive philosophies of public colleges and teaching-intensive universities in British Columbia (United Nations Educational, Scientific and Cultural Organization, 2012).

In North America, "higher education" is sometimes used in the same sense as how "postsecondary" is employed here. However, in such countries as Australia and England, higher education is often taken to mean baccalaureate and post-graduate studies, as distinct from the sub-baccalaureate education for adults, which is known as further education or technical/vocational education. The use of the term "higher education" is relatively recent in the United Kingdom; the Robbins Report (Committee on Higher Education, 1963) introduced it to embrace three previously unco-ordinated sectors – the traditional universities, advanced further education, and teacher training (P. Scott, 2009).

Even in Canada, Fallis (2013) uses "higher education" to refer only to colleges and universities, noting that it is just one component of postsecondary education. Because of the variation and exclusions in the definitions of tertiary and higher education, I prefer the word "postsecondary."

However, its meaning can vary in the literature. Dennison (1992) comments that "postsecondary" is often used in western Canada to typify the status of the learner (i.e., students who have left secondary or compulsory education), whereas in Ontario it reflects the content of the program (i.e., the curriculum is beyond that offered in secondary schools). Jones (2009) provides a Canadian example of using the word in the Ontario sense, whereas I focus on the learner by using the BC approach.

The levels encompassed in my definition of "postsecondary" include everything from adult basic education and the various forms of vocational education through to graduate studies. Continuing education, some of which does not involve formal evaluation of student learning, is the most problematic program area to define (Cowin, 2010). In the interest of simplicity and because greater refinement provides no substantial benefit for my purposes, all offerings that BC colleges and universities provide under the continuing education rubric, regardless of whether they carry academic credit, fall within the scope of this study.

System

I concur with Sheffield's (1982) use of the term "postsecondary system" to describe structures, relationships, and interactions among individual institutions, even where formal governance and co-ordination are weak or nonexistent.

British Columbia's postsecondary system exists not so much in the formal sense of centralized and co-ordinated administration but more informally in terms of interaction and interdependence, wherein students move among institutions, and the actions of one sector or institution affect others. Dennison (1997) argues that the province had more of a postsecondary system than elsewhere in Canada, with the exception of Quebec and perhaps Alberta.

Institution

"Institution" is employed here in the typical sense to refer to a formal postsecondary organization, such as a college or university, that enrols students and provides instruction. When the word is used in the sociological sense of generalized norms and ways of seeing and organizing the social world, it is italicized to distinguish it (see the section on *institutional* theory in Chapter 2).

Organization

"Organization" is sometimes used here in a specialized sense, although drawing upon the everyday meaning of a group of people who come together to achieve a purpose. Whereas an institution enrols students, an organization in my specialized sense does not. It consists of a group of educators who meet formally on an ongoing basis regarding a topic (such as facilitating the acquisition of information technology or to advocate for funding). In British Columbia, when government creates such bodies to perform tasks that it assigns, they are known generically as agencies even though their name might include such words as "council."

Credentials

In British Columbia, a bachelor's degree is always the equivalent of at least four years of study beyond secondary school, regardless of whether a general or, much less frequently, an honours degree is awarded. Whereas the BC government regulates the use of the words "university" and "bachelor," it does not regulate "college" and a number of other credentials. In the public sector, a certificate usually entails a program of no more than a year's duration, whereas earning a diploma normally requires two years (occasionally up to three). In the private sector, "diploma" and "certificate" have no standardized meaning.

Graduates of post-basic programs may be awarded such credentials as an advanced or post-baccalaureate certificate or diploma, a master's degree, or a doctoral degree. The Red Seal is an interprovincial designation conferred upon the completion of an apprenticeship program.

University Transfer

In addition to full programs equivalent to first and second year at universities, BC colleges and institutes offer an extensive array of courses that are individually equivalent to courses at specific universities. Universities may grant students credit towards their bachelor's degree for one to twenty such courses. The BC university transfer system consists mainly of course equivalencies, frequently bundled into complete feeder programs of one or two years' duration that allow college students to transfer into second or third year at university.

Types of Institutions

Until 2002, publicly funded colleges, regional colleges, and community colleges in British Columbia were synonyms for open-admissions, comprehensive, teaching institutions that offered up to two years of university transferable courses as well as an extensive set of preparatory and applied programs. Applied programs, sometimes incorporating a few university transferable courses, ranged in duration from three months to three years and were designed for graduates to enter directly into the labour force. Since 2002, public colleges have offered a limited number of baccalaureate degree programs in applied subjects.

Junior colleges provide only the first two years of baccalaureate studies (i.e., university transferable courses) rather than comprehensive programming that includes applied and preparatory programs. Their presence in British Columbia has been small, lying entirely outside the public system since Victoria College became the University of Victoria in 1963.

Unlike most Canadian provinces, British Columbia adopted an American comprehensive community college model and developed the university transfer function to become as robust as any in the world (Bahram, 2004). As a result, up to 60 percent as many college transfer students were admitted annually to BC research universities as were admitted directly from BC secondary schools (Cowin, 2004).

Outside the public sector, a college could be almost anything: an institution offering programs at the sub-baccalaureate, baccalaureate, or graduate level. In a few cases, faculty were required to conduct research as well as teach. With the use of "university" restricted by BC legislation, "college" became the default label for many institutions.

In 1989, a handful of public colleges were granted the authority to offer some third- and fourth-year university programming, with bachelor's degrees originally conferred under the auspices of a partner university and subsequently in the college's own name. These university colleges had all become teaching universities by 2008, although they continued to offer their original comprehensive range of college programs.

Public special-purpose or teaching universities all originated as community colleges or public institutes. They retain an open-access admissions philosophy – open access to the school, not necessarily to individual programs and courses – and offer a few employment-oriented master's programs. They are not funded for faculty to conduct research as part of their regular duties.

Doctoral programs are offered at research universities. Faculty are expected to undertake research as part of the tenure process, and the universities' operating grant from the provincial government supports some of this research.

In the public sector, institutes have a province-wide, rather than regional, mandate to offer instruction to a particular type of student or in particular fields of study (i.e., they do not provide a comprehensive curriculum). They originally offered only sub-baccalaureate programs, and this remains their emphasis today. Aboriginal-governed, private institutions often refer to themselves as institutes, a more generic use of the term "institute" than in the public sector College and Institute Act. The Aboriginal community sometimes avoids using the word "institution" because of its connotations of the institutionalization of Indigenous children in special residential schools, a system that some see as an attempt at cultural genocide.

Vocational schools are public postsecondary institutions that were merged with public community colleges in the 1970s. They are distinct from the private career colleges that lie outside the public system but are regulated by government, and from vocational secondary schools.

Private institutions operate under different legislation than do public universities, colleges, and institutes. They may or may not be for-profit; the faith-based and Aboriginal-governed examples are not profit seeking, whereas many, but not all, career colleges are businesses that attempt to make a profit. With the occasional small-scale exception, private institutions do not receive operating grants from government. However, subject to some accreditation and other requirements, students who attend them may be eligible for government financial assistance in the form of loans and grants.

In contrast to the more co-ordinated, planned, and school-based models of northern Europe, British Columbia's apprenticeship system falls firmly in the market-oriented Anglo tradition, where individual employers give priority to their immediate labour market needs rather than the educational needs of society. Apprentices, who are often in their twenties, typically spend four weeks per year in classroom settings, in either public or private postsecondary institutions, but most of their learning occurs on the job. A number of apprenticeable trades require four years of training.

Although continuing education is not a separate sector, it functions in many respects as if it were. It is a component of public education that operates in a market-oriented, entrepreneurial manner to deliver courses and programs that may or may not involve a formal evaluation of student learning. Legislation has consistently required BC public institutions to offer continuing education, but the term remains undefined, with the result that anything and everything could potentially be considered continuing education. The common threads in the widely varying continuing education units in public institutions are that course offerings are contingent on short-term enrolment demand and cost-recovery financing, and that instructors have short-term, course-specific contracts that are subject to a minimum level of enrolment being met for the course to proceed. Instructors and institutions typically have no further obligations to each other beyond the specific course. Continuing education is sometimes called adult education.

Distinctive Features of BC Community Colleges
The various types of private postsecondary institutions may be less known in British Columbia than those in the public sector, but it is the public colleges that are the most frequently misunderstood because "college" means different things in different jurisdictions.

Although hierarchical stratification among postsecondary institutions is increasing (Marginson, 2016b, 2016c), BC community colleges have historically had a strongly egalitarian, progressive character. Rather than serving as a dumping ground for academically or socially disadvantaged students, they have been leaders in implementing what is sometimes termed the community college philosophy (Vaughan, 2006)[1] – partly, but by no means entirely, because many areas of the world have nothing comparable. The United Kingdom's Higher Education Policy Institute concluded that BC public colleges had developed what is possibly the most extensive credit accumulation and transfer arrangement in the world (Bahram, 2004).

Because community colleges were conceived in British Columbia as comprehensive institutions, rather than junior colleges or vocational schools, and were often intended to address geographical rather than social and academic barriers for students, their student bodies have been more representative of the general population than in many jurisdictions. The handful of BC colleges that have participated since 2010 in the Community College Survey of Student Engagement (Center for Community College

Student Engagement, n.d.) all had lower rates of remedial coursework in English and mathematics than the American average. The majority had a student body with higher levels of parental education than the American average. Public college students in the United States are less consistently prepared in secondary schools than their BC counterparts due to greater variations in funding levels and educational standards in those schools. Also, the US public college sector is proportionately smaller than that of British Columbia (OECD, 2016) and more racially segregated.

It is the university transfer function that has been the greatest success of BC colleges. As a result, BC universities admitted three transfer students from college for every five who entered directly from high school in the 1990s (Cowin, 2004). Transfer students graduated from university with approximately the same number of course credits as direct entry students (Pendleton, 2010) and, despite an initial drop in grades during their first term, achieved similar grade point averages at program completion (Lambert-Maberly, 2010). One study found that high school graduates with just average grades who took the college transfer route to university performed as well as or better than their peers with average grades who went directly to university (Heslop, 2004).

Two findings in the American literature on community colleges are sometimes incorrectly generalized to BC colleges. Clark's (1960) articulation of the cooling-out function of community colleges has not, to date, been a particularly good description of BC colleges, according to the extensive research program of the BC Council on Admissions and Transfer.[2] Furthermore, Grubb's foreword in Beach (2011) mentions statistical evidence showing that even in the United States, warming up has actually been more frequent than cooling out. The second inapplicable generalization concerns vocationalization. Since 1989, some BC community colleges have transformed into universities, and the remaining colleges have maintained a strong academic component, unlike the opposite trend toward vocational education in American colleges observed by Brint and Karabel (1989).

Structural forces have helped shape the distinctive features of BC colleges, from the purposes for and ways in which they were established through to the evolution of some into teaching universities and the addition of limited degree-granting authority to the remainder. If one sector were to be taken as emblematic of the value of structural and system-interaction perspectives, the public college sector in British Columbia is a good candidate.

Inventory of Public Institutions

The public sector enrols the most students in British Columbia and is especially important outside the large cities of Vancouver and Victoria. Although sectors rather than individual institutions are the focus of this book, the latter are frequently mentioned if not described. Table 1 provides an inventory of public institutions in the province, classified by region and type, as a general orientation for readers who are unfamiliar with the landscape. Summaries of their history are available in the appendix of Cowin (2007).

TABLE 1
BC public postsecondary institutions, 2015

Region and type	Name	Opened	Notes
VANCOUVER			
Research university	Simon Fraser University	1965	
	Technical University of BC	1999	Merged into SFU to become Surrey campus
	University of British Columbia	1915	Predecessor affiliated with McGill University
Teaching university	Capilano University	1968	Originally Capilano College
	Emily Carr University	1933	Originally Vancouver School of Art, then Emily Carr College of Art and Design, then Institute
	Kwantlen Polytechnic University	1981	Originally part of Douglas College, became Kwantlen College and then Kwantlen University College
	University of the Fraser Valley	1974	Originally Fraser Valley College, then University College of the Fraser Valley
College	Douglas College	1970	
	Langara College	1994	Originally part of Vancouver Community College
	Vancouver Community College	1965	Originally Vancouver City College
Institute	BC Institute of Technology	1964	
	Institute of Indigenous Government	1995	Absorbed by the Nicola Valley Institute of Technology
	Justice Institute	1978	
	Open Learning Agency	1978	Originally Open Learning Institute. Merged into Thompson Rivers University
	Pacific Marine Training Institute	1938	Originally Vancouver Navigational School. Merged into BC Institute of Technology
	Pacific Vocational Institute	1960	Originally part of BC Vocational School. Merged into BC Institute of Technology
	Vancouver Vocational Institute	1949	Merged into Vancouver Community College

Region and type	Name	Opened	Notes
VANCOUVER ISLAND			
Research university	University of Victoria	1963	Predecessor was Victoria College
Teaching university	Royal Roads University	1995	
	Vancouver Island University	1969	Originally Malaspina College, then Malaspina University-College
College	Camosun College	1971	
	North Island College	1975	
SOUTH INTERIOR			
Research university	University of British Columbia – Okanagan	2004	Originally part of Okanagan University College
Teaching university	Thompson Rivers University	1970	Originally Cariboo College, then University College of the Cariboo
College	College of the Rockies	1975	Originally East Kootenay Community College
	Okanagan College	1968	Okanagan University College for a period
	Selkirk College	1966	
Institute	Nicola Valley Institute of Technology	1983	Private institution became public in 1995
NORTH			
Research university	University of Northern BC	1994	
College	College of New Caledonia	1969	
	Northern Lights College	1975	
	Northwest Community College	1975	
MULTI-CAMPUS			
	BC Vocational School	1960	Campuses across the province. After 1970, merged into colleges and BC Institute of Technology

2

Policy Rationales

History is complex and multidimensional; a single interpretation rarely encompasses all the reasons why a particular postsecondary policy decision was taken. Sometimes, for example, the personalities and values of key actors are important: if W.A.C. Bennett had not been premier of British Columbia in the early 1960s, Simon Fraser University and the University of Victoria might never have been established as separate bodies but rather as undergraduate institutions tributary to the University of British Columbia. Yet it is also true that the precipitating factor leading to the creation of these two universities was a specific report, the Macdonald Report (Macdonald, 1962), which came about independently of the premier. But this document, as distinctive and important as it was, reflected trends and thinking in other parts of the country. And so the plot thickens, and the number of causal relationships grows, as one's gaze broadens.

I often think of the theoretical frameworks and analytical lenses used in making historical interpretations as spotlights, revealing what might otherwise go unnoticed but at the price of illuminating only what can be seen from a particular angle. Other spotlights are needed to examine phenomena from more angles and thereby permit fuller understandings to emerge. This study uses three spotlights, referred to here as public policy rationales (broad, enduring goals and theoretical understandings of government decision makers), to illuminate my subject matter. None of these spotlights is new, but their use together is unusual.

At the most general level, the aspirations of BC policymakers for postsecondary education over the past two generations reflected thinking in other parts of North America – namely, to find fair ways to improve the economic circumstances of individuals and the broader society, while simultaneously enhancing the social well-being and personal development of all groups in society. As postsecondary participation patterns progressed from elite through mass and into universal stages, and as the economy cycled through strong and weak periods, questions of affordability and financial sustainability resulted in growing attention to efficient and effective management. So, notwithstanding all the distinctive local and short-term circumstances that have shaped the structure of postsecondary education in British Columbia, a small number of general policy goals in the North American literature have been repeatedly relevant in British Columbia.

One contribution that postsecondary institutions make to society is the generation of new knowledge, a central mission of universities. Research, however, is not within the mandate of the majority of postsecondary institutions. I have therefore chosen not to explore this particular dimension, even though knowledge generation has been an enduring rationale of government to justify expenditure on postsecondary education.

My focus is instead on just three policy rationales, or spotlights. They differ sufficiently from each other to make distinctive contributions to our understanding of historical events, yet they are sufficiently complementary to enable a cumulative interpretation. Each rationale helps explain why governments decided to establish institutions and then steer them in certain directions (or, in the case of private institutions, why governments chose certain regulatory approaches).

None of the rationales is relevant at every point in the narrative, but each has played a significant role in propelling the development of the BC postsecondary system for more than half a century. The rationales do not explain every nuance or individual development and do not provide exhaustive explanations, but assessing their collective relevance helps in interpreting change over time.

The first rationale concerns _fair access to postsecondary education_, drawing upon evolving and multiple notions of social justice. I present the differing meanings of social justice as complementary, not contradictory, and I draw upon all of them in subsequent chapters.

The second rationale focuses on human capital formation – preparing people for paid employment – as the primary way that BC policymakers have thought about the contribution of postsecondary education to the economic development of the province. Regional economic development theory also considers the importance of a skilled workforce and of education as a quality of life consideration for retaining qualified labour. Thus, I review the connection between human capital theory and certain aspects of regional economic development theory.

The third rationale concerns theories that help in interpreting how marketization in postsecondary education was an attempt to achieve the efficient and effective allocation of resources. Neoliberal theory is my starting point in accounting for the global trend toward marketization. The literature about new public management is also helpful here. Finally, to round out the marketization discussion, some specific aspects of *institutional* theory, illuminating competition and imitation among postsecondary institutions, are noted.

To shift from spotlights to a different metaphor, these three policy rationales constitute an analytical grid that I overlay on the complex and messy historical narrative to make the presence and absence of certain forces in various periods more evident, albeit downplaying other forces. The analysis does not purport to tell the whole story, simply to draw attention to important components of it.

Fairness and Social Justice

A significant portion of policy discourse and scholarly literature in British Columbia has examined the enrolment-related topic of access, the Access for All initiative (Provincial Access Committee, 1988) being a prime example. Because schooling is a major route for social mobility, serving as an equalizing force that affords opportunities for the disadvantaged, postsecondary institutions have been seen to perform important enabling and gatekeeping functions.

Federal and provincial policies to ensure that people have appropriate access to postsecondary education have implicitly been informed by theoretical literature about justice in general and, more specifically, about social justice. The foundation of social justice lies in determining a fair way to allocate benefits and burdens among individuals and groups in society.

Social justice is one of the elastic and evolving constructs prevalent in the social sciences (Shoho, Merchant, and Lugg, 2011). Especially since the 1990s, the construct has expanded beyond the fair treatment of individuals to include consideration of how to represent, recognize, and promote the cultures of groups within society. Thus, social justice has become multi-faceted and is therefore invoked today in more varied ways than several decades ago. Currently in education, it is often used in only one of its senses, focusing on how people use power, especially with the goal of countering such forces as sexism, racism, and exclusion based on social class (Davis and Harrison, 2013).

In this discussion, I draw on a broad conception of social justice, one that has four components (as there is no standard taxonomy, I use my own terminology for each component):

- Individual justice – Fair and equal treatment of individuals (often expressed in postsecondary education as ensuring that everyone has equal opportunity to be admitted to an institution or program of study)
- Compensatory justice – Unequal treatment of groups to achieve equitable outcomes for individuals in the group (often expressed as providing a level playing field for marginalized or disadvantaged populations)
- Cultural recognition – Fostering and accommodating distinctive group identities (often embedded in discussions of what are sometimes called identity politics and in challenges to existing knowledge as reflected in curriculum and program structures)
- Spatial adaptation – Fair and appropriate treatment of individuals and groups in the hinterland.

The first three components appeared in BC postsecondary education in a sequential and cumulative manner, with spatial adaptation running on a parallel track since 1960.

Definitions
Social justice is sometimes defined as the effort to ensure that all individuals and groups enjoy fair access to what is beneficial and valued, as well as

equitably sharing burdens (Furlong and Cartmel, 2009; Singh, 2011). Fairness, a "good" society, and access are key concepts for social justice (J. Blackmore, 2013; Craven, 2012). Fairness, however, does not necessarily mean an equal or identical distribution of benefits and burdens, and thus questions of equity for diverse groups enter the discussion.

In some recent definitions of social justice, the outcome of nominally fair (and potentially unequal) access and burdens might not be sufficient. L.A. Bell (2007), for example, takes a stance that also considers the process for achieving social justice – namely, that all groups should participate fully and equally in mutually shaping a society that meets all their needs. In such a society, resources would be distributed equitably, and all individuals would be physically and psychologically safe.

Over the past generation, social justice has increasingly been viewed as addressing the topics of respect, dignity, and inclusion in order to foster a just society. For Lowen and Pollard (2010), dignity is at the heart of social justice, based on human rights and the equality of all people. Zajda, Majhanovich, and Rust (2006) argue that most conceptions of social justice refer to an egalitarian society with a sense of solidarity that echoes the cry of the French Revolution for liberty, equality, and fraternity.

Although some authors focus on the justice aspect of social justice, Novak (2000) comments on the social aspect. He draws attention to two social considerations: co-operating and working with others to achieve some type of justice that has as its primary focus the good of others. He contends that concentrating on the social, rather than attempting to define justice, has the advantage of being ideologically neutral, enabling the concept to be used in an uncontested manner across the political spectrum from the right to the left. Zajda et al. (2006) see true social justice as attained only through the harmonious co-operative effort of the citizens, who, in their own self-interest, accept the current norms of morality as the price of membership in the community.

Units of Analysis

Some theories of justice focus on individuals, examining their rights and rewards within a free market economy, whereas others concentrate on group injustices and needs, which the state may be able to address only in more interventionist ways (Sturman, 1997). Anisef, Okihiro, and James

(1982), for example, argue that the ethical principle of individualism in education became a primary mechanism in legitimizing inequalities in a capitalist system because the affected individuals were seen as personally responsible for their own successes and failures. When the spotlight turned from individuals to groups, a social democratic emphasis tended to emerge (Sturman, 1997).

Earlier conceptions of social justice emphasized the individual. Although the landmark Truman Commission on higher education in the United States (Zook and United States, President's Commission on Higher Education, 1947) explicitly sought to rectify group barriers of race, religion, and curriculum content to postsecondary enrolment, its thrust was nevertheless on ensuring that qualified individuals did not encounter insuperable economic obstacles. Only in later years did its pioneering commentary on group barriers come to be viewed as a component of social justice (Thelin, 2011).

Some scholars have associated social justice not with individuals or even groups, but with entire social systems that arise from social structures (Zajda et al., 2006). These structures are defined as patterns of behaviour that have become so entrenched that they are no longer truly voluntary (Reiman, 1990). This conception of social justice is reflected in analyses of systemic discrimination.

Power and Marginalized Groups

Issues of power and identity have become increasingly prominent in the social justice literature (Gereluk, 2008). This is expressed in critical perspectives in which the fundamental purpose of education is seen as improving social justice (J. McArthur, 2010). In discussing the identity aspects of social justice – race, gender, sexuality, and so on – North (2008) starts from the premise that dignity, not rights and privileges, is usually what is at stake in human relationships.

Young (1990, 1992) suggests that social justice should be viewed as rectifying oppression and domination by majority groups that marginalize other groups, especially in the context of cultural justice and imperialism. She advocates a conception of justice that goes beyond the possession of goods to a wider context about the means to make decisions and to exercise capacities. Mills (2013) examines cultural domination using the example of a minority group having to subjugate its cultural ways of being and communicating to the often hostile norms of the dominant culture.

Fraser (1997) and Fraser and Honneth (2003) note that cultural groups frequently want recognition and acceptance of difference – calls for gay pride being an example – whereas distributive notions of social justice usually seek a reduction in difference, such as a more equal distribution of wealth and power. Fraser's work was formative in efforts to develop a theory of justice that incorporated consideration of both distribution and recognition, rather than treating them as separate understandings of social justice (Mills, 2013).

Social Justice in Education

Access for all individuals to equal forms of education has frequently been seen as integral to a fair and democratic society (J. Blackmore, 2013). Liberal and democratic philosophies stress the importance of providing abundant opportunities, such as through education, for people to improve themselves and better their circumstances (Anisef et al., 1982). Thus, a Canadian government report concluded that the goal of equal access to postsecondary education had helped propel a dramatic expansion of education throughout the Western world (Leblanc and Canada, 1987).

Burbules, Lord, and Sherman (1982) describe the concept of identical opportunities for all, emphasizing merit and assuming that most individuals are capable of making their own way in life, as formalism. Compensatory actualism acknowledges that people start from different places in life and encounter various barriers in accessing opportunities. It therefore seeks to bring everyone to the same starting point to ensure a fair competition. Alternative actualism does not provide alternative or compensatory routes to the same goal but rather furnishes different routes of access to differing end points. The varying goals are viewed as equally valuable, but groups and individuals should be allowed to choose among them. Formalism arises from a liberal/individualist tradition, and the two versions of actualism are associated with social democratic traditions (Sturman, 1997).

Burbules et al. (1982) see formalism as the earliest application of social justice to educational analysis and note its implicit or explicit assumption that equal opportunity entailed competing for unequal rewards (Porter, 1979). A meritocratic elaboration of the formalist view was that only a portion of the population has the academic ability to succeed in certain types of education (Furlong and Cartmel, 2009). Streaming and other mechanisms that enabled advantaged social groups to reproduce their privilege in their offspring thus managed to co-exist with what was seen as socially just, equal educational opportunity.

Studies in the 1960s began to question the efficacy of formal education in reducing societal inequities. As the scholarly gaze broadened from equality of initial opportunity to encompass the results of education, schooling came to be seen as both a sorting mechanism and a means to foster equality of condition (Anisef et al., 1982). In other words, education could be both a tool for social control and a means of emancipation. Against this backdrop, compensatory actualism became the new orthodoxy with respect to social justice in education. The argument was that an open-door philosophy to admissions was insufficient for students who faced barriers in passing through that door (Burbules et al., 1982). In practice, however, remedial educational policies still emphasized equality of access and participation, rather than equality of outcomes in the long-term social and economic conditions of former students (J. Blackmore, 2013; Sturman, 1997).

Gradually, equal access was understood as helping the disadvantaged overcome obstacles so that they truly did have equal access. For example, student financial aid was introduced to help address financial barriers. Special programs emerged to encourage the enrolment of under-represented groups, such as women in trades and engineering.

Government policy in Canada used the language of ensuring that postsecondary education was available on an equitable basis to all Canadians who were qualified and who wanted to study (Andres, 1992). The caveats regarding qualification and desire provided space for a differentiated postsecondary system under the rubric of equity. Thus, a provincial report (Alberta Advanced Education, 1984) asserted that equal opportunity to access postsecondary education meant that students should be offered different types and levels of education, with varying starting points and outcomes.

Policy discussion of what constituted a socially just postsecondary education system tended to stop at this point – namely, fair access using compensatory mechanisms. Other components of social justice theory entered public policy discourse less frequently. J. Brennan and Naidoo

(2008) argue that the typical discussion of educational access in terms of participation and whether certain groups were under-represented (a focus on the private benefits of education) begged the question as to who in society ultimately benefits and who pays for postsecondary education (public benefits).

Social justice in terms of identity and cultural recognition – of valuing and fostering distinctive subcultures in contrast to including more individuals from minority groups in the dominant educational culture – has garnered substantial attention in both the scholarly literature and within the curriculum and operating procedures of postsecondary institutions (e.g., accommodation of the holy days of religious minorities and indigenization initiatives). It has been less common, however, to find governments explicitly addressing the cultural identity aspect of social justice in public postsecondary policy, although the advancement of Aboriginal cultures has strengthened since the 1990s. One noteworthy exception is the long-standing recognition of rural communities in such countries as Canada, the United States, and Australia, where vast physical distances, not just social and economic characteristics, distinguish rural communities from urban centres.

Rural Recognition through Spatial Adaptation

The literature discusses the special challenges facing rural communities, but not necessarily in terms of social justice. Nevertheless, the needs of rural populations from a social justice perspective were at least an implicit policy rationale in BC postsecondary education. Some portions of the community development literature help elucidate what social justice in far-flung rural areas, or what I have called spatial adaptation, might mean.

"Community" has multiple meanings. My emphasis here is on the older notion of a geographically bounded place in which a group of people shares a common interest (Garkovich, 2011). Community differs from the geographical concept of place in that an essential attribute is its social relationships that link people together. When, as frequently occurs, community is defined independently of physical space to refer to a common identity, a shared set of values and norms that is reflected in social relationships, it provides the foundation for the social justice concept of cultural recognition. My usage with respect to rural communities, however, remains anchored in physical space and is not decoupled from geography (Bradshaw, 2013). When I discuss faith-based and Aboriginal-governed institutions, however, my use of "community" shifts to a decoupled definition.

Chaskin (2013) argues that there are three lenses for viewing community: social, spatial, and political. In BC government policy for public postsecondary institutions, the emphasis has been strongly on the spatial dimension. Nonetheless, the origins of policies leading to postsecondary structural change often lay in political communities. Social communities were factors in the emergence of the faith-based and Aboriginal-governed institutions.

Development can be defined as planned change that is intended to benefit the community, at least in the eyes of certain people (Garkovich, 2011). In the community development literature, development has the connotations of capacity building and of empowering individuals and groups to bring about changes that enhance their circumstances or make their communities more resilient (Ife, 2002; Nel, Hill, and Binns, 1997). Hustedde and Ganowicz (2013) emphasize solidarity (a deeply shared identity and code of conduct) and agency (the capacity to intervene effectively) in their definition of community development. The focus on empowerment, agency, and capacity building, in contrast to the delivery of goods and services to a passive citizenry, distinguishes community development from some other types of distributive justice initiatives.

Rural populations do not always have the capacity to bring about change and may therefore look to their local postsecondary institution, perhaps the largest organization in the community, for assistance as a partner or leader (A. Thompson, 2014). The institutions are seen not only as providers of educational services and brokers with other components of the education system (S.R. Robinson, 2012), but as mechanisms for improving the local quality of life; Miller and Kissinger (2007) use the term "social engine" to describe this type of capacity building. College and university activities that facilitate local community development include comprehensive continuing education offerings of a general as well as a professional nature, consulting and business development services, a wide array of cultural activities, and broad access to library, fitness, and other facilities (Garza and Eller, 1998).

In reviewing models of lifelong learning, Schuetze (2008) concludes that the earliest of the four models, one that was supported by UNESCO and the OECD into the early 1970s, was primarily a social justice and emancipatory proposition, with a strong emphasis on the advancement of an equitable society. A second model, a cultural one, aimed at fostering the life fulfillment and self-realization of the individual. Both these philosophies are reflected in policy rationales for rural community development.

Spatial adaptation involves elements of the three other forms of social justice in education: individual justice (as equal access to education as possible, given the constraints of critical mass, regardless of where one lives), compensatory justice (making allowances such as extra funding per student and providing special services to achieve equity), and cultural recognition (fostering a desired style of community life in small settlements). The way in which all three elements are invoked concurrently and then expressed spatially makes for a distinctive manifestation of efforts to achieve social justice.

Human Capital Formation

Among the numerous rationales for the state's interest in and support of postsecondary education, one set of benefits – the economic – has been persistently advanced to justify devoting public resources to it. Along with consumer protection, the economic implications for the broader community have provided a rationale for regulating it even when it is privately funded. Grubb and Lazerson (2004) suggest that the evolution of the economic purposes for schooling was the single most important educational development of the twentieth century in North America.

With only universities having a mandate for research and knowledge creation, the primary way in which public policymakers have viewed postsecondary education's contribution to the economic well-being of society has been in preparing students to enter the labour force. Since the late 1950s, understandings of this role have been informed by theory about human capital formation.

Human capital, a more concrete and bounded construct than that of social justice, refers to any knowledge, skill, or ability that increases the productivity of a worker and, by extension, that of society (J. Scott and

Marshall, 2009). It augments the classical economic understanding of the three factors of production: land (including all types of natural resources and raw materials), labour (human effort), and capital (expenditures used to provide means, such as factories, for producing goods and services).

If social justice is concerned with ensuring that everyone receives a fair share of the pie, human capital theory focuses on increasing its size. Whether everyone benefits equitably from its growth is not seen as particularly important; what matters is that everyone receives a larger slice than would otherwise have been the case.

As will be evident in the following chapters, theory about human capital formation has continually informed federal Canadian postsecondary policy since 1960. Its role and meaning have been more variable in BC government policy, both over time and across fields of study.

Two theoretical literatures undergird the economic rationales for state expenditure and regulation in BC postsecondary education: a general one about human capital formation that is applicable throughout developed countries and, to a much lesser extent, regional economic development literature that concerns the well-being of smaller and remote communities (Stimson, Stough, and Roberts, 2006). Regional economics is concerned with more than just education and the characteristics of workers, but enhancing the capacity and stability of the labour force for economic purposes is one argument that has been used to justify postsecondary development throughout the province.

Origins

Although its associated concepts have a longer history, the term "human capital" was introduced only in the 1950s. The concept was then developed by economists from the Chicago school, such as T.W. Schultz and Becker, in the early 1960s (Tan, 2014). Even though it concerned the development of skills and abilities in people – that is, in labour – the reference to capital drew attention to the investment that individuals and organizations make in people by providing learning opportunities to increase future rewards or returns. The concept of human capital shifted attention away from the accumulation of physical capital as a factor of production and toward the development of the labour force (Savvides and Stengos, 2009).

T.W. Schultz (1961) critiques the classical economic view of labour as fostering a notion of manual work in which workers resemble each other and are therefore relatively interchangeable. Instead, Schultz notes the role of specialized or innovative knowledge and skill in economic development. Since the early 1960s, economists have increasingly seen entrepreneurship, or enterprise, as a fourth factor of production, with human capital falling within this fourth category. Notions of human capital and the knowledge-based economy have become mainstream in economic and public policy discourse (OECD, 2004).

T.W. Schultz (1960, 1961) identifies human capital formation exclusively in terms of formal education, an attribute that is easy to measure and that frequently appears as a proxy for more encompassing ways of forming human capital. Becker (1964) broadens the scope to include both general and specific on-the-job training, informal learning, and other investments that improve the well-being of employed persons, such as in support of physical and mental health.

Adoption

The contribution of such researchers as Mincer (1958), Denison (1962), and Becker (1964) was to change the way in which education was viewed. Rather than being seen as an expenditure or a form of consumption, it came to be perceived as a long-term investment that benefitted individuals through increased earnings and society through increased productivity and innovation (Russell, 2013).

In an influential report in the United States, Denison (1962) points out that not only were increased levels of education among the largest sources of past and prospective economic growth for the nation, but schooling was one of the most amenable factors to government influence in the macroeconomic equation. Within a few years, human capital theory had attracted the attention of Canadian policymakers, championed by the Economic Council of Canada.

From the United States and Canada, the first countries to introduce mass higher education, human capital theory spread around the world in the 1980s and became a rationale for expanding postsecondary education; the perceived importance of human capital as a determining factor of economic success prompted numerous countries to invest heavily in education and training (P. Brown, 1999). More recently, Metcalfe and Fenwick (2009) observe that Ottawa has continued to follow encouragement from the Organisation for Economic Co-operation and Development (OECD) to formulate policies that promote the capacity of the citizenry to learn, adopt technology, and embrace informal learning as an accompaniment to formal learning.

Human capital formation, along with innovation theory and attention to the role of information and communication technology, has been an important component of the discourse concerning the knowledge economy (Jorgenson, 2012). Drucker (1969) popularized the term "knowledge economy," with writers such as Porter (1971) and D. Bell (1973) further promoting post-industrial theory. This school of thought argued that an implication of a shift in Western economies from materials handling to the processing of information was that much of the labour force would become knowledge workers, who would need to pursue lifelong learning to meet the growing knowledge demands of their jobs (Livingstone and Guile, 2012).

By the 1980s, economists increasingly realized that the connection between research/knowledge production and social and economic development was complicated (Sörlin and Vessuri, 2007). Despite lacklustre empirical evidence at the societal, as opposed to the individual, level, advocates of the knowledge economy nevertheless continued to assert the importance of scientific knowledge and a well-educated workforce in post-industrial societies (Livingstone, 2012). Powell and Snellman (2004) contend that the worldwide transformation of many polytechnics into universities was part of an upgrading movement to signal membership in the knowledge economy, even though substantive measurement of the knowledge economy remained elusive.

Concepts

A key concept in human capital theory is that of the differing private and public returns to investments in people. Individuals spend money and forego income to acquire learning that they hope will raise their incomes in the future. The comparison between their initial investment and future income represents the private rate of return. Though the technical details of empirically estimating private returns may be complex, this task is less challenging and controversial than the literature regarding public returns.

The notion of public returns rests on the proposition that a higher skill level in the workforce increases production capacity and the ability to gain a competitive advantage through innovation (Lindahl and Canton, 2007). Thus, investment in human resources is not only crucial for individuals but is seen as the key to economic success of regions and nations in the contemporary world (Tan, 2014). Whereas the claim is that human capital accumulation will make a country richer in the long run, theoretical and empirical verification of this logic has been difficult to achieve and the findings inconsistent (Savvides and Stengos, 2009). The embracing of human capital formation as a rationale for the state's expansion of postsecondary education persisted throughout, and sometimes despite, the emerging empirical studies.

The economic literature refers to the non-economic benefits of human capital formation – the social, cultural, intellectual, and aesthetic benefits – as positive externalities (Tan, 2014). They seem especially likely to be mentioned when economists attempt to estimate the social or public returns to human capital investment. Thus, for example, De la Fuente and Ciccone (2003) conclude that education becomes an attractive investment for society, not solely for the individual, when non-market returns such as social cohesion are brought into the calculation.

As will be described later, human capital theory in BC postsecondary policy has appeared in two forms: a generic usage about a well-educated workforce in a knowledge economy and, especially in vocational education, a usage that is more occupationally specific. These two variations arise as much from the ways in which governments have used human capital theory as from the theory itself.

Critiques

Although at the most general level, human capital theory has persisted and become influential, its significance has fluctuated over time. The academic discourse about it has been considerably more nuanced and skeptical than the popular discourse, at least in North America. Its early proponents explicitly acknowledged the lack of empirical studies to either confirm or refute their ideas (Becker, 1964; T.W. Schultz, 1961).

Two considerations seem to have constrained the empirical basis of human capital theory. One is that several aspects of human capital formation are difficult to measure. The most frequent measure of human capital in international comparative studies is the level of formal education (Savvides and Stengos, 2009), a relatively robust and easily obtained measure. However, the quality of that education and other ways of developing the skill level of labour – such as on-the-job training, the role of informal education, and even the general health of the working population – tend to be ignored because obtaining reliable, much less comparable, data on those topics is difficult.

The second research challenge is that both theoretical and empirical studies of human capital are often very technical and not accessible to those who seek policy applications of the resulting insights (Hartog and Maassen van den Brink, 2007). So, although the theory is straightforward at the general level, and the theoretical foundations have not changed much since the 1960s (Tarique, 2013), systematic research on how best to incorporate human capital in theories of economic growth really started only in the late 1980s (Lindahl and Canton, 2007).

Research has confirmed robust private returns to individuals for their investment in education, but findings about macro returns to the public at large have been inconclusive at best (Lindahl and Canton, 2007; Russell, 2013). The optimism of early theorists waned as massive increases in educational expenditures failed to rectify the slow economic growth of the late 1970s and early 1980s (OECD, 1989).

The OECD found that investment in human capital seemed to be effective only when made in conjunction with other policies as part of an overall strategy that included establishing an appropriate social context, as well as restructuring and modernizing the economy (OECD, 1989). The challenge that it saw in 1989 was not to determine whether education and training are factors in economic performance but rather to identify the means, directions, and responsibilities of the various parties to improve their provision. Nevertheless, the Organisation for Economic Co-operation and Development (OECD, 2012) continued to assert that investment in human capital was the single most effective way of promoting not just economic growth but also of distributing its benefits more fairly.

Other critiques of human capital theory have noted the assumption that though the state may seek to foster and shape certain types of human capital formation, ultimately the decision to engage in learning is taken by individuals seeking to maximize their interests (Tan, 2014). In this respect, the theory is a form of rational choice theory to which the sociological critiques of individualistic explanations of behaviour apply (J. Scott and Marshall, 2009).

Human capital theory operates according to supply and demand, leaving it to employers to decide how to reward people for acquiring learning (Davies and Guppy, 2010). P. Brown (1999) maintains that it either ignores interpersonal, teamwork, and creative skills or defines them in technical ways that see them as individual competencies that can be taught through formal education.

Regional Economic Development

Spatially oriented theory is more relevant in BC postsecondary education than in a number of other jurisdictions. Unlike in some regions, spatial considerations, often expressed in terms of providing better geographical access for students, have constituted a key theme in the province – a reflection of its vast distances and the existence of only two urban centres with a population over 150,000. Questions of geography and skill formation overlap in British Columbia, furnishing a link between the human capital discussion above and the regional economic development discussion below.

The trend in regional economic theory has been to go beyond simply attracting employers to a region to also consider how to foster a skilled, entrepreneurial population there and how to otherwise enhance its quality of life (Blakely, 1994). Especially with the ascendency since the late 1980s of endogenous growth theory (Romer, 1990, 1993) and the recognition of knowledge-based economies, "soft" or "smart" infrastructure such as information, education, amenities, environmental quality, entertainment, venture capital, and flexible institutions have been emphasized (Stimson et al., 2006). Topics ignored by classical economics – the quality of life in a region, a diversity of employment opportunities, greater social and financial equity, and sustainable development – have entered the literature of regional economic development.

Many theories have been proposed since the mid-1950s to explain why regions vary in their amount and types of economic growth (Dawkins, 2003; Szajnowska-Wysocka, 2009).[1] Most are not relevant to the educational policy rationales being examined here. Nevertheless, a certain aspect of regional economic development concerns labour force skills, touching on social and cultural capital (Bourdieu, 1977) and bringing a spatial dimension to human capital theory.

Nijkamp and Abreu (2009) conclude that regional development policy has moved increasingly toward knowledge and innovation policy, with leadership and institutional qualities having a great impact on regional welfare. They state that the spatial distribution of knowledge is accepted as an important success factor for regional development in an open competitive economic system and that a remaining debate in endogenous growth theory is simply whether the relationship between knowledge and development is unidirectional or circular.

Marketization

My rationale for grouping several topics from diverse literatures about neoliberalism, public administration, and *institutional* theory into a marketization category is that they all help to explain how a market approach has permeated the means, and even the taken-for-granted expectations, by which postsecondary institutions garner resources to operate. Competition is the theme throughout the disparate discussion: intentionally fostered or otherwise, for tangible items such as money and students as well as for intangibles such as prestige and legitimacy, and whether directly induced or the consequence of some other action. When considering competition for intangibles, the following discussion sometimes turns from what governments have done to the behaviour of postsecondary institutions to help with interpreting the impact of government actions.

The policy goals throughout this section are efficiency (maximizing output relative to inputs) and effectiveness (actually achieving goals). Whereas social justice and human capital rationales embody notions of what is desirable to accomplish, and despite the values embedded in market approaches, this section primarily addresses questions of means rather than ends (how to achieve social goals, rather than what those goals should be).

To return to the metaphor of a pie, if social justice seeks to divide it fairly, and human capital formation tries to increase its size, marketization attempts to provide a sharp knife and well-shaped server to obtain the most precise slices.

This discussion of marketization is presented in three sections. The first, about neoliberalism, examines theoretical concepts. Neoliberalism as an ideology, however, must be operationalized in some way if it is to affect postsecondary institutions. The second section thus explores how states have implemented neoliberal tenets through a body of public administration theory known as new public management, which in turn has been influenced by public choice theory.

With respect to research universities, neoliberal analyses can be compelling, but they do not illuminate as much as I would like about the growth of market forces, such as increased competition and efforts to enhance institutional prestige (P. Blackmore, 2016) in other postsecondary sectors. Moving beyond the mainstream literature about academic capitalism and neoliberalism in higher education (Slaughter and Rhoades, 2004), the third section presents selected concepts drawn from *institutional* theory – *institution* in the sociological sense of norms of social life and worldviews – to complete the marketization discussion.

Neoliberalism

Neoliberalism is one of the most significant social developments of the past century (S.C. Ward, 2012), an overarching worldview in which other ideas about social and cultural life have come to exist (P. Roberts and Peters, 2008). Based on principles that see the free market as the best way of preserving the rights of individuals, it has become so pervasive that alternative ideologies have diminished or disappeared from general public discourse (Boas and Gans-Morse, 2009). In contemporary postsecondary discourse, it is frequently associated with discussions of academic capitalism, globalization (e.g., Levin, 2001), commodification (e.g., Ball, 2012), the knowledge economy (e.g., P. Roberts and Peters, 2008), and managerialism (e.g., Marginson and Considine, 2000).

The many variations of neoliberalism, differing especially in the ways and extents to which it has been implemented, share the ideological principle of preferring the market (understood as a non-political, non-cultural machine) as the way to organize political and economic life (Mudge, 2008). The market is seen as not only efficient on a technical level, but also as a morally superior way of expressing the desires of individuals and resolving divergent opinions (Peters, n.d.).

Larner (2000) proposes that five values underpin neoliberalism: the sanctity of the individual, freedom of choice, market security, a laissez faire economy, and minimal government. Harvey (2007) concurs with this list but claims that if just one had to be chosen as the cardinal virtue, it would be that individual freedoms are best guaranteed by the freedom of markets and trade. This approach draws upon notions of human dignity and individual freedom as foundational, rather than on social or collective considerations.

Individuals, in the neoliberal view, are rational and self-interested. Every social transaction is seen as an entrepreneurial activity for personal gain. Competitiveness is viewed as a mechanism for quality and efficiency, governments should rule from a distance, services should be privatized as much as possible, and the economy should be open (Olssen, Codd, and O'Neill, 2004).

Although neoliberalism is strongly associated with marketization, the free market is seen as merely the means of protecting individual liberty and of fostering individual and collective initiative (Lilley, 2006). With this sort of freedom, according to the neoliberal argument, not only are society's resources allocated efficiently but the creative potential of humans is released, resulting in innovations and gains that ultimately benefit everyone (Thorensen and Lie, 2006).

The intellectual roots of neoliberalism are often traced back to Friedrich von Hayek (1944), but it was Milton Friedman (1962) who became the main scholarly proponent from the 1960s to the 1980s (Steger and Roy, 2010). With neoliberal ideology driving some profound economic reforms in Latin American countries such as Chile, developments that were often authoritarian and seen as unjust, neoliberalism shifted during the 1980s from being a moderate form of liberalism to acquire a radical connotation (Boas and Gans-Morse, 2009).

Supranational organizations such as the International Monetary Fund and the World Bank have imposed neoliberal reforms in less developed countries as a condition of financial aid, with negative results, and the consequences of neoliberal policies have been critiqued in more developed countries as well (see below). Thus, Thorensen and Lie (2006) observe that the term "neoliberal" is sometimes used to denigrate almost any recent economic or political development that is seen as undesirable, stripping the word of meaning. W. Brown's (2003) assessment of why it became pejorative arises from instances where it has deepened local poverty, enabled some wealthier nations to dominate less developed ones, and been compatible with authoritarian and even corrupt regimes. As a result, few if any proponents of neoliberalism use the word to describe themselves (Boas and Gans-Morse, 2009).

Classical liberalism and neoconservatism share with neoliberalism the economic presuppositions of rational, self-interested individuals, the allocative efficiency and effectiveness of markets, laissez faire, and a commitment to free trade (Olssen and Peters, 2005). However, neoliberalism differs from them in the relation of the state to the individual; it provides a distinct social-political analysis despite its vague and contested variations.

Although classical liberalism seeks to protect the individual from the state (Olssen et al. 2004), it attempts to do so on an egalitarian basis that ensures essential human and civil rights for all (W. Brown, 2003; Thorensen and Lie, 2006). It envisions an activist state that redistributes wealth and power to foster a more equitable society.

Neoliberalism rejects the notion of an activist or welfare state. Rather, it sees the state's role as simply ensuring that the laws and other conditions are present for markets to operate efficiently (Olssen and Peters, 2005). The market is assumed in the long run to bring about optimal social and economic equity.

The distinguishing feature of neoconservatism concerns personal and collective morality, a rejection of the moral permissiveness than can flow from individualism. Harvey (2007) claims that neoconservatives share the neoliberal tolerance of dominant class power, but that they attempt to legitimize that power through a climate of consent around a coherent set of moral values. Without morality, neoconservatives fear that unbridled individualism can undermine the market and create ungovernable situations. Lilley (2006) quotes Harvey in an interview where he described neoconservatives as control freaks sitting on a neoliberal agenda.

In contrast, neoliberalism eliminates the distinction between market and non-market activities, embedding and permeating market thinking and values into all social activities (S.C. Ward, 2012). The image is of people who are either operating as consumers (of health services, for example) or as investors (in education, for example), making private choices in a game-structure controlled by government but with providers from around the world competing to supply the best and cheapest service (Marginson, 1997b).

Neoliberals do not see markets as arising naturally or flourishing on their own, and thus the distinction between government and governance becomes important (Larner, 2000). Direct regulation may be reduced, but central government sets the rules as to what can and cannot be done, governing or steering from a distance (S.C. Ward, 2012). The result is that the neoliberal state leads and controls citizens without feeling responsible for their well-being (Lemke, 2001). Government workers shift from seeing themselves as public servants, entrusted with furthering the public good, to becoming responsive to market conditions and contributing to the success of government enterprises (Steger and Roy, 2010). More discussion of the role of public employees and of public administration under a neoliberal regime appears in the following section on new public management.

A substantial literature criticizes neoliberalism, often seeking not so much to refine concepts or to present alternative formulations as simply to inventory perceived deficiencies or to halt its advance. One area of critique concerns values with respect to social connections and responsibilities. Bourdieu (1998) argues that neoliberalism leads to a destruction of universal values and a suspicion of collective structures. S.C. Ward (2012) expresses these ideas as people being conceptualized less as socially connected citizens and moral members of a culture, and more as self-interested competitors, self-actualizing entrepreneurs, and rational consumers. W. Brown (2003) claims that the weakening of non-market morality erodes the foundations of democracy. The cult of the winner sees life as a struggle for everything (Bourdieu, 1998) in which the weak – those with lower incomes and less social and cultural capital – are disadvantaged (Rhoades and Slaughter, 2004).

Setting aside values and the desirability of democracy, Harvey's (2007) assessment at a technical level is that neoliberals favour governance by experts and elites, relying on the judiciary more than parliament and insulating key organizations such as central banks from democratic pressures. In this respect, individuals may be free to choose, but they are not supposed to construct strong collective organizations or to resist class power and governance by expert elites. Harvey also notes that the market premise that all participants have equal and sufficient access to information is often not met, with better-informed and more powerful actors therefore having a self-reinforcing advantage.

After two decades of hegemony, some commentators have suggested that a post-neoliberal period may be arising (Hunter, 2013), drawing upon such evidence as Craig and Porter's (2003) term "inclusive liberalism" and the United Kingdom's "third way" politics (Giddens, 1999). The argument is not that neoliberal economic ideology is being abandoned but rather that a balance is now being sought between right-wing economics and left-wing social policy. The view of P. Roberts and Peters (2008) is that by the late 1990s, the dogmatism of the neoliberal right was being questioned as a serious threat to social justice, national cohesion, effective public administration, and even democracy itself.

Public Choice Theory

Public choice theory, especially the portions of that literature dealing with bureaucracy, helps explain the receptivity of North American governments to using neoliberalism in the administration of postsecondary education – not hitherto a particularly problematic or contentious aspect of public administration.

Public choice theory uses economic methods and concepts to analyze the political process with respect to the workings of politicians and bureaucrats. It concludes that government is inherently inefficient and that free riding and the strategic concealment of individual preferences undermine the legitimacy of democracy (Mueller, 2004). Although public choice theory examines how political decision making can lead to results that do not seem to be what the electorate wants, my emphasis in this review is on the subfield that studies bureaucracy and the public officials who either provide or regulate postsecondary education.

The seminal works on public choice were written in the 1960s. Subsequent literature tended to build on those foundations, rather than to shift them. It did not seek empirical verification of its theoretical conclusions, at least not in the early years (Devine, 2004). Buchanan and Tullock (1962) became the leading proponents (Butler, 2012), concluding that the public interest cannot be derived from the aggregation of individual preferences and that any coherent social welfare approach will always involve some groups imposing their will on others (Olssen et al., 2004).

Tullock (1965) and Downs (1967) portray bureaucracy as shaped by employees acting in their own self-interest, a sharp departure from the way that rational choice had previously been applied to organizations (Moe, 1997). However, it was the work of Niskanen (1971) on bureaucratic growth and budget maximization that became the most influential (Moe, 1997). Stigler (1971) concludes that regulated groups have incentives to co-opt their regulators. The stage was set for the adoption of new public management techniques based on the conclusions that regulation does not work very well, bureaucrats are self-serving, and special interest groups dominate politics.

Scruton (2007) encapsulates the negative attitude toward the public sector that is evident in many public choice articles:

> By adopting an ideology which favors the needy, the minorities, and the powerless, the bureaucrat legitimizes the transfer of funds to his own profession, and makes available to himself and his colleagues the means to live comfortably at public expense while enjoying enhanced social status as a purveyor of official charity. (p. 568)

With public choice theory providing respectability to skepticism about the efficiency and effectiveness of bureaucracies, and with Keynesian economics withering under global recessions and neoliberal critiques, governments across the Western world became increasingly receptive in the 1990s to ways of reforming public administration. The approaches that emerged came to be known collectively as new public management.

New Public Management

Neoliberalism is an ideology involving many concepts and principles that need to be operationalized. Political rhetoric and official policy rationales may espouse a neoliberal philosophy, but these do not guarantee that what is implemented is consistent with neoliberal tenets. Conversely, neoliberal actions can be quietly taken with no accompanying verbiage. The resulting question concerns the markers that can be used to identify neoliberal actions with respect to postsecondary policy, regardless of what is or is not being said. My answer is that although new public management (NPM) is not a direct outcome of neoliberalism, and although proponents of other political and economic approaches can use many of its techniques, NPM has been a primary means by which Western governments have expressed neoliberalism in the public sector (Marginson, 2012).

"New public management," a term popularized by Hood (1991), is an ideology that brings neoliberal ideas about marketization and the state into the public sector. It is also a set of practices and techniques. The ideological aspect of NPM seeks to foster six behaviours (Christensen, 2008; Gültekin, 2011; Lynn, 2006; Pollitt and Bouckaert, 2011; Tolofari, 2005):

- a focus on outputs, performance, and results rather than inputs, effort, and procedural compliance
- attention to customer service and a user orientation
- cutting costs and red tape to increase efficiency
- promoting the benefits of competition and quasi-markets
- empowering employees to be problem solvers and to find innovative ways of achieving goals
- taking a business-oriented approach to government.

Several techniques are viewed as especially helpful for achieving these goals (Lynn, 2006; Pollitt and Bouckaert, 2011; Tolofari, 2005):

- deregulation and privatization
- decentralization and detaching policy formulation from policy execution
- creation of small, single-purpose organizations that do not overlap with other organizations

- contracting and the use of principal-agent arrangements, with the monitoring of performance targets
- competition for funding
- performance pay.

Table 2, excerpted and paraphrased from N. Roberts (1999, July), highlights some of the differences between NPM and previous Weberian conceptions of public administration.

Hood and Peters' (2004) assessment of NPM reformers is that they were selective, casual, and uncritical in the type of administrative theory and evidence they employed. From this viewpoint, the NPM movement was essentially ideological, consistent with an implementation driven from the top by politicians (Tolofari, 2005). In some countries, NPM seems to have been adopted partly just to join an international trend and was used to address issues from the perspectives of practitioners rather than theorists (Lynn, 2006).

The Canadian federal government, after making some pragmatic reforms and mild efforts to downsize, was lukewarm to NPM. Haligan (2011) calls Canada the most enigmatic of the anglophone countries with respect

TABLE 2
Public administration principles

Dimension	Traditional model	New public management
Agency	Laws and political processes	Competitive markets, individualistic self-interest, customer orientation
Key success	Equity, responsiveness, political appropriateness	Efficiency, effectiveness, customer satisfaction
Values	Public interest, consistency of bureaucracy with the electorate	Service quality, accountability, valuing of the private sector
Structure	Hierarchy	Networks of self-organizing teams
Jobs	Standardized, formalized	Multi-tasked, outcomes oriented
Techniques	Routinized, sequential	Customized, co-operation with private sector
Rewards	Rule-based	Incentive-based
Culture	Follow rules, minimize risk, maintain stability	Manage risks, solve problems, make improvements

to NPM in that it was the first to explore management reforms but slow to adopt them. He sees public service in Canada as remaining unmanagerialized in several respects. Managerialism in this context is the belief that organizations function best when power, control, and decision making are centralized among professionally trained and supposedly objective managers (S.C. Ward, 2012).

Lorenz (2012), writing about NPM in universities, claims that neoliberalism in the public sector was characterized by just two features: free market rhetoric and intensive managerial control practices. His view is that NPM promoted the takeover by distant managers of activities that were formerly run by professionals in accordance with their own standards, resulting in a loss of autonomy. As something of a counterpoint to Lorenz's perspective, Christensen (2008) finds that, worldwide, the decentralizing management techniques of NPM, by which managers were empowered to choose the appropriate way of meeting government goals, have been more prevalent than centralizing ones.

In reviewing the literature about the effects of NPM on public sector efficiency, Andrews (2011) concludes that despite the many claims and counter-claims, there remains a dearth of compelling evidence to support any position about the effects of NPM. A theme in studies by political scientists has been that NPM undermines political control as the distance to subordinate units increases, as services become fragmented and therefore challenging to co-ordinate, and as administration becomes dominated by judicial processes (Christensen, 2008). The vertical separation of policy making and implementation, and the horizontal splitting of agencies into single-purpose agencies, has made co-operation across organizational boundaries more difficult (Christensen and Lægreid, 2007; Lynn, 2006). Thus, post-NPM concepts such as joined-up government and whole-government have emerged (Bogdanor, 2005).

Institutional Theory

Neoliberalism creates competitive, uncertain environments for public postsecondary institutions in which little can be taken for granted, and self-interest is rewarded. If postsecondary institutions have experienced such environments, one would expect to see them engaging in competitive quasi-market-like behaviours.

Institutional theory helps explain change and stability in institutions by examining their relationship with other *institutions* and the broader environment. It also helps explain why competition and market behaviours do not necessarily focus on increasing efficiency in organizations. Among its many concepts, three are useful for understanding competitive behaviour in educational organizations: attempts to enhance organizational reputation (external legitimacy), the copying of high-status competitors that results in organizations looking similar (mimetic isomorphism), and the adoption of high-level goals that have little impact at the frontlines (loose coupling).

An *institution* is a sociological concept concerning sets of norms that are generalized across a group of people as a common way of acting, thinking, and feeling; they entail power relationships that help entrench them (J. Scott, 2007). Examples include private property, marriage, democracy, and professionalism. Lincoln (1995) emphasizes that *institutions* acquire meaning and stability in their own right rather than as means to an end. They are widely followed without debate and are long lasting (Tolbert and Zucker, 1983); indeed, they may be so taken for granted that alternative ways of seeing the world are unthinkable (Zucker, 1983).

Political science, economics, and sociology have all developed large literatures with differing emphases on and analyses of *institutions*. It is from the sociological stream, particularly as it interacts with organizational studies within administrative science, that the following material is drawn. Selznick (1949), especially, brought *institutionalism* into organizational studies through his work on the Tennessee Valley Authority (Gray, 2008).

Organizations sometimes behave in ways that defy economic logic or seem irrational; *institutional* theory offers a way of making sense of these situations (Suddaby, 2010). It provides an intermediate-level explanation, more than simple description or isolated case studies but less than universal generalization (W.R. Scott, 2014). Increasingly, under the rubric of neo-institutionalism, scholars seek to contextualize their analyses, situating organizations in their wider environment and social context, using an open systems approach (Pedersen and Dobbin, 2006). Gray (2008) sees the old *institutionalism* more as a theory of stability, whereas neoinstitutionalism incorporates attention to change.

According to Gray (2008), the term "neoinstitutional" was introduced in the mid-1990s, shifting attention from what happens inside an organization to also consider the broader environment in which it operates. The defining characteristic of neoinstitutionalism, in the view of Powell and Colyvas (2008), is a focus on the organizational field, which W.R. Scott (2014) defines as a collection of diverse, interdependent organizations that participate in a common meaning system. If we take into account both competitive and co-operative pressures that shape organizations, their repertoire of possible options is bound by the rules, norms, and beliefs of the multiple organizational fields in which they function (W.R. Scott, 2014).

Neoinstitutionalism considers questions of the legitimacy of an organization within its relevant organizational field. C. Carter and Clegg (2011) propose that legitimacy is the master concept of neoinstitutionalism, with the goal being to understand the ways by which the socially constructed external world shapes how people and organizations structure their categories of thought and resulting actions. Legitimacy is the first concept I draw from *institutional* theory.

In addition to material resources and technical information, organizations require social acceptability and credibility if they are to survive (W.R. Scott, 2001). Organizational legitimacy helps in accessing resources and markets easily, especially as some stakeholders will engage only with organizations they view as legitimate (A.D. Brown, 1998). Meyer and Scott (1983) describe a completely legitimate organization as one about which no questions could be raised. In a similar vein, Suchman (1995) defines legitimacy as a generalized perception that actions are desirable, proper, or appropriate.

Legitimacy is the basis on which prestige, a favourable (and often culturally conservative) social evaluation, emerges. In contrast, reputation (a generalized expectation about future performance) and status (a competitive ranking) may concern organizations that are not viewed as especially legitimate (Deephouse and Suchman, 2008).

Meyer and Rowan (1977) provide a linkage between legitimacy and organizational form: sometimes innovations are adopted not because they are seen as improving performance but because they enhance the reputation of the organization as a progressive, responsive entity. When the best means of producing desired outputs are ambiguous, as is the case in education, signalling credibility and legitimacy to key stakeholders becomes an important consideration (Morphew and Huisman, 2002). Organizational structure and nomenclature are means of sending such signals, which leads to the second concept from *institutional* theory, namely mimetic isomorphism.

Isomorphism is a similarity in form or structure, sometimes with the implication that the corresponding entities may have had different origins. In *institutional* theory, this type of conformity among organizations can arise from external cues in the organizational field about effective ways to enhance legitimacy and compete for resources. DiMaggio and Powell (1983) identify three mechanisms that lead to isomorphism: coercive (requirements from regulatory bodies, such as legislation to establish the governance structure of universities), normative (such as professional standards and expectations generated by the shared formal education of workers), and mimetic (imitative). DiMaggio and Powell (1983) propose that mimetic responses usually result from standard reactions to uncertainty, especially where goals are ambitious (Levy, 2006) and the means to achieve them are unclear; if an organization is uncertain of what to do, it may opt to copy a high-status peer. Also, an organization that looks similar to others is more likely to get a positive evaluation based on improved comprehensibility (Karlsson, 2008).

Despite efforts to foster legitimacy by adopting recognizable forms, an organization may simultaneously maintain some distinctive characteristics to gain a competitive advantage through differentiation and as its culture evolves (Pedersen and Dobbin, 2006). In an article about academic drift – the tendency among postsecondary institutions toward the structures and norms typical of prestigious universities – Morphew and Huisman (2002) consider the countervailing forces of homogenization and heterogenization from the point of view of *institutional* theory. More recently, Tight (2015) and Holmberg and Hallonsten (2015) have drawn upon concepts of legitimacy and isomorphism in neoinstitutional theory to help explain academic drift, including the related concepts of vertical extension (e.g., R. Schultz and Stickler, 1965) and mission creep (e.g., Gonzales, 2012).

Loose coupling is the third concept from *institutional* theory. Another tension within organizations is that the technical activities to achieve goals may vary from the expectations of policymakers and external stakeholders, so that actual practices do not match official positions (Parsons, 1960; Weick, 1976). Meyer and Rowan (1977) provide several explanations as to why the structural elements of organizations may be loosely linked, rules ignored, decisions weakly implemented, and evaluation systems feeble. Burch (2007) posits that loose coupling is one of the core constructs in analyzing educational reform.

Loosely coupled organizations may nevertheless perform well and may represent a functional compromise when change is externally imposed, rather than internally accepted. Loose coupling may also arise where there are high symbolic or legitimacy gains to acceding to external pressures but where implementation is expensive or difficult (Meyer and Rowan, 1977).

My use of *institutional* and neoinstitutional literature helps to explain the responses of particular postsecondary institutions and groups of institutions to competitive pressures. The responses may include increased efforts to cultivate prestigious images through such means as membership in high-status postsecondary organizations and strategies to improve rankings in national and international league tables. The theory suggests that postsecondary institutions will be apt to copy the forms and terminology of other institutions in their current sector and of other sectors into which they aspire to move. As inconsistencies materialize between market pressures and the technical and values bases of educators, instances of strategic decoupling will become more commonplace.

3

Clear Intentions (1960–79)

The three periods I use to depict the contemporary history of postsecondary education in British Columbia are examined in this and the following two chapters. Each chapter begins with a period overview to set the stage for analyzing one or two significant historical moments within the period. (Historical moments are much shorter than periods, involve at least two postsecondary sectors, and mark disjunctures in developmental trajectories.) The overviews also provide a vehicle for highlighting developments in the smaller postsecondary sectors that figure less prominently in the historical moments and that have received little attention in the literature.

The system of public postsecondary institutions that began emerging in the early 1960s developed along a consistent trajectory for two decades, during which the intentions of the provincial government regarding postsecondary education were clear and widely shared. Then, in the 1980s, a second period emerged as the original assumptions and certainties began to fade, first with respect to non-academic education and then in the academic sphere. The 1990s became a complex and sometimes perplexing decade.

The election of a new provincial government in 2001 led to a number of changes in postsecondary education that marked the beginning of a third period. By 2010, the new era seemed to be losing momentum, and in the past few years, it seems that the pendulum may be swinging back toward policies from the past. Nevertheless, many of the reforms and developments of the previous decade (since the early 2000s) have persisted.

It is sufficient to view changes since 2010 as constituting modifications within a period, rather than to divide the years since 2000 into two periods.

Following the period overview, each chapter continues with a detailed depiction of one or two historical moments, each of which I analyze from the perspectives of the three policy rationales: fairness and social justice, human capital formation, and marketization.

Period Overview

Although it was not evident in 1960 what the future scope and size of the BC postsecondary system would be, a few important actions by the provincial government, such as its response to the Macdonald Report of 1962 and its 1971 decision to meld postsecondary vocational schools with community colleges, resulted in an unambiguous and shared vision that endured until the early 1980s. These decisions provided the foundation for the postsecondary system as it exists today.

Victoria's response to growing public pressure for better access to postsecondary education was to massively expand university and college education after the Macdonald Report. It was the federal government, however, that took the lead in expanding the vocational sector, with the BC government again in a responsive mode (its default position regarding postsecondary education).

For fifteen years following the Macdonald Report, the public system grew significantly. Although it diversified, the diversification was along a fairly consistent trajectory that saw gaps filled more than new directions taken. Although smaller, the private sector has nevertheless played a significant role in the province. It, however, was fairly stable from 1960 to 1980 and was concentrated in the southwest, whereas public postsecondary education expanded across the province.

Public Sector

Dennison and Gallagher (1986) describe the 1960s as a golden age for public education in Canada. In British Columbia, the Macdonald Report (Macdonald, 1962) ushered in both an expansion and a new structure for the postsecondary system. Macdonald recommended increasing undergraduate education through the creation of two four-year colleges in the metropolitan southwest and the formation of comprehensive two-year community colleges throughout the province. Influenced by the tiered and co-ordinated system in California (Johnston, 2005), the proposal for a university transfer component in the community colleges was an American feature that was emulated in only one other Canadian province, Alberta.

Victoria reacted favourably and rapidly to the Macdonald Report but not entirely as recommended. Whereas it launched new universities, its legislation for the two-year college sector was merely enabling, providing a mechanism by which one or more school districts could establish regional colleges. Due to this lack of leadership and the dependence on regional coalitions to create colleges, more than twelve years elapsed before the system of fourteen (later fifteen) colleges was completed. In contrast, the system of three research universities was established within three years.

Colleges and school districts eventually became separate legal entities under the Colleges and Provincial Institutes Act of 1977. By 1983, school trustees no longer sat on college boards (Beinder, 1986), and the divide between the K–12 and postsecondary sectors became more complete.

Institutes under the Colleges and Provincial Institutes Act were sub-baccalaureate bodies with a province-wide mandate to focus on particular applied fields (e.g., the Pacific Marine Training Institute), distinctive delivery methods (e.g., the Open Learning Institute), or specific student populations (e.g., the Institute of Indigenous Government). Four were continuations or modifications of previous institutions, and two were created in 1978.[1]

It is difficult to categorize the provincial institutes, which reached a maximum number of seven in the early 1980s. They were founded over a period of more than fifty years in an unsystematic, opportunistic manner. They did not fit within the planned structure of the public postsecondary system that emerged in the early 1960s, but rather co-existed with it. Nevertheless, the policy convention eventually came to treat colleges and institutes as comprising a single sector, especially with respect to funding.

As new universities and colleges were being created in the 1960s, a parallel development was occurring in vocational education due to the federal Technical and Vocational Training Assistance Act of 1960. British Columbia drew upon federal funding for capital facilities to expand the rudimentary system of postsecondary vocational schools. By 1970, this consisted of the Vancouver Vocational Institute, operated by the Vancouver School Board, and eight campuses of the Department (later Ministry) of Education's BC Vocational School (Cowin, 2012b), which were spread across the province. Two planned campuses of the BC Vocational School were never opened, cancelled by a new provincial government in 1972, who opted for community colleges in those regions.

The BC Vocational School was highly centralized, with campuses administered directly by the Department of Education in Victoria. Whereas vocational and trades training has been tightly controlled in British Columbia, universities have been as independent as any public postsecondary institution in the Western world (see Skolnik and Jones, 1992, for a comparison of Canada and the United States). Colleges have occupied an intermediate position in terms of centralization, with provincial government influences fluctuating over the decades (Gaber, 2002).

Between 1971 and 1976, Victoria merged the vocational schools with their neighbouring community colleges, providing a boost for the latter.[2] The official rationale for this was to reduce the status gap between academic and vocational studies by co-locating them and to provide better opportunities for introducing general education into job training. Dennison (1997) observes that the policy was also partly prompted by the unwillingness of voters to pass referenda to build permanent facilities for colleges.

Some instructors in both vocational and academic/technical programs resented the mergers (Goard, 1977). Despite occasional government pronouncements about the need for trades training, and regular anxieties expressed by academics about growing perceptions of vocationalism in higher education, indicators such as funding for equipment replacement, enrolment patterns, and scholarly and professional publications would suggest that vocational education has in fact become a less significant component of the postsecondary system.[3] Whereas vocational education peaked in terms of its health and status in the late 1960s, the university sector continually thrived and was less complicated than the other postsecondary sectors until the late 1980s.

In the apprenticeship world, where several years of on-the-job training are interspersed with short classroom components in public or private institutions, the federal-provincial Apprenticeship Training Agreement of 1964 provided funding to expand apprenticeship training across the country.[4] Partly as a result of technological change, though, the BC Department of Labour, the government branch that administered apprenticeship, indicated in its 1971 annual report that technical training (the classroom component of apprenticeship) was in a state of flux.[5] The Goard Report on vocational education (Goard, 1977) noted a profound lack of co-ordination among the multiplicity of competing agencies (public and private, federal and provincial) that were involved in vocational, pre-apprenticeship, and apprenticeship training. Expressing the ongoing uncertainty about direction, the Provincial Apprenticeship Board, an advisory body, issued a report in 1984 on the future of apprenticeship, but little resolution was achieved (Provincial Apprenticeship Board, 1984).

By the end of the 1970s, the province had a three-pronged strategy for bringing postsecondary education to its far-flung regions. The foundation was a network of comprehensive, two-year colleges providing university transfer courses, career preparation programs, and developmental (secondary-level upgrading) offerings. The Open University in England influenced the philosophy of the second prong (Moran, 1993) – namely, the new Open Learning Institute, which offered distance education.[6] The third prong consisted of special funding from the province to universities to provide upper-level courses, sometimes leading to degree completion, in communities outside the urban southwest. This non-metropolitan programs initiative involved the continuing education departments of universities, a component of the postsecondary system that merits separate mention.

Continuing education offerings in public institutions have been extensive, but good enrolment data have proved elusive, and the activities have tended to be on the margins of institutions. As a result, continuing education has been characterized as an invisible giant (G.R. Selman, 1988). Except for a period in the 1970s, when the Ministry of Education established a continuing education branch, the attitude of the provincial government has been one of benign neglect.

M. Selman (2005) divides postsecondary continuing education across Canada into three periods: a social movement from the 1920s to the 1950s, professionalization and institutionalization in the 1960s and 1970s, and commercialization and competition since the 1980s. Differing BC institutions have moved through the phases at various times and rates, with the rural instances most resistant to losing a social and community development mandate in favour of marketization.

Private Sector

The for-profit, private career college sector was relatively stable until the early 1980s, notwithstanding the number of registered schools that grew gradually from 100 in 1963 to 165 in 1980. The first enrolment reports for the sector were not generated until 1978, at which time nineteen thousand students were listed (Cowin, 2013b). The trade schools section of the new BC Apprenticeship and Training Development Act of 1977 allowed regulations to be made by the minister of labour, rather than requiring cabinet approval.

Postsecondary education for BC Aboriginal students has two streams that span the public and private sectors: the larger-scale programs and services within public institutions and the small-scale offerings of the not-for-profit, Aboriginal-governed institutions (Cowin, 2011). Until 1970, Aboriginal students as a group were largely invisible in BC postsecondary education. A few isolated initiatives had started, such as the private Native Education Centre (now College) in Vancouver in 1967 and UBC's Native Indian Teacher Education Program in 1974, but it was the 1980s that saw the beginnings of broader-scale activity.

Like education for Aboriginal students, faith-based education is driven by cultural and other values. Both sectors have faced financial challenges, but these differed in that faith-based postsecondary institutions have received no public operating or capital funding and are therefore very sensitive to tuition fee and enrolment levels.[7] A major financial hurdle facing Aboriginal institutions, on the other hand, is that though funding has often been public, from both federal and provincial governments, it has tended to be short-term or project-based rather than ongoing.

The faith-based sector in British Columbia occupies an awkward space where provincial policy seems to have no shared principles or guidelines – a more extreme case of the situation experienced by provincial institutes.

Decisions were made on an ad hoc basis as situations arose, and the sector developed largely on a separate track with only a few points of convergence or overlap with the public system. Federal postsecondary policy was relevant only with respect to student financial aid and, rarely, institutional eligibility for research grants.

The BC attitude to faith-based institutions can be traced back to at least the 1908 act that established the University of British Columbia as strictly non-sectarian (though a clause did make provision for affiliated theological schools to grant a post-baccalaureate bachelor of divinity degree, and land was set aside on the UBC campus for a theological precinct). The background to this part of the act was that churches had established a number of denominational colleges in central and eastern Canada, and these institutions had proven challenging for provincial governments, especially when it came to questions of public funding for university education (see Jones, 1997, and Christie, 1997, for the flavour of these challenges in Ontario and Nova Scotia respectively; see Harris, 1976, for details). British Columbia managed to avoid similar difficulties but never did articulate the basis on which it would permit faith-based institutions to operate. The practice emerged of conferring degree-granting authority to individual institutions through specific acts introduced as private member's bills.

In the faith-based sector, a handful of Bible schools for lay people and seminaries for training clergy, Notre Dame University College, and Trinity Junior College existed at the time of the Macdonald Report in 1962. In 1963, the BC legislature passed the Notre Dame University of Nelson Act, and Notre Dame became the first private university in the province with the authority to grant baccalaureate degrees. The legislation for Trinity Junior College was amended in 1971 to rename it Trinity Western College and then again in 1979 to permit it to grant bachelor's degrees. Whereas Trinity Western flourished and is now a university that grants master's degrees, Notre Dame struggled and closed in 1977 (Universities Council of British Columbia, 1976).[8]

Several small theological schools opened during the 1960s and 1970s. The most interesting was Regent College in 1968, the first graduate school of theology in North America to focus on educating the laity. It quickly established a world reputation, albeit in a small field.

TABLE 3
BC postsecondary system, 1960 and 1979

Sector	1960	1979
Public universities	UBC	UBC, SFU, University of Victoria
Public colleges and institutes	3 vocational schools Continuing education through school districts Grade 13	14 community colleges 6 institutes Continuing education at all institutions and some school districts
Private academic (small institutions)	Notre Dame University College	Trinity Western College Some external institutions beginning to deliver niche instruction Some high school completion and ESL colleges
Private career colleges (small)	100 registered colleges	137 registered colleges
Aboriginal-governed (small)	–	Several, with a combined enrolment of fewer than 1,000
Faith-based (small)	About 12, although some were residential at UBC and not instructional	Mergers, closures, and openings resulted in a net increase of 6
Apprenticeship	3,000 apprentices	13,800 apprentices

Summary

Table 3 summarizes the dramatic change and growth over two decades in the BC postsecondary system.

Historical Moment: The Macdonald Era

This historical moment lasted from 1960 to about 1964. I present a fair amount of earlier material to help explain why events unfolded as they did in the early 1960s and mention a few subsequent developments to bring closure to certain topics.

Although there is no doubt that the Macdonald Report of 1962 was of seminal importance, and it is a convenient shorthand explanation for the rise of the contemporary BC postsecondary system, the forces propelling educational change were rather more complex than a single report. They also evolved over many years. The report was silent about several postsecondary sectors, and its existence does not account for developments in them. Furthermore, the issues raised by Macdonald were not unique to British Columbia and were in fact being considered in other jurisdictions. Macdonald's genius lay not so much in generating new insights and ideas as in drawing together the work and discussions of the previous years to encapsulate a growing consensus in British Columbia.

What I am calling the Macdonald era was the source of a societal accord that lasted throughout the 1960s and into the 1970s regarding the character and desirable development of the province's postsecondary institutions. Although never articulated in a comprehensive and systematic manner across all sectors, the vision was firmly established in the early 1960s, and it served as a touchstone for two decades.

Macdonald Report

The Macdonald Report of 1962, initiated by UBC's new president, John Macdonald, and not commissioned by government, marked a substantial departure from the approach of his predecessor, Norman MacKenzie. The report's background lies in the late 1950s, although some commentators have contended that the seeds were planted decades earlier.

Thirty years prior to the report, a UBC graduate completed a master's thesis at Stanford University (Knott, 1932), proposing that British Columbia should adopt the junior college concept of California and Texas. He suggested Victoria College, the two normal (teacher training) schools, and Grade 13 senior matriculation as the nucleus from which to launch a college system.[9] He discussed future enrolment demand and proposed seven centres in the BC hinterland where colleges might best be located. Three decades later, Macdonald also used California's approach to higher education as a model for British Columbia, recommended the establishment of community colleges, argued for enrolment growth based on demographic data, and proposed locations for colleges and universities arising from geographic considerations.

Knott felt that echoes of the Putnam-Weir Report (Putnam and Weir, 1926) regarding the BC school system had been evident in discussions about the potential for junior colleges in the province. Beinder (1983) perceives precedents for college development in two subsequent commissions of inquiry. In his view, the Cameron Report (M.A. Cameron, 1945)

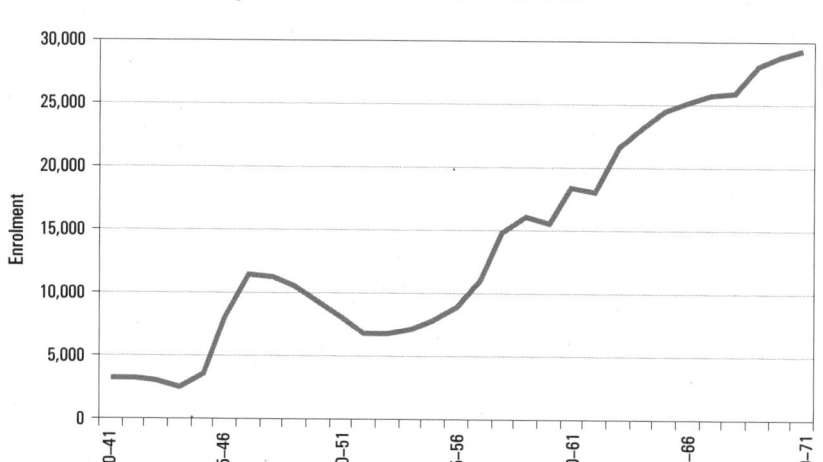

FIGURE 3
UBC enrolment, full- and part-time combined, 1940–41 to 1970–71

Source: University of British Columbia (2017)

on educational finance was focused on inequalities in educational opportunity in rural communities, a concern that emanated from grassroots citizens around the province rather than from government officials. In a similar vein, Beinder notes that the Chant Commission (Chant, 1960) recommended equalizing educational opportunity throughout the province.

The more proximate precursors to the Macdonald Report, both internal and external to UBC, emerged in the mid- to late 1950s. Internally, enrolment at UBC had soared after the Second World War, with an influx of returning veterans, and then dropped in the early 1950s as the veterans completed their studies (Figure 3). Enrolment recovered by the mid-1950s and, with a postwar baby boom and rising postsecondary participation rates, some faculty and administrators at UBC were becoming concerned that it was about to face unprecedented and overwhelming enrolment demand (Johnston, 2005). Their fears proved justified.

Macdonald's predecessor, Norman (Larry) MacKenzie, had put considerable effort into advocating for more funding for universities nationally and for UBC provincially. Worried that any new academic institutions in British Columbia could further restrict provincial grants to his own university, he thus suggested that they be affiliated with and tributary to it. Waite (1987) bluntly describes this approach as the "UBC empire principle" (p. 186), contrasting it with the stance taken by Victoria College that it should become a full-fledged university in its own right. Initially, MacKenzie's position seemed to be endorsed in that a 1958 amendment to the Public Schools Act enabled school boards to establish colleges on the condition that they were affiliated with UBC. The amendments reflected a concern for equitable educational opportunity across the province (Beinder, 1983), but the requirement that colleges be affiliated with UBC was unappealing. No action ensued.

This did not indicate a lack of interest by school districts in forming colleges, but rather unease about the conditions under which they should operate. The BC School Trustees Association had struck a committee in 1961 to consider its responsibility for continuing education, given growing enrolments in Grade 13 and in upgrading and applied courses for adults in night school (Beinder, 1986). In their brief to Macdonald, the school trustees were clear that colleges should be extensions of the school system and that they themselves were dismayed by the existence of public vocational schools that were separate from it (Dennison, 1979a). Macdonald incorporated their wishes into his recommendations, decoupling the proposed colleges from UBC and instead calling for a province-wide academic board to guarantee educational standards. Something of a parallel development occurred in Alberta, where the Public Junior Colleges Act of 1958 was amended in the early 1960s to give colleges more independence from the University of Alberta (Berghofer and Vladicka, 1980).

If a single event were to be selected as marking the prelude to the Macdonald Report, a national Canadian university enrolment projection made in the mid-1950s (Sheffield, 1955) is a strong candidate. The predicted dramatic increase in enrolment over the ensuing decade was seen as credible, and it spurred university presidents, who were already preparing an advocacy campaign for more federal funding, into planning for a massive expansion of academic education in Canada (D. Cameron, 1991).

UBC was thus not alone in anticipating large enrolment demand during the coming years and in seeing the need for a system-wide plan. In the United Kingdom, for example, the Robbins Committee had been established in 1961 to examine such topics as access to higher education and the competitive advantages of an educated workforce (Committee on Higher Education, 1963).

In Canada, 1961 was also proving to be a significant year for postsecondary planning. In Quebec, the highly influential Parent Commission was launched that year, issuing five volumes between 1963 and 1965 (Royal Commission of Inquiry on Education in the Province of Quebec, 1965). Responding to the demands for democratization of education and for mass education, it recommended the creation of a distinctive college system, the Colleges d'enseignement general et professionnel (Cegeps), which was accepted by government. In New Brunswick, a royal commission on higher education, chaired by John Deutsch, was also established to study issues of funding and access (Royal Commission on Higher Education in New Brunswick, 1962). Alberta founded an advisory committee, the Survey Committee on Higher Education, in existence from 1961 to 1965, to assess future enrolment demand and to recommend responses (D. Cameron, 1991). One of the first actions of Ontario's Advisory Committee on University Affairs, formed by the government in 1961, was to prepare some enrolment projections. The response to these, the Deutsch Report of 1962 for the university presidents of Ontario (Committee of Presidents, 1963), became the blueprint over the next decade for expanding universities in Ontario (D. Cameron, 1991).

Against that national and international backdrop, Johnston (2005) describes some of the planning that UBC faculty had done for BC system expansion in the years prior to Macdonald's arrival in 1962. Walter Hardwick, for example, was a geographer who had prepared a report that he took to the UBC Senate about a location for a second university campus in the Vancouver area. He had also been promoting the American community college model as desirable for British Columbia, following his exposure to such colleges during his year's study in Wisconsin. Macdonald, who had been the nominee for president of the UBC Faculty Association, incorporated the prior work of such faculty into his report.

Response to the Macdonald Report

Well received, the Macdonald Report led to a shared vision for college and university education in British Columbia, but the vision that government enacted was not identical to what Macdonald had proposed. With respect to universities, he had recommended that Victoria College, which by then was offering some four-year programs leading to a degree conferred by UBC, be given the option of determining whether it wished to become an independent, degree-granting undergraduate college. He also proposed that a new four-year degree-granting college be created in the western Fraser Valley area of Greater Vancouver. In other words, expensive professional programs (such as engineering), graduate studies, and research should, in the view of Macdonald, all remain the exclusive purview of UBC. Rejecting the notion that UBC should be the flagship university in British Columbia, the government instead created the University of Victoria and Simon Fraser University as full-fledged research universities that could offer master's and doctoral programs and that, in principle, were identical to UBC. (As an extension of the former Victoria College, the University of Victoria was able to open quickly in 1963, and Simon Fraser was an "instant university" that opened in 1965.)

With respect to two-year regional colleges, Macdonald had proposed that the first three should be located in Greater Vancouver and the southern Interior towns of Kelowna and Castlegar, with four additional colleges to be established by 1971. He expected that Kelowna would become a four-year college by 1970. The provincial government accepted the American comprehensive community college model, with its university transfer component, but remained silent about any of them ever becoming four-year, degree-granting colleges.

It endorsed the concept of community colleges providing both geographical and social access, and retained the 1958 concept of close association with school districts that Macdonald had also espoused. Amendments to the Public Schools Act enabled school districts to hold plebiscites (approval in principle) and referenda (authorization for capital construction) to form colleges (Dennison, 1979a). The college boards consisted of representatives from locally elected school boards, and half the operating funds of colleges came from local property taxes and tuition fees. Whereas the universities were independent institutions with province-wide mandates and provincial funding, colleges were regionally controlled and only partially funded by Victoria.

Beinder (1986) describes the approach of the province to the new college sector as unbelievably casual, with little evidence of any sort of planning. Provincial politicians seem to have vaguely expected that colleges would easily share secondary school facilities and equipment, a weak assumption. The first community college, Vancouver City (now Community) College, opened in 1965. Nine additional colleges, some with multiple campuses, had been launched by 1974.[10] The Department of Education's Task Force on the Community College (Department of Education, 1974) then considered the needs of isolated communities. This resulted in the establishment of the final four colleges,[11] serving the rural areas farthest from the southwest, directly by government and without the use of local plebiscites.

Macdonald's planning concerned higher education, which, though not explicitly defined in his report, essentially meant university education. Colleges, with their "unique character" (Macdonald, 1962, p. 51), fell within the scope of his study in that they would have a university transfer component. In recommending that they provide technical, career, and adult education (continuing education) programming, he did not elaborate what this might mean and did not discuss the implications for the postsecondary system as a whole. He briefly mentioned one vocational school (in Kelowna) and the BC Institute of Technology simply in the context of locational considerations for new colleges, but he did not comment on the existing or future vocational and apprenticeship aspects of the public postsecondary system. His emphasis set the tone for historical scholarship on BC postsecondary education ever since.

Public Vocational Schools and Technical Institutes

Although vocational institutions were established over a longer period than the five or so years that I have designated the Macdonald era, the early 1960s were a critical period for this sector, with the creation of the BC Vocational School and the opening of the first few of its permanent campuses by 1964. Also during this historical moment, the BC Institute of Technology, now the third or fourth largest postsecondary institution in the province depending on the enrolment measure, came into being.

Whereas the impetus for expanding universities and establishing college education came from within the province in the form of the Macdonald Report, the evolution of the postsecondary vocational school system, which reached its highpoint around 1970 and did not entirely disappear until

1986 (with the amalgamation of the Pacific Vocational Institute into the BC Institute of Technology), was in large measure spurred by federal government priorities.

Ottawa's interest in postsecondary education, a provincial responsibility, arose from the importance of education to the economic performance of the nation. The federal government presented its direct funding not as in support of *education* but either as *training* for adults who were already in the labour force (Sheffield, Campbell, Holmes, Kymlicka, and Whitelaw, 1982), the fostering of research, financial assistance to students, or contract training purchased for its clients (often unemployed individuals or those facing barriers to employment). The evidence of the enactment of federal educational policy has always been financial, sometimes supplemented by related verbiage in legislation, official documents, and public relations material (Trilokekar, Shanahan, Axelrod, and Wellen, 2013).

Federal legislation in support of vocational and apprenticeship training dates back to 1913, but it is the Technical and Vocational Training Assistance Act of 1960 that is the most germane for the Macdonald era. This act was the means by which Ottawa assumed a major role in occupational training, in response to national unemployment and a growing awareness of job obsolescence. At least three-quarters of the funding under the act was devoted to capital funding for provincial training facilities.

Prior to the mid-1950s, a variety of private institutions and school district night courses for adults provided the bulk of vocational and apprenticeship technical training in British Columbia. A small public postsecondary facility, the Dominion-Provincial Youth Training Centre, had opened in Nanaimo in 1936. In 1949, the Vancouver School Board opened what quickly became the province's centre of vocational training for the following decade, the Vancouver Vocational Institute.

Because of the urgent need for vocational training in the late 1950s – eventually, double shifts and even around-the-clock training occurred in a few instances at the Vancouver Vocational Institute (Rerup, 1993) – a temporary campus of the Federal-Provincial Trades and Technical Institute in Burnaby opened in 1958, with a permanent campus announced in 1959, to open officially in 1960. This school, first known locally as the Burnaby Vocational School and later renamed the Pacific Vocational

Institute, became the largest, and in some ways the flagship, campus of the network of BC Vocational School campuses across the province.

Several other campuses of the new BC Vocational School opened in 1963, taking advantage of federal funding under the Technical and Vocational Training Assistance Act for 50 percent of the capital costs. The campuses were sometimes situated on former military land owned by the federal government. The last of them opened in Dawson Creek in 1966, Terrace in 1968, and Kamloops in 1971 (Cowin, 2012b). They were centrally administered by the Department of Education in Victoria, and thus their governance contrasted with the local and independent control enjoyed by colleges and universities.

At the height of their enrolment in 1970, just prior to the government's decision to begin merging them with community colleges, the BC Vocational School and the Vancouver Vocational Institute enrolled a joint total of about twenty-six thousand students (Department of Education, 1971). To put this number in context, the University of British Columbia, by far the largest of the three universities in the province, reported twenty-nine thousand students that same year.

The origins of the BC Institute of Technology are most clearly seen in a needs assessment, the Bridge/White Survey, conducted in 1959 for the provincial government, with assistance from Ottawa (A. McArthur, 1997). With the introduction of federal funds for the capital construction of technical and vocational schools, planning for the new institute began in 1961, and the first students enrolled in 1964.

Apprenticeship

The fourth of the public postsecondary sectors of the 1960s (in addition to universities, colleges and institutes, and the vocational schools) was the apprenticeship system. It too fell outside Macdonald's vision. In fact, apprenticeship has been something of a stepchild in the BC public system, displaying a lineage and characteristics that differ from those of the other three sectors. As with other forms of vocational education, federal funding was more visible and directive than for academic education.

British Columbia's first Apprenticeship Act in 1935 was intended not to promote apprenticeship but rather to regulate and curb abuses in apprenticeship training through such means as ensuring wage increments, limiting the duration of apprenticeships, and specifying ratios of supervising journeymen to apprentices (Cowin, 2012b). Within a few years of the federal Vocational Training Co-ordination Act of 1942, British Columbia began using some of the resulting federal funding to establish classes that enabled apprentices to obtain co-ordinated theoretical instruction in classrooms throughout the entire period of their apprenticeship. The BC Department of Labour, which administered the apprenticeship system independently from the Department of Education, was at that time contemplating some pre-apprenticeship training to shorten apprenticeships. It was not until 1957, however, that pre-apprenticeship classes, ranging in duration from five to ten months, were introduced.

The federal-provincial Apprenticeship Training Agreement of 1964 was intended to expand apprenticeship. Figure 4 shows that registrations did in fact increase greatly in subsequent years. (The number of registered apprentices plateaued during the quarter century after 1975, growing only from 13,000 in 1975 to 16,000 in 2000. Pre-apprenticeship enrolment, on the other hand, increased from 2,200 to 6,200 over the same period.)

FIGURE 4
Registered apprentices and pre-apprenticeship enrolment, 1945–75

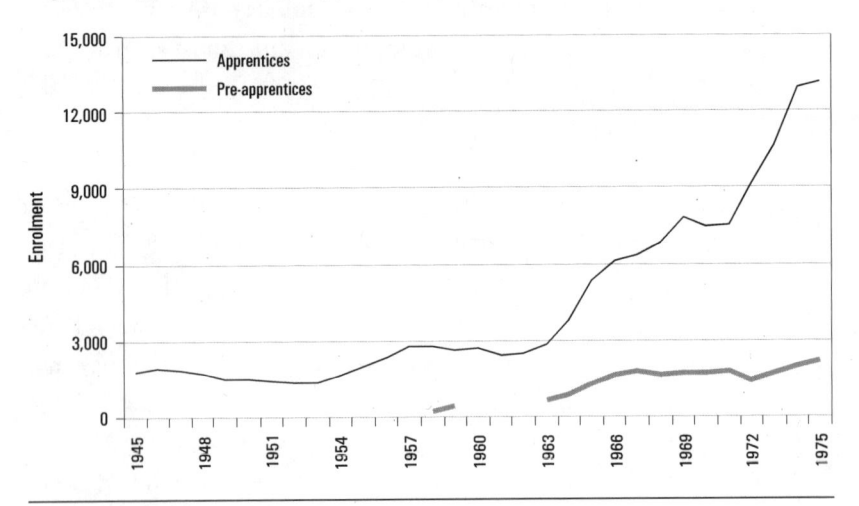

Source: BC Department of Labour annual reports, 1945–75

The BC Apprenticeship Act was amended at much the same time as the 1964 federal-provincial Apprenticeship Training Agreement came into effect, broadening provisions for the optional examination of apprentices. The primary method of ensuring educational standards remained inspections of worksites by BC government officials.

Despite receiving large amounts of funding from Ottawa, British Columbia was dissatisfied with several aspects of federal involvement with apprenticeship (Cowin, 2012b). The province complained that the 1967 federal Adult Occupational Training Act neglected co-ordination at the national level and that it treated apprenticeship as an afterthought. It argued that Ottawa should pay training allowances to all apprentices, not just to some. (By 1973, all BC apprentices received either federal or provincial funding, depending on who was sponsoring them.)

The apprenticeship system grew and became increasingly complex during the Macdonald era. The federal presence was large and sometimes at odds with BC government priorities. Technical classroom instruction was delivered by a variety of public and private institutions, some optional pre-apprenticeship training was introduced, and employers and unions influenced the availability of apprenticeships. Co-ordination became progressively more difficult across the BC Departments of Labour and of Education, especially with respect to pre-apprenticeship training, where the Department of Labour did not have exclusive jurisdiction. Whereas public universities and colleges enjoyed operating under a clear vision in the 1960s and 1970s, apprenticeship became complicated and difficult for any part of government to steer. Its boundaries were well defined and accepted, however, even if what occurred within the sector seemed chaotic at times.

Private Sector

Private postsecondary education in British Columbia has served a modest number of students dispersed among a large number of generally small institutions. During the 1960s and 1970s, it consisted of two sectors: the not-for-profit, faith-based institutions (which offered certificate and diploma programs, with the only degrees being in theology at institutions other than Notre Dame University) and occupationally oriented career colleges (which were generally profit seeking and which offered certificate and diploma programs).

The changes arising from the Macdonald Report and from federal postsecondary policy in the 1960s had little, if any, direct impact on the private career college sector. These colleges had to wait another two decades for a policy change that approached the significance of the Macdonald Report for the public college sector. In the meantime, they followed a steady path of slow net growth as institutions opened and closed, operating uncontested in parallel to the public system.

When British Columbia passed the Trades School Regulation Act in 1936, the first such legislation in Canada, the number of registered institutions, including business and correspondence schools, was about 70. The sector grew slowly and it took until the early 1960s before there were 100. In 1967, the total had reached 107 (Department of Labour, 1967).

The small faith-based sector developed independently (Cowin, 2009), yet a case can be made that Macdonald helped increase its legitimacy. In surveying the higher education landscape, he included Trinity Junior College, even though it had just opened that year, 1962, with a mere seventeen students, and treated it with the same respect as Notre Dame University College (then affiliated with St. Francis Xavier University in Nova Scotia to offer degree programs in arts and science). Likewise, he mentioned Prince George College, although it never did really get beyond providing some Grade 13 classes due to the establishment of the public College of New Caledonia. Immediately after describing these institutions, Macdonald (1962) noted "some of the greatest universities in the world are private. They have become great because they are free to meet the special demands and beliefs of their founders and supporters" (p. 45). Whatever subsequent controversies arose on other matters, Trinity quickly became a credible member of the BC transfer system, and its academic rigour was not questioned by the universities that received its transfer students.

Analysis: Macdonald Era

Social Justice
As analysts in the 1950s and 1960s examined demographic trends and postsecondary participation rates, it was taken for granted that everyone

who was motivated to pursue an academic education and could benefit from it should be able to access it. The question was not so much whether to accommodate enrolment demand but the means for doing so. It was, in part, a matter of fairness, of distributive justice, that there should be sufficient spaces for all and that those spaces should be as close as possible to the homes of students.

In structuring BC colleges as a way to respond to growing enrolment pressure, the early proponents were apt to view them as special types of institutions designed to meet the needs of students, rather than the needs of the economy, government, or educational personnel. Beinder (1983) was eloquent in describing the community colleges as a "social invention," the "crystallization of a dream of service to people" (p.1). The Assistant Deputy Minister for postsecondary education, Andrew Soles (n.d.), concurred in the early 1970s with the community service mission, explaining that "their dedication must be, as it is, to improve in every way they can, the quality of life in their region" (p. 4). He added that the college "would open the door to all who can benefit from it ... It takes away the exclusiveness – the mystery – the snobbery – the retrograde and obscurantist ways of higher education" (p. 9).

Universities, in contrast, were less likely to think of access in egalitarian and universal terms, viewing it instead in terms of meritocracy and access to the type of institution commensurate with the abilities and aptitudes of students. Macdonald (1962) bemoaned the number of unsuccessful students at UBC who were "neither suited for nor interested in university education" (p. 50). In commending the California Master Plan, he was endorsing a scheme in which the community college was seen by at least one influential California university president as the first line of defence for protecting elite education from the masses (Kerr, 1978). Whether elite and stratified postsecondary education (sometimes framed as the pursuit of educational excellence and access for qualified students) ultimately promotes or hinders social justice remains contested, but proponents of both positions claim that they seek to serve students and society in the most appropriate and best ways possible.

Exactly what benefits were expected to accrue to society as a whole from a college or university education were less clearly spelled out in much of the BC postsecondary discourse of the 1960s. With a backdrop of ideas as to how human capital formation could benefit the economy and increase the earning power of individuals, and optimism about the role of education in promoting a democratic and civil society, it did not seem essential to enumerate in any detail the advantages of expanding the postsecondary system. Rather, what seemed to propel its development was simply a perceived need for more student spaces that should be geographically accessible.

This conception of social justice was framed in individualistic terms. The closest it came to recognizing the aspirations of special groups concerned access for people living outside the metropolitan southwest. Even in this discourse, and it was a powerful one, the goals were more to replicate the opportunities of urban populations as much as possible rather than to cultivate distinctive experiences that would foster particular non-metropolitan subcultures – although the latter was not precluded, just not advocated.

An instance of social justice conceived as recognizing and respecting cultural groups was with respect to faith-based institutions. The provincial government did not seem able to articulate a position or policy about this sector, but neither was it prepared to stand in its way. It acknowledged the special interests of religious groups and continued to use the backdoor route of private member's bills to charter degree-granting institutions and to allow sub-baccalaureate schools to incorporate as non-profit societies.

In the apprenticeship world, Weiermair (1984) indicates that only in the late 1970s did apprenticeship and industrial training come to be seen nationally as important to industrial productivity, as opposed to social policy for the economically disadvantaged. This suggests that apprenticeship policy in British Columbia shifted from more of a social justice orientation in the Macdonald moment toward today's entrenched emphasis on human capital formation.

Victoria did not articulate its views about private career colleges. Such institutions were neither encouraged nor discouraged, but simply allowed to exist (provided they followed basic rules). It is not clear why they were permitted to exist. Perhaps they were seen to meet needs that the public system was not serving. (In the growing economy of the 1960s, when postsecondary participation rates remained modest, the use of private providers as a cost-saving measure for government does not seem a likely explanation.) If career colleges were viewed as complementing the public system, perhaps they could be taken as another example of a social justice interest in ensuring that everyone had access to the type of postsecondary education that he or she desired.

If social justice concerns propelled the development of the vocational school system, documentary evidence is lacking. The presence of these schools, however, may have contributed to the strong liberal education orientation of BC colleges – a contrast to the vocational orientation of colleges in some other jurisdictions. With a vocational sector already well established, the new colleges had the freedom to address other needs, such as supporting disadvantaged students across the curriculum rather than relegating them to particular programs.

Human Capital Formation

By the mid-1950s, government and the public had begun to see universities as a dependable route to economic growth and individual prosperity (D. Cameron, 1991). The Royal Commission on Canada's Economic Prospects (W.L. Gordon, 1957), for example, recommended strengthening and expanding universities as a core strategy for economic development in Canada. The launch of Sputnik by the Soviet Union and the resulting frenzy in the United States to build up scientific capabilities reinforced the notion that high levels of postsecondary education were essential to the competitive economic position of a nation. It took several more years, however, until theoretical articles such as T.W. Schultz (1960, 1961) and Becker (1964) encapsulated the emerging orthodoxy.

Johnston (2005) claims that Canadian university presidents were quick to adopt human capital perspectives as they promoted their institutions in the late 1950s:

> In selling universities to a federal government and a Canadian public that in the past had been largely indifferent, university presidents, with striking ease and assurance, adopted the argument of utility. They encouraged parents and young people to see a university education as a route to better-paying jobs and more security. And they promoted the idea of the modern university as an engine of economic growth. (p. 16)

Macdonald (1962) echoed this theme, beginning his report with a human capital argument to warn that an inadequately educated citizenry would lead to "a nation doomed to economic distress at best, and economic disaster at worst" (p. 6).

Human capital formation became the fertile ground in which the seeds of change – concern about access for a growing number of students seeking education – could blossom into an expanded public university and college system. To switch metaphors, a social justice concern for access was the spark, but human capital theory provided the fuel. The human capital rationale for state investment in public education paralleled the social justice call for more postsecondary seats.

Despite the importance of human capital formation, it does not seem that the role of colleges in fostering regional economic development in the hinterland through a skilled workforce was an especially important argument in favour of creating them. The BC resource economy was still strong in the 1960s, and rural populations, at least males, could earn good incomes and maintain a secure life with minimal levels of education. It was only since the 1980s, as employment in the resource economy declined, that interest grew in the linkage between human capital formation and regional economic growth in the non-metropolitan parts of the province. In the 1960s, the emphasis seemed to be on regional access for quality of life considerations and on the vocational education of workers rather than on what were then flourishing regional economies.

Whereas social justice themes intertwined BC government postsecondary policy, human capital arguments have been the driver for federal government initiatives. This has been evident in federal vocational and apprenticeship legislation, not only in the Macdonald era but also in the decades leading up to it:

1913	Agricultural Instruction Act
1919	Technical Education Act
1939	Youth Training Act
1940	War Emergency Training Act
1942	Vocational Training Co-ordination Act
1945	Vocational Schools Assistance agreement

1960   Technical and Vocational Training Assistance Act
1967   Adult Occupational Training Act

The importance of non-academic postsecondary education in the development of Canada's human capital can be seen in educational attainment statistics: in 1965, 48 percent of the nation's adult population age twenty-five and over had only an elementary school education or less. The situation was improving, though, and the proportion of twenty- to twenty-four-year-olds in 1965 who had not progressed beyond elementary school had dropped to 24 percent (Whittingham, 1966). These data notwithstanding, Canadians generally followed the British tradition of valuing academic education and had been resistant to vocational education for the first half of the twentieth century, with some exceptions such as during the First World War (D. Bell, 2004; Lyons, Randhawa, and Paulson, 1991).

The federal role in occupational training prior to the Macdonald era had mainly consisted of minor conditional grants (McBride, 1998). With Ottawa's overhaul of unemployment insurance in 1955 (Pal, 1988) and rising unemployment in the late 1950s, it had begun by 1960 to take a more active interest in retraining its unemployed clients for stable, long-term jobs in technological fields (D. Bell, 2004). This active interest in education in support of labour market strategies manifested structurally in funding for new vocational and technical facilities in British Columbia and other provinces, and figured prominently in the next historical moment to be analyzed.

Marketization

Marketization was the least explicit of the three policy rationales in the Macdonald era, but elements of a competitive market philosophy were nevertheless present in this Keynesian age that preceded the 1980s shift toward neoliberalism. Marketization was certainly emerging during the 1960s in the internal culture of universities as competitive research grants from the federal government, starting in the sciences, moved the emphasis from undergraduate teaching toward graduate education and knowledge generation. By the end of the 1960s, the publish-or-perish ethos was well established in BC universities, despite voices at the beginning of the decade that had cautioned against the dominance of research (Damer and Rosengarten, 2009; Johnston, 2005; MacPherson, 2012).

The expression of a market philosophy in the structure of the postsecondary system was subtler. In arguing against a centralized or unified higher education system, Macdonald (1962) claimed that institutional competition was desirable for educational excellence: "Free enterprise here, as much or more than elsewhere in society, is the essential key to progress" (p. 23). Although he wanted UBC to maintain a monopoly on graduate and professional education, Macdonald also sought institutional autonomy.

The BC government's decision to make SFU and the University of Victoria full research universities rather than undergraduate teaching colleges reflected its uneasy relationship with UBC by providing UBC with competitors, not feeder institutions. Giles (1983) quotes Minister of Education Leslie Peterson as subsequently explaining that a visit to California had shown him the desirability of competition. Macdonald (2000) himself acknowledges Premier W.A.C. Bennett's "desire to establish competition for UBC which to some degree he mistrusted" (p. 88).

The literature often frames the mechanism chosen by government for establishing public colleges in terms of local control (Dennison and Gallagher, 1986; Gaber, 2002), but it can also be viewed as a form of laissez faire, with colleges to be founded only once the local market demonstrated sufficient demand. The funding arrangement until 1977 was that local taxpayers contributed half the operating and capital costs (Dennison, 1979a), allowing for variation in the resources available to deliver the same service, depending on the local tax base and priority placed on college education. For their first decade, the provincial government maintained a hands-off approach to colleges, with no central planning or co-ordination.

The colleges, described from their inception as a unique educational setting in the Canadian context (Academic Board for Higher Education in British Columbia, 1965), faced challenges in the academic marketplace of status and prestige in establishing their legitimacy for funding and student recruitment purposes. The elitist, restrictive advice to colleges from the university-dominated Academic Board for Higher Education (Perry,

1969) – which the colleges ignored – was that "those who advocate an open-door policy fail to understand the primary purposes of colleges and the educational standards they must maintain ... or [those who enrol] too large a number of older students, will invariably interfere with the instruction of the students for whom the college is primarily intended" (Academic Board for Higher Education in British Columbia, 1966, pp. 18–19).[12] Both the types of students served and the educational philosophy of colleges meant that academic programs in colleges had to strive to establish and maintain their credibility with universities and the public.

With tight central control by the provincial government over the campuses of the BC Vocational School, and even the separate Vancouver Vocational Institute being gradually brought more within the ambit of the provincial government, it is hard to find evidence of a market philosophy in the vocational school sector. Certainly, the curriculum was sensitive to employer preferences, and enrolment demand reflected labour market conditions, but the structure and operations of the vocational schools were controlled by the state, not the market.

By definition, the private postsecondary sector – composed of faith-based institutions and career colleges in the Macdonald era – operates in a market environment. The public policy issues are how tightly government chooses to regulate these bodies, whether it generally encourages or discourages their existence, and whether students are eligible for government financial aid. During this time, the provincial government's default position seemed to be one of benign neglect. Students were not funded, and no attempt was made to foster growth. The policy seemed to be to provide only as much oversight as was needed to prevent problems from arising that would inconvenience government. This again was a laissez faire approach.

Apprenticeship is difficult to classify. It was tied to the market in that the availability of apprenticeships was dependent on employer interest and in that employers had a great deal of freedom in how they chose to deploy apprentices. On the other hand, apprenticeship was strongly regulated in certain respects such as wages and journeyman supervision. Its character was shaped by the interactions of four provincial interest groups – employers, unions, government, and educators – and not by local forces. With the availability of funding for living and travel expenses during the classroom portion of training each year, Department of Education or Labour officials sometimes assigned apprentices to vocational schools or colleges anywhere in the province depending on which institutions had unused seats, rather than on student preference or other market forces.

4

Assumptions Challenged (1980–99)

The postsecondary system in British Columbia was dynamic and growing in the 1960s and 1970s, but it was evolving in systematic ways that were easy for citizens and educators to comprehend. In the 1980s, some of the certainties and confidences about the future began to fade. In a number of areas, the ground rules for the system altered, and the postsecondary landscape became more complex.

Two historical moments are examined in this chapter, the first being unwelcomed by public institutions and the second applauded by them. The first involved a contraction in public education during the early 1980s, followed by a shift in vocational education from public institutions toward the private sector in the mid-1980s. The second moment, at the end of the 1980s, introduced a new type of postsecondary institution to British Columbia and expanded academic education in the public sector.

Period Overview

The change most commented upon in the scholarly literature on the history of BC postsecondary education from 1980 to 1999 was the transformation of five community colleges into a new institutional type, the university college. Although this development was not quantitatively significant, affecting relatively few programs and students, it blurred boundaries and altered perceptions of what had previously been a clear binary public system. The introduction of degree-granting authority to two provincial institutes was lower profile.

Even notions of the essential characteristics of a university were mildly challenged during this period by the establishment of two specialized non-traditional universities, Royal Roads and the Technical University of BC. The role of a faith-based university, Trinity Western, in liberal and professional education became controversial.

As federal training dollars shifted from public to private institutions, the career college sector blossomed while apprenticeship remained in the doldrums. The provincial government chose to move the oversight of both sectors to arm's length organizations outside of government proper.

Continuing education moved closer to the market and emphasized cost-recovery operations, in some cases competing directly with the private sector. Postsecondary education for Aboriginal students became an explicit priority in public policy.

Public Sector

An economic recession during the early 1980s resulted in both across-the-board and targeted cuts in public institutions, marking the end of the previous expansionary phase. It was in the continuing education departments of colleges that changing policy orientations, not simply questions of affordability, first became evident.

Over a two-year period beginning in 1982, the provincial government eliminated its designated funding to colleges in support of "general interest" continuing education, a term that encompassed all personal and community development courses that were not directly job-related. A further shock to colleges came in 1985, when Ottawa announced its new Canadian Jobs Strategy (CJS), explicitly promoting training by the private and voluntary sectors instead of by public colleges. This strategy resulted in a halving from 1986 to 1991 in the purchase of vocational training in public colleges by the federal government (Witter, n.d.).

One response of the public colleges to the CJS was to use continuing education departments to subcontract the delivery of training on behalf of private and non-profit organizations that were receiving CJS funds. These colleges increasingly bid on projects in partnership with private trainers and voluntary organizations (see the following section on private career colleges).

The Centre for Policy Studies in Education at UBC concluded that three distinct changes in continuing education at BC colleges had occurred in less than a decade: services to community organizations declined while those to employers increased; programming to assist disadvantaged people diminished; and priorities shifted from enfranchisement to training (Ministry of Advanced Education, Training and Technology, and Centre for Policy Studies in Education, 1992). This finding was consistent with the case made by Cruikshank (1990) that across Canada, notions of adult education as a vehicle for social change and development were being replaced by a focus on individual clients in which educators competed as businesses in markets.

At the end of the period, in 2000, the BC government withdrew funding for part-time vocational offerings (college continuing education courses and programs that were directly linked to the labour market). Thus, the public college sector faced a double funding blow from 1985 to 2000, one federal and one provincial. This funding disappeared permanently, in contrast to the temporary reductions from the recession of the early 1980s. Some colleges and institutes chose to subsidize continuing education from other operations, some made it fully cost-recovery, and some greatly reduced or eliminated it.

Developments in the university sector were mainly cyclical in the 1980s and 1990s, involving first contraction and then expansion, whereas colleges experienced both cyclical and structural change. When the small University of Northern British Columbia opened in Prince George in 1994 – more the result of local lobbying to support the economic and community development needs of the region than an attempt to meet the educational needs of individuals – its innovations such as thematic graduate programming and aspirations (only partially realized) for collaboration with local colleges were still well within the bounds of the conventional research university paradigm. It was not until the formation of Royal Roads University in 1995, followed by the Technical University of BC in 1997 (although it did not open to students until 1999), that taken-for-granted notions of the nature of BC universities were unsettled.

The establishment of Royal Roads was opportunistic, taking advantage of a beautiful military college site that the federal government had recently vacated. It was a small niche institution, using mixed mode delivery to serve adult learners.[1] It had no bicameral governance system and only a small core of permanent faculty – something of a continuing education model. The Technical University was assigned a specific mission but enrolled students for only about three years, before a new government had it absorbed by Simon Fraser University. It too featured an unusual governance structure, one that was challenged by the Canadian Association of University Teachers.[2] Subsequent changes to governance at other BC universities turned out to be traditional, not following the precedents set by Royal Roads and the Technical University, but governance structures could no longer be taken for granted.

A change in the public college sector, the creation of university colleges, captured the attention of scholars such as Dennison (2006), Dennison and Schuetze (2004), Fleming (2010), Fleming and Lee (2009), and Levin (1994, 2003). Whereas developments in the university sector tended to be variations on traditional structures, five community colleges were transformed into an entirely new type of institution, the university college. Unlike in some other jurisdictions in Canada and around the world, university colleges in British Columbia were autonomous, and they also offered a full range of non-university programs.

Victoria had struck an access committee in the late 1980s, when the economy was again expanding. The committee concluded that the province needed significantly more student spaces to meet the national average for postsecondary participation, noting that access was particularly difficult for those living in remote areas and for selected groups such as Aboriginal students (Provincial Access Committee, 1988). It recommended that upper-level (third and fourth year) programming be added to some larger community colleges outside the southwest.

In 1989, the province designated Okanagan, Cariboo, and Malaspina Colleges as university colleges.[3] They initially conferred bachelor's degrees in partnership with a university and then in their own name within a few years. In 1990 and 1995 respectively, the BC government also designated Fraser Valley and Kwantlen Colleges as university colleges, to their mild surprise. Both lay on the outskirts of Vancouver, serving residents who lived south of the Fraser River, a natural barrier that made attending UBC or Simon Fraser University inconvenient for them.

The university college model was largely unfamiliar to Canadians. Questions arose about the acceptance by the general public and by graduate schools of the quality of university college degrees, the status of preparatory and vocational programs in these schools, and the workload and scholarly expectations for upper-division instructors. The authorization in 1994 for the BC Institute of Technology to offer a new credential, the bachelor of technology degree, and for the Emily Carr Institute of Art and Design to grant conventional degrees, went largely unremarked.

Instruction Spanning the Public and Private Sectors

A cluster of small Aboriginal-governed institutions began emerging in non-metropolitan areas during the early 1980s: for example, the Nicola Valley Institute of Technology (public since 1983), the Chemainus Native College, and En'owkin Centre. Public institutions began to develop custom programs and services in the 1980s. Then, in the 1990s, programming for Aboriginal students began to build momentum, as reflected in the creation of the province's Aboriginal Post-Secondary Education and Training Policy Framework in 1995 (Ministry of Education, Skills and Training, 1996). Another initiative in 1995, the public Institute of Indigenous Government, did not thrive and closed in 2007.

Elsewhere in the public sector, the presence of Aboriginal students was most noticeable in the smaller rural institutions. Adult basic education, First Nations studies, and programs up to two years in duration were popular (Cowin, 2011). Several more private, not-for-profit Aboriginal colleges were established, bringing the total to more than twelve. Lacking authority to grant credentials, they frequently partnered with public institutions and often served as a bridge for students into public institutions.

Apprenticeship in Canada resembles British and American models in that it is embedded in the market, with apprentices sponsored and laid off partly in response to the economic prospects of employers. In British Columbia, the number of apprentices had crested at nineteen thousand in 1981 but fell back to ten thousand during the economic recession of the early to mid-1980s. The peak number of nineteen thousand was not reattained until 2004 (Cowin, 2012b).

In the 1960s, the Department of Education came to fund a parallel stream of trades training, known as pre-employment training, for students who were not eligible for apprenticeship (because they were too old, for example) or who did not want to follow the Department of Labour's apprenticeship route. As administrative tensions among the parties grew throughout the 1970s, and complaints were voiced that employers were not providing enough training through apprenticeship, provincial politicians decided in 1982 simply to terminate pre-apprenticeship and pre-employment training offered by either department (L. Thompson, 1983).

Aghast at this decision, government bureaucrats convinced the politicians to embark on a major reform instead. The result, the Training Access program, was a self-paced, competency-based, modularized program that began with a common curricular core and allowed students to gradually specialize (Dwyer, 1983). Innovative and progressive, it was so hastily implemented in 1983 with so little support from instructors or employers that it faded away within a few years as the former system resurfaced. In the meantime, the rising political tension about apprenticeship since the late 1970s had subsided.

The federal government's 1989 Labour Force Development Strategy was an unsuccessful attempt to import a more collaborative, northern European model of apprenticeship (Haddow, 2000). It led to the establishment in 1994 of an advisory BC Labour Force Development Board, which lasted only until 1996.

In 1995–96, the BC Ministry of Labour, Citizens' Services and Open Government, began consultations that resulted in the February 1997 report, *Revitalizing Apprenticeship: A Strategic Framework for British Columbia's Apprenticeship Training System*. At much the same time, in late 1996, the Ministries of Labour and Education jointly struck a Committee on Entry Level Trades Training and Apprenticeship. The result of these studies was to move the oversight of apprenticeship out of government in 1997 to an arm's length body, the Industry Training and Apprenticeship Commission.

Private Sector
The implementation of the federal Canadian Jobs Strategy may have harmed public institutions, but it led to a major expansion of their private sub-baccalaureate counterparts. Government was concluding that private institutions were both cheaper and more flexible than public ones (Culos, 2005). Entrepreneurs seized the opportunity as Ottawa announced

that it would direct more of its funding for seat purchases to private institutions, and the number of career colleges registered under the BC Apprenticeship Act doubled from 250 in 1984–85 to 500 in 1990–91 (Ministry of Labour, 1985, 1991). Although enrolment statistics for this sector have not been especially reliable, enrolment appears to have been around thirty-five thousand in 1983–84, just prior to the continuing education and Canadian Jobs Strategy historical moment.

Responsibility for the Apprenticeship Act shifted in 1986–87 from the BC Ministry of Labour to the Ministry of Advanced Education and Job Training. Despite the dramatic growth of the career college sector in the late eighties, the ministry devoted few resources to this new aspect of its mandate. This was arguably the least transparent and accountable period for private career colleges (Cowin, 2013b).

Following some adverse publicity about a few problematic career colleges, the province moved the regulation of career colleges out of the government bureaucracy in 1992. The new Private Post-Secondary Education Commission became responsible for all private institutions, not simply those providing career training. Close to 1,000 institutions had achieved their required registration by 1996, and the total stabilized at 1,100 shortly thereafter (Private Post-Secondary Education Commission of British Columbia, 1996).[4]

The legislation that created the commission also provided for voluntary accreditation of private institutions (compulsory registration by this time was little more than consumer protection for prepaid tuition fees). Little happened with respect to accreditation until the late 1990s, when both levels of government indicated that it would soon become a requirement for an institution's students to remain eligible for such government supports as financial aid (Cowin, 2013b).

In the faith-based sector, the BC government in 1985 extended the authorization of Trinity Western College to grant bachelor's degrees in any subject to include graduate degrees (at which time it was renamed as a university). By then, it was a member of the Association of Universities and Colleges of Canada, a membership that was controversial. Trinity Western subsequently endured other accreditation controversies and legal challenges based on its Christian worldview as it introduced new programs, but it prevailed in each instance.[5]

Roman Catholics opened two tiny liberal education colleges in 1999: Corpus Christi College affiliated with UBC, and Redeemer Pacific (now Catholic Pacific) College affiliated with the Protestant Trinity Western University.

The Associated Canadian Theological Schools formed in 1987 as a partnership of what now consists of six seminaries, with graduate degrees awarded jointly by Trinity Western University and each seminary. This arrangement differed from what had occurred on the UBC campus in 1970 with the formation of the Vancouver School of Theology in that UBC did not jointly confer degrees (Cowin, 2009).

Organizations and Agencies

Although the structure of the BC postsecondary system was not determined by the advisory and co-ordinating organizations and agencies associated with it, these bodies influenced its development. They are not the focus of this study, but they merit a brief discussion.

During the 1970s, the provincial government had created several intermediary bodies to help guide the young public system. The three councils for colleges and institutes lasted only from 1977 to 1983, but the Universities Council existed from 1974 to 1987. Other groups (for students, for faculty, to forecast enrolment, to conduct institutional evaluation, and so on) formed as the system matured (Cowin, 2012a).

From 1985 to 2000, new organizations tended to be specialized. The BC Council on Admissions and Transfer (established in 1989) made a large contribution to supporting student mobility among institutions and emerged as a principal source of research about public colleges and universities in the province. The Advanced Education Council of BC (founded in 1990) included all public institutions except the universities. It started to fragment as the new university colleges sought to stake out their own territory, and it disbanded in 2001 (Cowin, 2012a).

By and large, the universities were wary of participating in BC system organizations. They tended to co-operate among themselves and not be part of such bodies as the Centre for Curriculum, Transfer and Technology (1996–2003) or the Centre for Education Information Standards and Services (also 1996–2003). The Electronic Library Network (created in 1989) is one exception to this generalization.

Historical Moment: Continuing Education and the Canadian Jobs Strategy

Unlike the Macdonald era and the subsequent Access for All historical moment, the continuing education and Canadian Jobs Strategy (CE and CJS) moment has no single document that marks a decisive turn. Rather, changes evolved gradually following an economic slump in the early 1980s, with the exact nature and implications of new provincial and federal policies becoming evident only after several years. It was a moment characterized by financial restraint and attention to labour market strategies.

The policy changes in this historical moment, ones that did not directly alter the sectorial structure of the postsecondary system but did have indirect consequences for its scope and balance, affected only two sectors: public community colleges and private career colleges, with the latter benefitting at the expense of the former. Linking the sectors, and complicating the narrative, were continuing education offerings, both credit and non-credit, in the public colleges. Although continuing education was formally a component of the public college sector, its distinctive operational style and structures made it, for practical purposes, a quasi-sector.

The outcomes of the CE and CJS moment were a dramatic expansion in the number of private colleges and modified internal structures and emphases in public colleges, especially regarding non-credit programming, that significantly reduced their service to non-traditional clienteles in terms of geographical and social reach. Some temporary overlap between public and private colleges also developed as public continuing education departments partnered with private institutions to access federal funding. The credit programs in public colleges that suffered from federal cutbacks were academic upgrading at the secondary-school level (developmental or adult basic education) and non-academic applied programs.

The backdrop to the CE and CJS moment was a worldwide recession ending the economic boom that had supported public sector expansion in British Columbia throughout the 1970s. In the early 1980s, the recession had become the deepest since the 1930s, and British Columbia, with its dependence on commodities, was affected more severely than other provinces (Fisher et al., 2014). As a result of this recession, BC public colleges and institutes experienced a mid-year reduction in their provincial operating grant in 1982. For the 1984–85 fiscal year, they received a

5 percent decrease and advance notice that a similar cut was possible the following year (Beinder, 1986). The BC economy began to improve in 1985, however, and was again growing by 1986.

The federal government had concluded that the recession was more than a cyclical downturn. Due to structural changes in the economy, it was realizing that some of the lost jobs would not return and that new approaches for stimulating the economy were needed. It commissioned several studies, such as the Allmand parliamentary task force report, *Work for Tomorrow* (Allmand, 1981), to examine, among other topics, the dilemma of simultaneous high unemployment and shortages of skilled workers. The task force determined that what were then termed manpower training programs were not achieving their objectives. Likewise, the federal Nielsen Task Force on Program Review called for better training of the long-term unemployed and a better matching of skills with the needs of the economy (Prince and Rice, 1989; Task Force on Program Review and Nielsen, 1986).

Government thus faced two problems: a short-term decline in revenues due to the recession and a long-term shift in the character of the labour market. These pressures in and of themselves may not have been sufficient to cause modifications in public educational policies, but they were a strong incentive for any government that was inclined to consider making changes – and governments were indeed disposed to do just that.

Both British Columbia and the nation had recently elected right-wing governments. Promising a regime of fiscal restraint, the BC Social Credit Party was re-elected in 1983 and immediately introduced a harsh restraint budget that sought (unsuccessfully) to reduce the provincial public sector by a quarter through dismissals, privatization, and reorganization (Fisher et al., 2014). Federally, the first Conservative majority government in over two decades was elected in 1984, with a promise to lower the deficit.

Indications that policy changes were under consideration had been evident during the mandates of each government's predecessor. At that time, the BC Ministry of Labour was responsible for regulating private career colleges. In its 1981 annual report (Ministry of Labour, 1981), the ministry hinted that the private vocational sector could be a viable complement to the public system. It also stated that a modest number of grants (325 of up $500 each) had been made available to students in private colleges by way of financial assistance. Then in its 1984–85 annual report, it explicitly said that a further expansion in the number of private training institutions was foreseen and that students from all parts of the province were increasingly finding individualized instruction at private colleges to be a major attraction.

Federally, concern about Canadian labour market policy (McBride, 1998) had led to three major assessments in rapid succession: Allmand (1981), Canada and Dodge (1981), and the Economic Council of Canada (1982). The emerging consensus was that Canadian occupational training programs were unable to provide training in the middle- and high-skill areas (Witter, n.d.), that labour demand and supply were disconnected, and that institutional training needed to be more aligned with high-demand occupations to rectify or prevent skills shortages (Fisher et al., 2006).

With the above economic and governmental considerations as context, I now turn to specific provincial policy changes regarding continuing education and then to the federal Canadian Jobs Strategy. Finally, the overlap and interactions between the two will be discussed.

The first change in this historical moment was a shift in the BC government's approach to continuing education, namely the abandonment of its short-lived interest in policy development for the field and the withdrawal of a certain type of funding over a two-year period. The federal initiative that followed was more a redirection of funding from the public sector to the private sector, with the repackaging of programs and grants making it difficult to know if funding levels actually remained the same.

"Continuing education" has been a complex term in British Columbia, with each postsecondary institution defining and structuring it according to its own vision and circumstances. It had been seen as serving two basic purposes: technical empowerment and access to basic education as a civic right (Ministry of Advanced Education, Training and Technology, and Centre for Policy Studies in Education, 1992). Its association with volunteerism and learner autonomy linked it with entrepreneurial activity, and its social activism connected it with equity and compensatory education (Ministry of Advanced Education, Training and Technology, and Centre for Policy Studies in Education, 1992).

For the purposes of this analysis, the only distinction that needs be noted about the continuing education activities of the various institutions was the difference in the late 1970s and early 1980s between continuing education in the university sector and in the public colleges and institutes sector. This difference explains why the forces described below did not affect universities (in the long run, though, dissimilar dynamics have brought the college and university sectors to a similar entrepreneurial, cost-recovery orientation for continuing education).

Universities did not receive targeted funding from government for continuing education, so changes to their continuing education operations arose from causes other than financial exigency. UBC reorganized its continuing education operations several times, with tensions surfacing about the role of liberal education versus cost-recovery programming.[6] The UBC Senate modified its definition of a diploma program in 1994 so that continuing education could offer and credential post-baccalaureate programs. Simon Fraser University and the University of Victoria used continuing education as a vehicle for opening facilities in the central business districts of their respective cities and, especially in the case of the University of Victoria, to provide leadership in the delivery of post-secondary distance education for the province.

In the mid-1970s, both federal and provincial governments began to fund adult (continuing) education in school districts, colleges, and institutes (Ministry of Advanced Education, Training and Technology, and Centre for Policy Studies in Education, 1992). The provincial grants to BC colleges in support of continuing education were unrestricted, provided that the courses and activities fell within the vague category of continuing education. Colleges used some of this funding for technical and professional development courses, but much was allocated to general interest and personal and community development purposes, where registrants may have had less ability to pay the full costs of tuition (Ministry of Advanced Education, Training and Technology, and Centre for Policy Studies in Education, 1992).

Community colleges took seriously the emancipatory and democratic function of continuing education, ranging from basic literacy through community development courses and activities. Universities at that time also had personnel who embraced a popular and social justice conception of continuing education, but with no earmarked funding from government, continuing education at universities differed qualitatively from college offerings.

The introduction of continuing education funding for colleges and institutes led to a new continuing education division in the Ministry of Education, formed in 1976, to provide leadership and co-ordination for the colleges and institutes (Cowin, 2010). By 1982–83, BC colleges and school districts were serving almost 400,000 students annually,[7] an increase of 53 percent in seven years (Ministry of Advanced Education, Training and Technology, and Centre for Policy Studies in Education, 1992). A Statistics Canada study of adult education participation in Canada found that community colleges were the largest providers of continuing education in British Columbia, followed by voluntary organizations, employers and school boards, and then other organizations, in that order (Devereaux, 1984).

With the onset of financial restraint in the early eighties, the provincial government trimmed postsecondary budgets across the board. Along with this undifferentiated quantitative reduction, it made more severe targeted cuts that qualitatively changed public colleges.

According to Beinder (1986), Ministry of Education officials felt that the college system was overextended. They therefore clamped down on funding for facility leases in 1983 to encourage greater use of large campuses and to foster distance education. With minor leases (facilities that were located away from a main campus in areas with small populations) no longer funded, many storefront operations in small towns and on First Nations reserves that were run by college continuing education departments could no longer afford to remain open. The geographic reach of colleges was sharply curtailed, although the number of students affected was small. Colleges argued, unsuccessfully, that many of their storefront classrooms served at-risk populations whose members were not likely to attend a distant, larger campus or to succeed in distance learning environments.

A more profound change to college continuing education came in 1981, when a new minister of education (and subsequently premier), Bill Vander Zalm, called a halt to the provincial policy development process for continuing education. Eventually, he dismantled the continuing education division and publicly announced that the ministry intended to stop providing leadership in the field (G.R. Selman, 1988). In addition, over a two-year period beginning in 1982, funding for general interest continuing education was eliminated. The only BC government funding for continuing education that remained was for job-related courses, known as part-time vocational training.

Colleges responded in differing ways to the funding cuts, in several cases drawing upon other revenue sources to varying degrees to maintain at least a skeleton of general education offerings. By the late 1980s, when the economy was healthier, all colleges were again providing some non-government-funded continuing education programs and services. In aggregate, they then served a little over five thousand full-time equivalent (FTE) students, where one FTE represented between six and eight hundred hours of instruction, depending on the nature of the instruction (Ministry of Advanced Education, Training and Technology, and Centre for Policy Studies in Education, 1992). This volume of instruction was similar to that delivered by a medium-sized college but involved many more students because most registrants were enrolled in very short courses.

On the national scene, the federal government had introduced the Canada Manpower Training Program under the Adult Occupational Training Act of 1967 and then replaced it with the National Training Program in 1982 (McBride, 1998). These programs enabled Ottawa to purchase training, mainly from public community colleges, of a vocational nature as well as English as a second language and adult basic education instruction. The original emphasis was on public providers of training because the government feared that on-the-job training could easily become just a subsidy to industry (Dupre, Cameron, McKechnie, and Rotenberg, 1973).

By the mid-1980s, Ottawa had come to perceive public colleges as slow in responding to new labour market demands and in winding down programs for which demand had declined (McBride, 1998). Furthermore, it felt that an inordinate amount of the training was being devoted to the Basic Training for Skill Development program, an upgrading of basic academic skills. Federal officials viewed the program as simply rectifying deficiencies in provincial secondary education (Rubenson and Gaskell, 1987). Ottawa was also seeking to shift funding from lower-level to higher-level skills training (Fisher et al., 2006).

The new Conservative government of 1984 introduced the Canadian Jobs Strategy in 1985, with full implementation coming in mid-1986. The strategy replaced all former training employment programs and represented the largest reform in labour market policy since the introduction of employment training programs in the 1960s (Prince and Rice, 1989). It consisted of a set of programs targeted to specific clienteles, such as Aboriginal persons and the long-term unemployed. The implication was, according to Prince and Rice (1989), that all previous job creation programs were little more than short-term, ad hoc, make-work schemes.

The CJS explicitly promoted training by the private and voluntary sectors, reflecting the skepticism of the federal government about the cost effectiveness and responsiveness of public colleges. This fostered dramatic growth in private career colleges as public training funds were redirected to them (Auld, 2005; Sweet and Gallagher, 1999). In the five years following 1986, direct federal purchase of training in public colleges halved, destabilizing their vocational programs, especially in the first few years of the new regime (Witter, n.d.). In the private sector, in contrast, BC Ministry of Labour annual reports indicated that the number of registered private career colleges in the province tripled in a decade, from 165 in 1980 to 500 in 1990–91 (Cowin, 2013b).

Along with reducing and refocusing their programming, one response of BC colleges to the CJS was to use their continuing education departments to serve as subcontractors to deliver training on behalf of private and nonprofit organizations that were receiving CJS funds. Public colleges also increasingly bid in partnership with private trainers and voluntary organizations; lacking educational expertise and capacity, these other organizations fronted bids but turned to public institutions to actually deliver significant portions of the contracts that they were awarded (Cowin, 2010).

Vocational instructors in BC community colleges were dismayed by the change in federal policy, claiming it had deprived, betrayed, and devalued the public postsecondary vocational education system (Vocational Instructors Association of BC, 1991). Other criticisms of the CJS were that it reduced the absolute amount of funding for training, weakened quality assurance (audits by the federal government concerned financial propriety, not educational standards and outcomes), and increased the possibility of duplication of services across providers (McBride, 1998; Witter, n.d.).

Analysis: Continuing Education and the Canadian Jobs Strategy Moment

Social Justice

It is difficult to find evidence that any concern for social justice influenced the actions of the BC government in reducing public expenditures, especially with respect to continuing education, in the early 1980s. The government seems to have sacrificed portions of the emancipatory and democratization mission of community colleges in light of financial exigencies. Nevertheless, a couple of considerations slightly temper this stark conclusion.

While causing the closure of many storefront college facilities through a refusal to continue funding minor leases, the government claimed that affected students had an alternative – to make greater use of the relatively new Open Learning Institute and the Knowledge Network of the West educational television service. When educators suggested that the students who accessed storefront centres tended not to perform well in distance education settings and that such settings were inappropriate for them, their advice was considered suspect in that college employees were seen as having a vested interest in keeping the storefronts. Regardless of the sincerity of either government or college personnel, or even the soundness of their arguments, the point is that Victoria felt it had to offer a substitute means of accessing postsecondary education for the vulnerable students who would be affected by storefront closures.

The withdrawal by the BC government of funding for non-vocational continuing education greatly reduced the ability of colleges to equip and empower marginalized populations. Possibly reinforcing other factors leading to this decision was a perception in government that some continuing education activities were becoming more political than educational. This view was exacerbated by the belief of the ministry's executive director for continuing education, Ron Faris, that school districts and colleges were not making sufficient efforts to serve disadvantaged persons (G.R. Selman, 1988). His continuing education division attempted to change institutional priorities and, in some instances, was seen by field personnel as interfering with local programs and priorities. Receiving mixed messages from constituents around the province about the accomplishments of general continuing education and knowing that he had to make financial cuts somewhere, a new minister of education, Bill Vander Zalm, was not predisposed to protect this particular budget item.

The picture at the federal level was more complex, and it is too facile to conclude that a transfer of funds from the public to the private post-secondary system automatically meant that the welfare of needy or vulnerable citizens was unimportant to government. Perhaps the bigger concern is the inconclusively documented suspicion that the Canadian Jobs Strategy ultimately reduced overall training funds across all sectors, but it is difficult to unwind the budgetary strands to confirm this.

When the Mulroney government came to power in 1984, it explicitly established social justice as one of the four overarching priorities to dominate its decisions for the next few years (Prince and Rice, 1989). It did not necessarily agree with its political opponents as to what constituted social justice, but it nevertheless felt that its conception of social justice was worthy and important.

Under the CJS, a right-wing government, which might have been expected to be concerned with promoting individual rights, chose to define social justice and equity in terms of groups of disadvantaged people for whom compensatory efforts were needed: the strategy explicitly focused on women re-entering the workforce, youth, the long-term unemployed, Native people, disabled persons, visible minorities, and social assistance recipients. Whereas the Macdonald era in British Columbia had emphasized social justice as access to education for all individuals, the federal emphasis in the CJS was on compensatory programs for specific groups of people. Whether the federal goals were ever actually achieved is irrelevant to the policy intent that ultimately drove the reshaping of the private career college sector in British Columbia.

Human Capital Formation

Having come to view the economic recession as heralding a structural change in the economy, not merely a cyclical downturn, the BC and federal governments made improving the skill level of the workforce generally, and helping displaced workers retrain for participation in the new economy in particular, key policy goals. The province's concern for human capital formation prompted it to keep funding the part-time vocational component of continuing education in public colleges and institutes, despite rapidly phasing out all other types of continuing education funding as a cost-saving measure. The priority accorded labour force development over other educational purposes was clear.

The involvement of the federal government in postsecondary education has been driven by economic and labour market considerations, but its actions during this historical moment were more nuanced than those of the BC government. Rather than providing general funding for vocational programs as the province had done, leaving individual colleges free to choose whatever specific programs to offer for whatever reasons they thought important, Ottawa tried to target its funding. In addition to targeting certain groups that were disadvantaged in the labour market, as discussed above, it abandoned temporary make-work programs and attempted to invest in medium- and long-term skills.

The federal government's shift in the mid-1980s from a focus on public postsecondary institutions to private ones and the workplace marked the beginning of a turn from previous notions of human capital formation as both a public and a private good, reorienting policy from public investment in education toward individual investment (Haddow, 1998; G. Stewart and Kerr, 2010). By the early 1990s, Ottawa was backing even farther away from a national role in skill development as it began decentralizing administrative control of federal expenditures through labour market development agreements negotiated on a province-by-province basis.

Reflecting on the mid-1980s from a college perspective a decade later, Knowles (1995) claimed that postsecondary resource allocations in Canada were increasingly determined by perceived demands for vocational and occupational training. She noted that for most colleges, their initial forays into the contract-training market (a subset of cost-recovery continuing education where a third-party funder determines which students are eligible to enrol in the course) had emerged in the 1980s, often beginning with computer and technology training.

In short, notions of human capital formation were important in the CE and CJS moment, but they seemed to be taking on new meanings in terms of the role of the federal state.

Marketization

Marketization, another significant theme in this historical moment, seemed less an ideological driver of educational policy than a pragmatic response to a changing international environment and an opportunity to save money. The federal government had sought a new job-training strategy not only to foster what it perceived as more relevant curriculum for helping the Canadian economy adjust to the changing global economy, but also in the hope that it would get the instruction it wanted in a more responsive and cheaper manner. The government itself, as the funding body, was also an important intended beneficiary.

By the mid-1970s, global economic problems such as stagflation (persistent unemployment during high inflation) had made it clear that Keynesian policies were not working (Harvey, 2007). The first wave of neoliberalism in the English-speaking world had been prefaced in Australia under Prime Minister Malcolm Fraser in 1975, but it was the election of Margaret Thatcher in Britain in 1979 and Ronald Reagan in the United States in 1980 that brought this ideology to the forefront. The election of Brian Mulroney in 1984 resulted in a campaign in Canada to end Keynesian-style "big government" (Steger and Roy, 2010). By the mid-1980s, neoliberalism had arrived in Canada as a powerful political ideology.

In British Columbia, the 1983 Speech from the Throne announced the government's intention to downsize by eliminating some activities and transferring others to the private sector (British Columbia, 1983, June 23). It declared that the road to economic recovery lay in the private sector. The brief mention of education stated that any initiatives would occur in the context of fiscal restraint and enhanced productivity.

Despite the privatization rhetoric, BC public colleges experienced mainly financial restraint – funding cutbacks that forced continuing education, for example, to become more entrepreneurial and cost-recovery, emulating the private sector. Only a few programs, such as customer relations training for taxi drivers and hairdressing programs, were actually transferred to the private sector (Beinder, 1986). It remained for the federal government, a few years later, to start a large-scale shift of instructional funds – that is, designated funding that was separate from transfer payments to the provinces for education (Leblanc and Canada, 1987) – from public to private colleges.

The BC government reduced its grants to public colleges, quit collecting continuing education data, stopped providing leadership in that field, and stood back to observe the consequences. It let colleges and institutes do whatever they wanted with respect to general continuing education and storefront campuses; the institutions just would not receive government funding for these purposes.

Continuing education had always operated in something of a market environment in that a significant portion of instructional costs were offset by tuition revenue, with government grants used more for infrastructure and to subsidize specific courses. With the loss of the grants, institutions reduced or eliminated offerings that were not cost-recovery and generally treated continuing education as even more of a market commodity than a public service (Ministry of Advanced Education, Training, and Technology, and Centre for Policy Studies in Education, 1992). The long-term structural impacts were to create pseudo-private-sector divisions within public sector institutions and, depending on the bidding rules of various training contracts that have come and gone over the years, some overlap between public and private sectors to develop programs in partnership, with continuing education personnel serving as the bridge between the two sectors.

The federal government was ideologically sympathetic to neoliberal approaches, and its practical experience was that provincial education systems were neither responsive, flexible, nor informed about the skills that were actually used in the workplace (Witter, n.d.). It wanted to introduce competition in adult training to address these perceived shortcomings. In doing so under the new and sweeping Canadian Jobs Strategy, it not only shook up public colleges and prompted some co-operation between private and public institutions, but it led to the tripling of the number of private career colleges in British Columbia. Marketization was an important component of this labour market and educational policy.

Historical Moment: Access for All

As this chapter turns from analysis back to the historical narrative, the timeframe shifts almost a decade to the late 1980s and early 1990s. This second historical moment concerns two postsecondary sectors – public universities and colleges. A new form of institution, the university college, emerged from them. Some commentators have suggested that it constituted a distinct sector of its own.

Like the Macdonald Report of 1962, what became known as the Access for All Report (officially *Access to Advanced Education and Job Training in British Columbia: Report of the Provincial Access Committee*) and strategy of 1988–89 appeared to arrive suddenly from nowhere, involving extensive but quick community consultations, receiving broad endorsement, and (moderately) changing the size and structure of the public postsecondary system. However, it too was actually the culmination of years of work and advocacy efforts. Once again, the primary beneficiary was academic education.

Unlike the Macdonald Report, Access for All was a government initiative – one of the infrequent occasions when the BC government showed systematic leadership in postsecondary education. Also unlike in the Macdonald era, politics took an unwelcome twist from the point of view of Ministry of Advanced Education officials: as will be discussed below, they saw the establishment of the University of Northern British Columbia as a departure from the government plan and feared that the new university would be doomed to low enrolments and high costs because the region's population was too small to support it.[8]

Two streams of complementary advocacy in the prior decade provide the backdrop to the Access for All moment. One concerned the performance of British Columbia in postsecondary education relative to the Canadian average. The other reflected community aspirations in the Interior of the province for a local university.

Around 1980, the institutional research office at the University of Victoria began analyzing per-capita degree and enrolment rates in British Columbia relative to other Canadian provinces and to the national average, including consideration of university transfer enrolment and what was then called career/technical education in colleges. (Vocational education, a separate data set at Statistics Canada that used different measures, was excluded from the analysis.) The results showed that British Columbia was not keeping pace with other provinces.

In 1981, the intermediary body for BC universities, the Universities Council of British Columbia, funded the University of Victoria to publish a report, *A Widening Gap*, to present interprovincial participation and credential data (Gallagher and Merner, 1981). Although the absolute numbers of students and credentials awarded were rising in British Columbia, the per-capita measures showed that the province had been "steadily declining over the last fifteen years. Currently the Province is at or near the bottom of the national ranking in almost every comparison" (Gallagher and Merner, 1981, p. 1).

Moreover, participation rates in the outlying regions were below even the BC average. Although geographic access was thought to be an important explanatory factor for the low rural rates, the report cautioned that it fell short of a complete account of the situation.

With an economic recession in full force during the early 1980s, the timing to rectify the "widening gap" was inopportune; the public finances were simply not available. Nevertheless, the Universities Council continued to advance variations of this theme in periodic submissions to Victoria until the government disbanded it (for other reasons) in 1987. When ministry officials began preparing background analyses in 1988 as part of the accessibility initiative of the BC government, they were thus familiar with participation rate and credentialing arguments as well as with the data available to make them.

The other prior stream of advocacy efforts, concerning aspirations for universities in the Interior, extended over a longer period and was more diffuse. The precedent was the private Notre Dame University of Nelson, in the southeast region of the province (Cowin, 2009). Closing in 1977 after years of financial struggle, it had garnered such strong local support that the BC government reopened the campus in 1979 as the David Thompson University Centre. When it permanently closed the campus in 1984 due to budgetary restraint and high costs per student, the local community was again upset.

In Prince George, in the central north of the province, the Catholic Church opened the tiny Prince George College in 1962 and offered Grade 13, drawing in part on federal funding for Aboriginal students. The aspiration of Bishop Fergus O'Grady was to eventually offer four years of university, and the young college did go so far as to have three small cohorts of students complete two years of university transfer studies (McCaffray, 1995). When the College of New Caledonia opened in 1964 with public funding, the Catholic college decided to withdraw from postsecondary education and to operate as a secondary school instead.

Not all Prince George residents supported the establishment of the College of New Caledonia, given that the city already had a postsecondary vocational school. Along with questions about its cost (under BC legislation at that time, locals were responsible for half of the operating costs), some feared that a new college would jeopardize the chance of the city ever having a full university (McCaffray, 1995). In 1978, the dean of university programs at the College of New Caledonia, Frank Gelin, suggested that it should become Prince George University (McCaffray, 1995). Prince George thus had a long history of wanting a university of its own.

In the Okanagan Valley, in the southern Interior, the three main cities pushed for a postsecondary institution during the late 1950s and early 1960s, each vying for the right to become a college or university town (Freake, 2005). Vernon had already purchased a hundred acres, and the mayor of Kelowna had hired a consultant in 1959 to do a feasibility study for a junior college. The Macdonald Report (Macdonald, 1962) recommended that a four-year college be established at Kelowna within eight years, emerging from a two-year college that should open immediately. This did not occur, but the dream of a degree-granting institution in the Okanagan did not die.

Against this backdrop of long-standing regional aspirations for universities in the Interior, and more recent concern that British Columbia was not keeping up with national postsecondary developments, the Access for All historical moment began at a political convention in 1986 at which the governing Social Credit Party chose a new leader to replace Premier William Bennett. Delegates were concerned about public complaints regarding overcrowding and lack of access to postsecondary institutions, fee increases, and inadequate student aid (Bullen, 1991). Institutions were complaining about the financial cutbacks they had endured in the earlier eighties.

The newly chosen premier, Bill Vander Zalm, gave his new minister for postsecondary education, Stanley Hagen, two tasks: to improve student financial assistance and to increase access to postsecondary education (Bullen, 1991). Sweeping changes to financial aid, to be implemented over three years, were announced in March 1987.

The process for enhancing student access proceeded more slowly. A former assistant deputy minister (and former president of Camosun

College), Grant Fisher had returned from a medical leave into a position as head of the policy and planning branch of the ministry. His task was to establish a base of information about postsecondary access and university transfer in British Columbia (Bullen, 1991). Working with a small team of ministry staff and consultants, Fisher produced a dozen papers, some of which picked up themes from the University of Victoria's work on participation and credential rates, mentioned above.

With the ministry uncharacteristically well briefed and proceeding in a well-orchestrated manner, the next step occurred in February 1988, when Minister Hagen struck one provincial and eight regional access committees to gather public input and to prepare a report (a government-wide regionalization plan was concurrently launched, mainly for economic development purposes). The goal was to complete the postsecondary report by the summer so that it would co-ordinate with the government-wide planning initiative. The Provincial Access Committee met this deadline, issuing its report in June 1988.

At the same time, two groups independently advocated for the establishment of Interior universities. In the view of Les Bullen, chair of the Provincial Access Committee, the report from Kelowna envisaged a natural growth from the existing college and harmonized well with his own committee's report (Bullen, 1991).

The Prince George initiative, on the other hand, did not harmonize either in process or substance with the Provincial Access Committee. In fact, the Prince George group came to view government officials as producing slanted briefings that steered priorities to southern regions of the province (McCaffray, 1995). The Interior University Society in Prince George, incorporated in the autumn of 1987, therefore chose to interact directly with provincial politicians, making an end run around the Provincial Access process.

In March 1988, soon after the launch of the Provincial Access Committee, community members from Prince George met directly with selected cabinet ministers to lobby for what was no longer framed as a Prince George university but rather as a university for the entire north. This regional approach increased the demographic base to over 300,000 people, although spread over vast distances. It also provided a way to differentiate this university proposal from others in non-metropolitan British Columbia by emphasizing the distinctive needs and character of northern regions. Drawing upon the work of a Swedish consultant, Urban Dahloff, a network university using a mix of face-to-face and distance delivery methods, working closely with the three northern community colleges, was proposed (McCaffray, 1995).

The Provincial Access Committee made many recommendations, with the key structural change to the public postsecondary system being a proposal to create university colleges: the offering of third- and fourth-year courses by community colleges in midsized Interior communities under the educational auspices of the existing universities. This would bring degree-level programs to the hinterland without incurring the attendant financial overhead of the research mandate of universities. The committee explicitly left the door open for university colleges to continue operating in partnership with universities, to develop into comprehensive degree-granting regional colleges, or to eventually become autonomous universities (Provincial Access Committee, 1988).[9] Victoria accepted this recommendation, announcing three university colleges in 1989 and later adding two more.

After receiving the report of the Provincial Access Committee, Minister Hagen agreed to a university in Prince George and struck an implementation planning committee in 1989. He and some of his staff visited Scandinavia and parts of Canada that had small, remote universities, eventually concluding that a centralized university model, such as at Lakehead University in Ontario, was more appropriate for British Columbia than the Scandinavian models that worked elsewhere (Bullen, 1991). The University of Northern British Columbia was thus established as a rather traditional North American university, to the chagrin of the Interior University Society (McCaffray, 1995).

The access work culminated in March 1989, when the provincial government announced the Access for All strategy (Hagen, 1989). Along with the creation of university colleges and the promise of a university in Prince George, fifteen thousand student spaces would be added to university programs in colleges and universities across the province. Three thousand of these were to be added during the first twelve months. In contrast to the expansion of academic education, only a thousand spaces would be added immediately to non-university programs, and no promises were made for expanding these programs in the following years.

Under the Access for All strategy, a special partnership would be explored by which the Open Learning Agency would grant degrees for the Emily Carr College of Art and Design (as it was then named). Among the other initiatives the government embarked upon, committees were formed to promote adult literacy and postsecondary education for Aboriginal students. A council on admissions and transfers was founded to facilitate student mobility among institutions. Hagen reminded his audience at the Access for All news conference that the government had recently committed some additional funding for adult special education, students with disabilities, and general student support services.

The creation of university colleges attracted a fair amount of scholarly attention because they represented a new institutional type that complicated binary models of postsecondary education and changed the internal operations and culture of institutions (Dennison, 2006; Dennison and Schuetze, 2004; Fleming and Lee, 2009; Gaber, 2002; Levin, 1994, 2003; Schuetze and Day, 2001; Skolnik, 2012). Whereas scholars focused on the implications of the university college model for educational providers – for postsecondary institutions and sectors – and how distinctions among institutional types were blurring and becoming complicated, the documents cited above from committees and government officials concentrated on beneficiaries, students, and communities. The goals of public servants and politicians were to find pragmatic ways of responding to educational needs, keeping costs manageable, and leaving the door open to further institutional evolution. The resulting ambiguity of institutional purpose and identity, and the development of an increasingly differentiated postsecondary system, were not prominent concerns for politicians or ministry staff.

Once the simple model of three types of public postsecondary institutions in two sectors – universities in one sector and colleges and institutes in another – had been complicated by the introduction of university colleges, other variations followed. The opening of Royal Roads University in 1995 and the short-lived Technical University of BC in 1999, and of two small Aboriginal-governed but publicly funded institutes in 1995 (the previously private Nicola Valley Institute of Technology and the new Institute of Indigenous Government) all introduced non-traditional components of governance and mission to the public system. The ambiguities associated with the university college model kept the door open to lobbying for a local university in Kelowna and Kamloops, lobbying that eventually resulted in the transformation of their two university colleges into a campus of the University of British Columbia and into a "special-purpose" university, Thompson Rivers (as discussed in the next historical moment).

Analysis: Access for All Moment

Social Justice

Social justice considerations undergirded the work of the Provincial Access Committee, whereas the concurrent lobbying in Prince George and the Okanagan was driven more by human capital considerations. Nevertheless, lobbyists for new universities advanced fairness arguments, especially in Prince George.

The unmet demand for postsecondary education and the desire that access be equitably distributed throughout the province resembled the situation in the Macdonald era – that the key issue was one of basic fairness for individuals. In this respect, Access for All can be seen as an effort to maintain the existing social contract.

The report of the Provincial Access Committee not only asserted economic benefits, but also claimed that investment in education had social and cultural benefits (Provincial Access Committee, 1988). Furthermore, the committee stated that increasing accessibility to all types of education, including personal enrichment, was a social imperative "for all who demonstrate the necessary competence, motivation and maturity to benefit from further education" (p. 10). In other words, postsecondary education was viewed as something of a human right. The minister presented it as a strong force in breaking the cycle of poverty and of social malaise, and as fundamental to the democratic process and to preserving the balance between human values and the technological world (Hagen, 1989).

A new aspect of social justice in the provincial government discourse on postsecondary education was the Provincial Access Committee's focus on under-represented groups (enumerated as people in small remote communities, "Native Indians," disabled students, and the prison population) and those needing literacy upgrading – a theme that was subsequently echoed in the government's announcement about its strategy in response to the access report (Hagen, 1989). How much was actually achieved for equity groups over the succeeding years is in some ways irrelevant from the perspective of policy intent; what mattered was that these groups were viewed as important and deserving of special attention from government.

This emphasis on social justice was a marked contrast to its absence in the continuing education and Canadian Jobs Strategy historical moment of a few years earlier. Not only had the economic recession ended and provincial revenues were rising, but a new premier and a new minister of advanced education were now in charge – a different environment with different actors that enabled the policy pendulum to swing back toward its historical balance among the various policy rationales.

A different way of framing social justice considerations in BC postsecondary education was forcefully articulated during this time. It arose from geographical considerations. The perspective was not new in itself, but it was distinctive in finally catching the attention of powerful politicians, ultimately persuading them of its merit.

The issue concerned differing values that could not be resolved on technical grounds and therefore appropriately belonged in the political arena. The particular political process ran independently and parallel to the Access for All initiative, which, depending on one's perspective, was either unfortunate or inevitable.

Government officials, whose duty was to ensure that public funds were used efficiently and effectively, recognized that government could provide only limited amounts of money to expand postsecondary capacity and that costs per student were generally lower in large institutions due to economies of scale. They strongly suspected that any additional capacity in rural areas would not be fully used, whereas the same amount of money spent in the more populated southwest would provide a greater number of places, all of which would probably be filled. It was difficult for them to justify not meeting a proven educational demand in metropolitan areas in order to fund more costly spaces in non-metropolitan regions, especially when some of those spaces might not even be occupied. Their focus was on students, not on the students' communities, and they seem to have viewed all students as needing to be treated as equally as possible.

The question of "getting the most bang for the buck" was seen differently in the north. It was not a technical issue about the efficient allocation of public resources, but one of values. For many northern residents, the fairness question was not how to get the most output in terms of graduates from the least input of money. It concerned who benefitted from the wealth generated in the north: northerners or southerners. As Prince George mayor John Blackhouse explained in the late 1980s, "we were tired of being treated like a colony, sick of exporting our resources, including our children" (McCaffray, 1995, p. 249).

Northerners felt it was only fair that they should enjoy the same quality of life as southerners, including local access to postsecondary education for their children and skilled workers who viewed northern communities as more than either temporary springboards for their careers or locales to be avoided altogether. If revenue from their region could fund local postsecondary spaces, resulting in a quality of life similar to that in the south, they considered it irrelevant whether those spaces were more expensive than in the south.

The University Advisory Council, a short-lived advisory group established by Victoria following its abolishment of the Universities Council of BC, articulated the divide in southern and northern perspectives by framing it in educational versus economic terms: "While recognizing that there are economic benefits which will accrue to a region in which a university is located, the Council feels that the educational need, not the economic benefit, should be the basis upon which university programing decisions are made" (Bullen, 1991, p. 27). Based in the metropolitan southwest, the council recommended against establishing a separate Interior university at that time.

By the time the Provincial Access Committee was writing its report, the northern university advocacy campaign was showing signs of success with provincial politicians. The access committee was not about to embarrass its political masters. It stated that although it had not been presented with justification for a new university based on enrolment demand, it was fully aware that the justification "may rest on much broader grounds" (Provincial Access Committee, 1988, p. 18). The government eventually accepted this broader justification, saying it was prepared to pay a northern premium for a new university in recognition of the long-term nature of investment in education (Hagen, 1989).

Human Capital Formation

Although not the only argument advanced by the Provincial Access Committee for expanding postsecondary education, human capital formation was certainly an important consideration. Both the committee and the minister in his subsequent announcement of Access for All articulated a comprehensive understanding of the purposes of postsecondary education, ranging from civic/democratic justifications through social and cultural to economic factors. With respect to labour market contributions, the Provincial Access Committee (1988) stated,

> Previous analyses, however, done in Canada and elsewhere, suggest that additional investment in advanced education and job training will have high pay-off value in terms of future economic, social and cultural benefits ... The relationship between levels of education and unemployment ... is particularly telling ... It seems clear that countries with a well-educated labour force will have competitive edge in the emerging world economy. (p. 6)

The provincial government took a similar stance. Although the minister explicitly stated in the press conference to announce the Access for All strategy that postsecondary education was important for reasons other than economic ones, he nevertheless began by referencing a consensus that the future prosperity of the province would depend on investments made in people: "Indeed, if we are to continue to prosper in an increasingly complex world, British Columbians must have access to relevant postsecondary education" (Hagen, 1989, p. 4).

Whereas the provincial government took a balanced view of the purposes of postsecondary education, the advocacy groups for Interior universities were much more focused on economic and labour market considerations. In fact, the Kelowna effort was spearheaded by the Chamber of Commerce. Its report noted that as well as providing better access for students and enhancing the quality of life in the community, a university would nicely benefit its seasonal economy; the quiet summer in the academic year would complement the employment cycles of the local agricultural and tourist industries (Bullen, 1991).

The Prince George community was well aware that not only did it have a cyclical, resource-based economy, but that the economy was changing structurally and the jobs lost during the recession of the early 1980s were probably gone forever. The Regional Development Corporation in Prince George saw a university as the single most important initiative toward stabilizing and growing the local economy (McCaffray, 1995). Similarly, Prince George mayor Blackhouse, reflecting back on the successful campaign for a northern university, commented, "a university would be a way to diversify the economy, changing the social fabric ... Indeed when I lobbied for the university, I rarely mentioned education – usually only economics, social change, retention of young people" (McCaffray, 1995, p. 249).

In assessing the Access for All policies, Fisher et al. (2014) identify two distinct but related sentiments at play: recognition of the instrumental benefits of education and a commitment to educational access as a democratic right. They conclude that the issue of social inclusion was not addressed by direct redistributive means but rather by investing in public postsecondary education as a spur to economic growth and general prosperity. Furthermore, they argue, this approach was in line with the human resource theory of the day. My view is that this conclusion is a little too narrow an interpretation. It does not adequately acknowledge the comprehensive purposes articulated for education or the explicit attention to under-represented groups in the Access for All moment. Nevertheless, it does highlight the implicit policy assumption that all segments of society would benefit from a well-educated labour force and from efforts to raise postsecondary participation rates generally.

Marketization

Several market-oriented forces were noticeably absent during the Access for All moment. The Social Credit Party, in power in 1989, was the same one that had announced in its 1983 throne speech that it intended to downsize and rely more on the private sector. Furthermore, this party had recently abandoned continuing education (except part-time vocational courses) to cost-recovery market forces. At the federal level, the Canadian Jobs Strategy of 1985 had also promoted the private sector. Yet these previous trends were interrupted for a few years during Access for All.

A healthier economy and different politicians – the BC government was now led by Bill Vander Zalm rather than Bill Bennett – do not seem to fully account for the absence of market forces. I suspect that a higher societal valuing of academic education than non-academic education – the former being the emphasis of Access for All – is also part of the explanation, but this hypothesis would require a study of its own to confirm or refute.

The way in which marketization is relevant to the Access for All moment is subtler, long-term, and not directly linked to money. It has to do with the gradual development of an institutional prestige economy in the public postsecondary system in which institutions and sectors increasingly competed with one another in more ways than the usual jockeying inherent in public sector budgeting.

The fifteen thousand seat expansion and the introduction of upper-level instruction in university colleges had the potential to introduce competition for students among institutions, but this did not really occur because enrolment demand was so strong. Neither does the encouragement of such competition, a neoliberal strategy, seem to have been a policy intent. (Both the intent and the reality of student competition came a decade or more later.)

What does seem to have occupied the mind of government at this time was a question of legitimacy: Would the degree programs delivered at university colleges be seen as credible and equivalent to those at universities? Its strategy for ensuring the legitimacy of the degrees was to have existing universities oversee the academic aspects of these programs and to award their own degrees to university college graduates, at least in the initial years. Whether colleges that had been successfully offering the first two years of a bachelor's degree for a decade or two actually lacked the expertise to expand into upper-division programming is moot, but the provision of the university quality assurance mechanism forestalled any possible debate. The new BC Council on Admissions and Transfer was given a mandate to address a variety of issues, one of which was to provide a confidential, neutral place where any issues of academic credibility among institutions could be discussed and potentially resolved before they escalated publicly.

Despite these proactive steps by the government, Fleming and Lee (2009) find that "the university colleges legitimately engage in isomorphic behavior – emulating aspects of traditional university programming, faculty workload, and governance – to ensure their recognition and credibility as degree-granting institutions and in deference to professional practice norms supportive of quality programs" (p. 96). In small and subtle ways, the university colleges were drawn into the zero-sum prestige economy of university education (Levin, 2003), leading first to the formation of their own advocacy group (which contributed to the dissolution of the Advanced Education Council of BC in 2001) and a campaign of their own for university status.

Throughout the early 1990s, status issues were an ongoing source of debate and conflict within institutions. Dennison (1995) concludes that university colleges were reinforcing the latent academic drift among other BC colleges and institutes – aspirations for degree-granting status. The scholarly interest noted above in institutional differentiation and the abandonment of a clear binary model is further indication of the beginning of reputational jockeying that emerged more fully in the next historical moment to be analyzed. The evidence does not suggest, however, that reputational or any other type of competition was a policy intent of Access for All; rather, it seemed more of a consequence.

5

Cynicism (2000–15)

Bolstered by a strong economy, idealism about the contribution of education to the betterment of society characterized the 1960s and 1970s. Beinder (1983), for example, describes the 1960s BC college movement as

> a unique social phenomenon bringing people together, creating a more tightly knit and understanding society ... There was truly an element of missionary concern in what they did. They were clearly concerned about the life chances of people. That's missionary business. (pp. 19-21)

As assumptions about the postsecondary system were challenged in the 1980s and 1990s, the world had changed by 2000. In the years that followed, competitive and market-like behaviours in an uncertain environment became more evident in BC postsecondary education.

Policymakers in the BC government and in educational institutions have continued since 2000 to seek better ways of serving British Columbians, both individual residents and society as a whole. Paralleling this ongoing mission, however, has been a growing awareness that the survival of their organization, at least in its current form, could not be taken for granted. Attention to self-interest intensified as funding and sources of student enrolment became more vulnerable in the globalized world of neoliberalism.

This environment came to be perceived as one that provided incentives for public relations messages to displace balanced reports,[1] for institutions to pay greater attention to enhancing their status, and for game playing to emerge in such aspects of public administration as the creation and reporting of key performance indicators. The co-operative working relationships of the 1990s between institutional personnel and government officials weakened, and suspicions grew as to what the hidden agendas of the other might be. None of this was explicitly acknowledged, but official announcements and expressed postsecondary policy rationales became more difficult to take at face value.

It is on this basis that I have chosen to label the period since 2000 as one of cynicism. Rather than openly debating the merits of alternative policy options for postsecondary education, government increasingly made its decisions behind closed doors, and its official explanations were viewed with skepticism by at least some stakeholder groups. Collaboration across public universities and colleges declined in favour of strategic alliances among subsets of institutions, all claiming to have student and societal interests at heart. Information and policy analyses about postsecondary institutions became less accessible, sometimes even becoming confidential, in order to maintain competitive advantage. Institutions dutifully repackaged their public plans and reports to reference the changing slogans of the provincial government.[2] I do not believe that this ethos was intentionally inculcated, but it developed nevertheless and stands in marked contrast to the heady, and in some ways innocent, days of the Macdonald era.

It may or may not be that the idealism of the 1960s served society better than the pragmatism since 2000 in British Columbia. I am not recommending that the province should return to the past. Rather, my argument is simply that the nature of educational policy discourse has shifted. In contrast to the missionary zeal – to use Beinder's term – of the past, the tone has become more multilayered, with some of the less savoury layers acknowledged only to selected audiences. Thus, in terms of policy intent, the "who ultimately benefits?" question at the heart of critical theory (Bohman, 2015) seems more germane today than half a century ago. (I am not arguing that the question has changed in importance in terms of policy outcomes.)

Period Overview

A new right-wing BC government in 2001 introduced some significant changes to the postsecondary system over the following few years, a few of which resembled developments in Alberta and Ontario. One change opened the door wider for private and out-of-province universities to operate in the province. A second set of changes completed the redefinition of the degree-granting sectors, eliminating some institutions, transforming university colleges into a new form of teaching university, and affording public colleges and institutes some authority to grant certain types of baccalaureate degrees. A third set of changes altered the oversight of the apprenticeship system and private career colleges, and deregulated English as a second language (ESL) training schools.

The changes during the period since 2000 occurred with little planning. The new provincial government of 2001 had abandoned the previous administration's Charting a New Course strategic plan of 1996 for the college, institute, and university college sector. Only after expanding degree-granting authority and changing apprenticeship and the regulation of private career colleges did Victoria retain one of its former cabinet ministers, Geoff Plant, to prepare a new strategic plan for the entire post-secondary system, public and private. The resulting *Campus 2020* report (Plant, 2007) did not sit well with the government. Though ministers made mildly supportive comments about the importance of the plan and acted on a key recommendation that probably would have been implemented in any event – the transformation of university colleges into teaching universities – the majority of the recommendations were quietly ignored.

As these alterations occurred, the government's leadership of public institutions and its accountability requirements were complicated by its sometimes contradictory actions (Fisher et al., 2014), making it harder to assess which changes were significant and which were superficial. Public institutions were granted more freedom to determine their own enrolment and program mixes, yet at times the provincial degree-approval processes and tuition caps imposed by government, along with central bargaining controlled by government, hamstrung institutions as they attempted to exercise this greater freedom. Victoria set annual performance targets for each one, but the consequences of failing to meet them were generally negligible. The messages from government have been mixed, often seeming more concerned with image than substance and exacerbated by a revolving door for ministers, deputy ministers, and assistant deputy ministers, some of whom had no background in educational administration (Cowin, 2012a).

Reliable enrolment data for institutions outside the public system are difficult to obtain and are not comparable across sectors (Plant, 2007). The survey in Table 4 may be crude and uneven, but it is the best that is currently available and does succeed in portraying the general contours of the system. Refinements to the table are an essential next step toward a better understanding of the system as a whole.

TABLE 4
BC postsecondary system, 2012–13

Sector	Enrolment	Notes

Public institutions (25):
  Colleges (11)
  Institutes (3)
  Research universities (4)
  Teaching universities (7)
	188,000 FTE:
	44,000 FTE
	16,000 FTE
	88,000 FTE
	40,000 FTE
		Serving 440,000 individuals who took at least one course of any duration during the year
		
		Includes sub-baccalaureate enrolment
		(*Source:* Ministry of Advanced Education, Skills and Training, 2018)

Apprenticeship	35,000 active apprentices	As of March 2013 (*Source:* Industry Training Authority, 2013)
Private career colleges (330 registered in 2011)	51,000 individuals	Took at least one course of any duration during the year (*Source:* Private Career Training Institutions Agency, n.d.)
Faith-based institutions (24)	5,000 FTE (estimated)	Actively delivering instruction, estimated (*Source:* Author's estimate)
Aboriginal-governed institutions (35 in 2011)	1,500 FTE (estimated)	Of which 500 were at NVIT (*Sources:* Indigenous Adult and Higher Learning Association, 2013; Ministry of Advanced Education, Skills and Training, 2018; and author's estimate)
Other private and out-of-province degree-granting institutions	3,000 FTE (estimated)	Operating in BC. Includes such institutions as Quest University, Columbia College, City University, and Adler Institute (*Source:* Author's estimate)
English-language training schools	Unknown	Approximately 40 institutions on the Languages Canada website, excluding public institutions and institutions potentially included in the private career colleges total above. Not all schools are listed on this website

Baccalaureate Education

The Degree Authorization Act of 2002 enabled new private universities based in British Columbia and external universities such as City University and the University of Phoenix to confer degrees in the province. Yet at the same time, Victoria retained a gatekeeping function under the concurrent degree-quality assessment requirements. Although the Degree Authorization Act initially caused some consternation among public institutions and a flurry of activity among potential private universities, the impact to date of private and external universities has been modest.

Following the lead of Ontario and Alberta, but unexpectedly as far as many BC educators were concerned, the Degree Authorization Act also signalled that all public colleges in the province would be empowered to grant applied degrees. Although these colleges now resemble the former university colleges, this later transformation resulted in far less discussion in either public or academic circles. The number of baccalaureate programs in colleges remains small but is growing.

With only two colleges (Vancouver and Northwest) using the word "community" in their names and a few others downplaying the traditional community college philosophy in favour of positioning themselves more as baccalaureate colleges, exactly what constituted a desirable ethos for public colleges became contested. Something of a parallel shift occurred in the rebranding of the national organization, the Association of Canadian Community Colleges, as Colleges and Institutes Canada in 2014.[3]

Responding to local advocacy, the BC government transferred the north campus of Okanagan University College in Kelowna to UBC in 2004. The University College of the Cariboo, in Kamloops, was designated a special-purpose university and renamed Thompson Rivers University in the following year. Then, in 2008, with little consultation and almost no implementation planning, Premier Gordon Campbell announced over a period of weeks that the four remaining university colleges, one college (Capilano), and one institute (Emily Carr) would receive university status, albeit as teaching universities that would receive no additional funding to support research or different teaching arrangements. The university sector thus expanded dramatically, but it now consisted of two classes of universities: teaching and research (with Royal Roads and Thompson Rivers in some ways spanning the boundary, even though they are not research intensive).

Competitive federal funding for research recovered from the cutbacks of the 1990s throughout the period since 2000. New types of funding, such as for research infrastructure and endowed chairs, were also introduced. Ottawa made the commercialization of academic science and linkages with industry a policy priority (Fisher et al., 2006). These changes blurred the boundaries of public institutions as they partnered with private organizations.

Sub-baccalaureate Education

Not only did baccalaureate education change dramatically in British Columbia after 2000, but so too did apprenticeship. In 2004, the provincial government replaced the Industry Training and Apprenticeship Commission with the Industry Training Authority, an industry-dominated agency in which the voices of unions and educators were greatly diminished. The Industry Training Authority was mandated to bring about several reforms, including competency-based (i.e., not time-based) qualifications and the modularization of certification, known as progressive credentialing. These proposed changes were controversial, leading to claims that they would result in deskilling, and relationships in the sector remained prickly.[4] Implementation was slow and not all reforms have been achieved (Cowin, 2012b).

The BC government reviewed the Industry Training Authority in 2013 and announced some changes to it in 2014 that made it more closely resemble its predecessor, the Industry Training and Apprenticeship Commission. Organized labour was again to be represented on the board, and the functions delegated to seven Industry Training Organizations over the previous few years would be returned to the parent Authority.

The marginalization of trades and vocational education generally and the persistent under-representation of certain populations such as women and immigrants have been themes in the apprenticeship literature since the 1970s (Canadian Apprenticeship Forum, 2004). This disregard for sub-baccalaureate education from both policy and societal perspectives may help explain the laissez faire approach taken to the private career college sector until 2014.

The Private Post-Secondary Education Commission maintained a lean staff, but some in the industry perceived it as bureaucratic and unnecessarily treating the majority of private institutions in the same manner as problematic ones (Culos, 2005). In 2004, the BC government switched from public regulation of the sector to industry self-regulation, when it replaced the commission with the Private Career Training Institutions Agency. The new agency originally consisted entirely of representatives from industry, with some limited representation from students and public institutions eventually added (Cowin, 2013b). The new legislation exempted the now substantial English-language training sector from any type of regulation. Oversight of private academic institutions switched to mechanisms specified in the Degree Authorization Act of 2002.

Private career colleges and English-language schools continued to attract controversy, with some institutions perceived as providing high-quality education and as good corporate citizens, whereas a few were seen as rogue operators that tarnished the reputation of the entire sector (a particular problem for international marketing). In 2014, Victoria announced that the Private Career Training Institutions Agency would be dissolved and its functions transferred to the Ministry of Advanced Education. Like the recent changes to the Industry Training Authority for apprentices, this change suggests that the transfer of regulatory authority a decade ago to the private sector did not achieve what had been envisaged.

Other Developments

The Indigenous Adult and Higher Learning Association formed in 2003, the third generation of a consortium of Aboriginal-governed institutions. The original consortium had been established partly due to a perception in the Aboriginal community that the public institutions with which Aboriginal-governed institutions were partnering were charging excessive amounts for programming. Today, the association has about three dozen members, one of which (Nicola Valley Institute of Technology) is public. The association lacks complete enrolment information, but the available data suggest that member institutions accept a combined total of around three thousand students each year. (In 2005, three-quarters of the institutions enrolled one hundred or fewer students.)

The province began in 2000 to make some short-term, project-based funding available to public institutions to support Aboriginal education. About 5 percent (twenty thousand headcount students) of BC public postsecondary enrolment has at some point in its educational career self-identified as Aboriginal, although many of these students would not see their Aboriginal heritage as a primary identity.

The Aboriginal Post-Secondary Education and Training Partners group formed in 2005. Including representatives from the federal and BC governments, First Nations and Metis groups, and college and university presidents, it was the first forum of its kind in Canada and it continues to meet a few times each year (Cowin, 2011).

The structure of the faith-based sector has been stable over the past fifteen years. Although evangelical Protestants, a group not known for its commitment to higher education, are just a small portion of the BC population, they provide the majority of students in the faith-based sector (Cowin, 2009).

The character and extent of continuing education – the most market-responsive aspect of public postsecondary education – varied considerably across institutions during this period, as, for example, in the amount of contract training conducted for the private sector and government.[5] In 2006, colleges and institutes were allowed to count most continuing education enrolment toward achievement of their FTE enrolment targets set by government. (Not coincidentally, these were rising as the result of the additional twenty-five thousand FTE spaces for the public system, which were announced in 2004 but proving difficult to fill.)

Unlike in the 1990s, British Columbia currently lacks province-wide groups with independent legal status that provide educational leadership or focus on improving the teaching and learning environment. Likewise, the list of groups that are collaborative across the entire public system and that concentrate on the student experience, such as the BC Council on Admissions and Transfer and the BCcampus online organization,[6] is short (Cowin, 2012a). The types of organizations that seem to have thrived are special or self-interest groups: constituency-based advocacy groups of institutions, labour relations groups, and so on. These tend to be groups seeking to enhance access to resources or, like the BCNet information technology group, to save money.

Historical Moment: New Era

This chapter discusses two historical moments. The emphasis is on the first because the second is so recent that events are still unfolding.

A right-leaning Liberal government replaced the left-leaning New Democrats in the BC election of May 2001. Campaigning on a New Era platform – that is, "a new era of hope, prosperity and public service" – the Liberals promised "an unflagging commitment to the principles and values that underpin our free enterprise society," vowing to "initiate a number of specific changes within 90 days of being sworn into office" (British Columbia, 2001, July 24, p. 40). Fisher et al. (2014) view the initial agenda as the most radical shift in postsecondary policy in both substance and philosophical orientation by any BC government in forty years.

The tenets of new public management were already making inroads in the BC government: one of the last acts of the New Democrats in 2000 had been to enact the Budget Transparency and Accountability Act that, among other things, required government to prepare performance plans, measures, and reports. The Liberals raised the stakes with the Balanced Budget and Ministerial Accountability Act of 2001, which immediately prohibited deficit budgets and implemented a 20 percent salary holdback for ministers who did not meet their performance targets.

The new government promptly established a task force of its legislators to conduct a core services review to evaluate the entire public sector, promising public input. By the end of August, just a few months later, Premier Gordon Campbell had taken the chair, and the review was proceeding entirely behind closed doors (Palmer, 2001, September 19). Educators were nervous and uncertain about the outcome.

The first change to the structure of the BC postsecondary system came with the passage of the Degree Authorization Act in May 2002. Several other significant changes came in subsequent years, ending with amendments to the University Act in April 2008 that transformed three university colleges, a college, and an institute into special-purpose and teaching universities. The New Era historical moment thus encompassed changes to public and private postsecondary education over a six-year period, 2002 to 2008.

As with the Access for All moment, federal postsecondary developments are not discussed in this analysis. Although federal initiatives with respect to research, innovation, and student financial aid were significant (Fisher et al., 2006), they affected the internal characteristics of institutions rather than the structure of the postsecondary system. Thus, the discussion in this section focuses on the BC government.

Baccalaureate Education

The following sections describe three major changes to baccalaureate education in British Columbia. Although the impact to date of a greater number and range of institutions authorized since 2002 to grant bachelor's degrees, and the transformation of five public institutions into teaching universities in 2008, has been modest, the academic postsecondary system has nevertheless been restructured and presented with the option of a significantly different path of development. For the most part, the institutions affected turned out to have already been operating in British Columbia. Whereas the structural changes to baccalaureate education were made in a rather revolutionary manner, the actual growth and shifts in degree-level enrolment have been more evolutionary.

Applied Degrees

One thrust of the Degree Authorization Act was to increase the degree-granting capacity of public institutions through two new credentials, the applied baccalaureate at colleges and the applied master's degree at university colleges. This change was ultimately reflected in modifications to the College and Institute Act as a result of the consequential amendments section of the Degree Authorization Act.

The introduction of applied degrees, a significant expansion of the college mandate, occurred with remarkably little public discussion or implementation planning. It nevertheless proceeded smoothly, with the gradual introduction of a small number of applied degrees over the following decade. Some clues as to the rationale of government can be gleaned from public comments made by the minister of advanced education in the legislature, in which she mentioned increasing access, offering students more choice, and finding innovative ways of doing so (Bond, 2002, April 29). The applied degrees policy framework of the Ministry of Advanced Education subsequently added the rationales of responding to increasing certification requirements in many occupations, the greater likelihood of learners staying in the communities where they were trained (the retention of a skilled labour force being an important factor for rural communities), and enabling public colleges to remain relevant and competitive (Ministry of Advanced Education, 2015).

Even though government stated that no additional funding was anticipated for institutions to offer applied degrees (Ministry of Advanced Education, 2015), implying that implementation would therefore necessarily be slow, the lack of public attention to the applied degree initiative is curious. Certainly, there was some precedent with the earlier transformation of some colleges into degree-granting university colleges and with the introduction of a new credential, the bachelor of technology, at the British Columbia Institute of Technology in 1995. Nevertheless, some important stories may yet emerge as to what happened behind closed doors in discussions between institutional presidents and others with government officials.

The mild controversy that did initially arise concerned neither the policy intent nor the merit of applied degrees, but rather their definition. Although there was a consensus that they were not general arts or science degrees, and that the credential had to be employment oriented, it was not initially clear whether the BC government envisaged the Alberta or the Ontario model. The Alberta model, introduced in a demonstration project in 1994, consisted of three years (six semesters) of academic studies followed by at least two semesters of related paid and supervised work experience (Alberta Learning Information Services, 2015). This model received little support from BC colleges. Within months, the model that Ontario had introduced in 2000 (Panacci, 2014) was the understood definition of applied degrees in British Columbia. This entailed traditional four-year bachelor's degrees in applied subjects (with the definition of applied subjects remaining vague).

Private and External Universities

The other thrust of the Degree Authorization Act, in addition to applied degrees, was to make it easier for private and external universities to operate in the province. Prior to 2002, universities outside the BC public system had three options. They could obtain special provincial legislation to confer degrees (the BC-based Quest University, originally Sea to Sky University, took this path). They could teach in the province but confer degrees from outside it (as City University did). Or they could partner with an existing BC university or university college, which would confer the degrees (this was the least frequently, if ever, used of the three options).

The Degree Authorization Act smoothed the regulatory path for private and external institutions should they desire to avail themselves of the opportunity. It provided for proposals for degree programs from institutions other than BC public universities to be reviewed by an independent Degree Quality Assessment Board and a recommendation made to the minister of advanced education as to whether the program met the expected standards of educational quality. The minister could then authorize delivery of the degree program by regulation, rather than through legislation. At the same time, the minister remained a gatekeeper; even educationally sound proposals were not automatically approved.

The act initially resulted in a flurry of inquiries, with the Degree Quality Assessment Board reviewing fifty-three degree program applications in its first four years from private and out-of-province institutions (Degree Quality Assessment Board, 2003-04 to 2006-07). Since then, a few institutions have come and gone, and a few that were previously operating in the fringes have gained a way to legitimize themselves.[7] Most provided small niche programming in professional fields (such as MBA programs or the Adler School of Professional Psychology) or served a degree-completion market (the University of Phoenix tended to enrol students with some previous postsecondary credits). Trinity Western University, the largest and most comprehensive of the private institutions in British Columbia, was unaffected because it was already operating under its own BC legislation.

Part of the reason why private and external universities have had less of a presence in the province than many anticipated when the Degree Authorization Act was passed lies in competitive enrolment pressure from the public postsecondary sector. In addition to public colleges recruiting and retaining students in new applied degree programs, the government funded public institutions to increase enrolments by 25,000 FTEs (on a base of 150,000 FTEs) over the six years from 2004 to 2010. This expansion in capacity started just as enrolment demand was weakening. Almost every public institution nevertheless received a portion of the funding, even those that already had excess capacity. Students now found it easier to enrol in the much less expensive public institutions.

Teaching Universities

In 2004 and 2005, with the transformation of two public institutions, followed by five more transformations in 2008, the BC government created a new postsecondary subsector, the teaching university. Despite the name change, the degree-granting powers of these new universities were only modestly greater than in their previous incarnation. They remained non-doctoral institutions that continued to offer a comprehensive range of adult basic education, trades, and diploma-level programming along with bachelor's and some master's degrees.

A curious artifact of the teaching university category, reflecting their origins as community colleges, is that the province now has five universities that offer trades training and other programs comprised of few if any academic courses,[8] whereas two of the colleges, Douglas and Langara, offer some bachelor's degrees but no trades programming. University and college nomenclature now provides but a weak indication of the program mix in BC institutions.

The background to these developments begins in 1998, when the presidents of the five university colleges retained the recently retired president of the University of Victoria, Howard Petch, to evaluate the success of their baccalaureate programs (Church, 2002). Finding university college degrees to be academically strong, Petch discussed expanding the mandate of university colleges to include graduate studies and research (Petch, 1998).

Responding in part to a more competitive environment, university colleges began lobbying for a name change. Their poorly understood name would be discarded, and they would become "universities," especially as the Degree Authorization Act had allowed them to offer applied master's degrees (a vague concept but subject to approval by the new Degree Quality Assessment Board). Later in 2002, the university college presidents formed their own advocacy organization, the University Colleges of British Columbia.[9] Fleming and Lee (2009), administrators at what had formerly been a university college, maintain that the new consortium effectively created a tripartite public postsecondary system.

Community aspirations for a local university in the southern Interior had not been extinguished by the creation of university colleges. The Society for Okanagan University Legislation formed in 1999, leading to a new community group, University 2000, to lobby for a full-status university. By 2000, the Kelowna Chamber of Commerce had taken up the cause (Freake, 2005).

In the spring of 2001, both Okanagan University College and the University College of the Cariboo publicly proclaimed their desire to come under the University Act (Gaber, 2002). The university college consortium prepared a position paper at that time, calling for all university colleges to become regional comprehensive universities (Church, 2002). In its submission to the government's core review, it argued in 2001 for separate legislation and the ability to grant graduate degrees (Gaber, 2002).

The first action, as opposed to talk, taken in response to advocacy for university status was decidedly unsuccessful for the advocates: the government dismissed the board of Okanagan University College for agreeing to a university-style contract with its faculty that introduced faculty ranks and differentiated salary levels (Fleming and Lee, 2009). Ministry officials communicated to other university colleges that, as budgets were tight, overtures about university status would be unwelcome for the next few years (Church, 2002). Nevertheless, lobbying persisted despite the renunciation of Okanagan's contract. Levin (2003) concludes that all university colleges had begun adopting a university ethos, with their emphasis on research and scholarship, academic rank, and desire to join the national university association, the Association of Universities and Colleges of Canada.

In March 2003, Victoria acceded to the Okanagan's request for a university, but not at all in the way that some had hoped.[10] Okanagan University College was not transformed into a university. Instead, its north campus in Kelowna was hived off and transferred in 2004 to the University of British Columbia. Whiteley, Aguiar, and Marten (2008) describe the UBC takeover as resembling a Third World coup d'état in their examination of forces in the Okanagan that had arisen from a particular strategy for regional economic development adopted by the local business community. The remaining components of the former university college reverted to being Okanagan College, a comprehensive public college that now, like all public colleges, had the ability to grant applied degrees and that maintained a university transfer function.

In Kamloops, also in the Interior of the province and something of a competitor with Kelowna, the Friends of the University College of the Cariboo continued to lobby for a name change to "university." Two years later, in 2005, the government acceded by designating the university college as a special-purpose university, under the Thompson Rivers University Act.

Lacking the convenient two-campus configuration of Kelowna, with only baccalaureate programs located on one campus, the Kamloops initiative involved transforming the entire University College of the Cariboo into a university that was to emphasize teaching, retain its comprehensive set of sub-baccalaureate programming, add master's degrees, and pursue research and scholarly activity. This mandate resulted in a broader curriculum than those of institutions in England and Australia that had also been granted university status (Dennison, 2006). Adding to the complexity of the new university was its inheritance of the Open University, a distance learning entity that had been part of the disbanded Open Learning Agency.

Finally, in a series of five announcements spread over the month of April 2008, the premier proclaimed that the three remaining university colleges, as well as Capilano College and the Emily Carr Institute of Art and Design, would all be designated as special-purpose teaching universities (Ministry of Advanced Education, 2008, April 29). They would join Thompson Rivers as a new form of university in British Columbia that encompassed non-academic programming and did not require permanent faculty to conduct research. The initiative was described in government press releases as arising from the recommendations of the *Campus 2020* report (Plant, 2007), but given the long history of advocacy for more universities and Victoria's general lack of enthusiasm for the Plant report, this seemed a convenient rationale for politically driven decisions and a way of politely acknowledging an otherwise unwelcomed document.

Whatever discussions may have been occurring in cabinet and the premier's office in 2008, postsecondary policy directions and plans had not been made publicly available. Fleming (2010) characterizes developments as piecemeal expansion. This final new era measure, the 2008 transformation of five institutions into teaching universities, occurred with no implementation planning or explicit vision for the public post-secondary system. With no extra funding to support the transformed institutions, it was not immediately clear to their personnel what steps would be needed or possible beyond creating new letterhead and changing academic governance from education councils to senates.

The other BC universities promptly distanced themselves from their new counterparts, renaming their advocacy organization from the University Presidents' Council to the Research Universities' Council of British Columbia in 2008. Thompson Rivers and Royal Roads lost their membership but were readmitted in 2011, given their limited research mandates under their respective legislation. In January 2010, the remaining (new) universities formed the BC Association of Institutes and Universities, with a staff of two (Cowin, 2012a).

Sub-baccalaureate Education

Whereas the above changes in the authority to grant degrees seemed to occur mainly for pragmatic reasons, increasing the degree capacity of the province at minimal cost to the public purse, new policy for sub-baccalaureate education seems to have been more ideologically driven. These latter changes were made to the governance structures that affected entire sectors, altering their character rather than directly modifying their constituent institutions. The specific changes involved the regulatory bodies for apprenticeship and private career colleges, as well as the deregulation of ESL schools.

Apprenticeship

In a 2002 discussion paper, the Ministry of Advanced Education served notice that in its opinion, the Industry Training and Apprenticeship Commission had failed to implement the sweeping changes that it viewed as necessary (Ministry of Advanced Education, 2002). The Industry Training Authority Act of 2003 replaced the commission with the Industry Training Authority.

Apprenticeship was vigorously promoted, and the fourteen thousand registered apprentices in 2003–04 rose to a peak of thirty-five thousand in 2008–09, dropping back to thirty thousand in 2011–12. Completion rates, however, fell to historic lows: only 40 percent of apprentices finished their studies within six years of first registration, compared to 75 percent in previous decades. Meredith (2012) concludes that the controlling interests, employers, were quite content to have the apprenticeship system serve as a high-volume source of low-wage, entry-level, and semi-skilled labour.

On the surface, some of the apprenticeship reforms the government was seeking fell well within the scope of normal educational discourse and reflected developments in such countries as Australia (C. Robinson, 2000): competency-based certification to replace time-based training, modularized training and certification, more involvement of employers in determining curriculum, and transferability of previous learning toward certification in another trade (Ministry of Advanced Education, 2003, April 30; Sharpe and Gibson, 2005). These proposals, however, were controversial and quickly became politicized (Cowin, 2012b). Some saw modularization as likely to lead to deskilling in the trades and to hindering interprovincial mobility. Quality assurance mechanisms were claimed to be at risk. Undergirding the alarm was the change in governance that saw organized labour removed from the new Authority, whereas unions had been one of four constituencies in the previous commission (along with business, government, and education).

The structure of the new Industry Training Authority had been influenced by open-shop, non-unionized employers (Coalition of BC Businesses, 2001; Fisher et al., 2014). The new legislation was silent as to the responsibilities of employers in workforce training, and it restricted the Authority to defining performance standards for trades certification and to distributing funds. The government hoped that the new Authority would expand the amount of training from twenty-four thousand individuals (sixteen thousand apprentices plus eight thousand in entry-level trades training at public institutions) to thirty thousand within three years (Ministry of Advanced Education, 2003, April 30).

Following its start-up period, the Industry Training Authority made two noteworthy changes to the training system. In 2005–06, it established the first of seven principal-agent arrangements whereby separate not-for-profit legal entities, Industry Training Organizations, came by 2011 to manage 95 percent of apprentices under delegated authority (Industry Training Authority, 2012). Each one represented a distinct industry sector, such as residential construction and automotive, and was governed by industry organizations.

The second change reflected the call in the ministry's 2002 discussion paper for a transformation of the Entry Level Trades Training program that was then consuming two-thirds of the budget of the Industry Training and Apprenticeship Commission (Ministry of Advanced Education, 2002). In 2006, the Industry Training Authority replaced the pre-apprenticeship Entry Level program in public institutions with the Foundation Program. The new program altered some registration and credentialing practices, but perhaps the most significant development was the introduction of standardized, centralized curriculum (curriculum in terms of learning outcomes, not necessarily lesson plans and instructional materials) that allowed program success measures to be tracked on a province-wide basis. Whereas apprenticeship itself was less centralized than in the recent past, pre-apprenticeship training had become more centralized. Meredith (2012) argues that the overall impact of the changes since 2003 under the Industry Training Authority was a retention of the terminology and institutional trappings associated with apprenticeship but the loss of the essential components for a well-functioning system.

Private Career Colleges

A parallel, but more extreme, development in sub-baccalaureate education occurred in the governance of the private career college sector. When the Private Post-Secondary Education Act had been passed in 1991, it brought all private institutions – not just career colleges – under the purview of a single regulatory body, the Private Post-Secondary Education Commission. By 2001, the commission was registering 1,100 institutions (Private Post-Secondary Education Commission of British Columbia, 2002).

The provincial legislation and associated regulations did not enable the commission to generate sufficient revenue to cover its costs, and some institutions complained that it was excessively bureaucratic. They asserted that it trapped legitimate colleges in regulations that were developed in response to the worst institutions (Cowin, 2013b). In evaluating the commission, Culos (2005) states that from the outset, half measures and ambiguity had hampered a policy environment that was intended not only to protect consumers but also to legitimize and foster the growth of the career college sector.

In addition to the 2001 core services review, a parallel administrative justice review by the government scrutinized the commission. It was the BC attorney general, not an education or labour minister, who announced early in 2002 that the commission would be replaced by a self-regulating industry board.

The 2004 press release announcing the formation of the Private Career Training Institutions Agency framed the issue in terms of tuition protection for students (Ministry of Advanced Education, 2004, October 25), but it was really the agency's reduced scope and new form of governance that were newsworthy. Private and out-of-province universities were excluded from its purview because they now fell under the Degree Quality Assessment Board. More startling was the complete deregulation of schools that provided only ESL instruction, a growing component of the private sector and one that was frequently the first contact that international students had with British Columbia. Although the deregulation was controversial, the government did not articulate its policy rationale, other than to note that the province had previously regulated far more private institutions than did Alberta and Ontario (Bond, 2004, May 3). The decision to establish thresholds in terms of program duration and tuition fees for regulation of the remaining career colleges is more readily understood.

The Private Career Training Institutions Agency was required to be cost-recovery from fees charged to the colleges that it regulated, and its board was composed entirely of industry representatives. In other words, the sector had been transformed from a publicly regulated one to a smaller self-regulated set of institutions that the government expected to be more efficient and that would rely extensively on market mechanisms to ensure quality.

Deregulated institutions could choose to register with the agency. Furthermore, institutions that wanted their students to be eligible for government financial aid had to take the additional step of becoming accredited by the agency. Thus, when the money at risk was that of the students, quality assurance mechanisms were minimal. When government money for students was at risk, a higher standard of quality assurance was invoked.

Several mergers of career colleges have occurred since 2006, partly accounting for the reduction of 400 registered schools in 2008 to 320 in 2012. In 2012, 60 percent of the fifty-one thousand students were in the 160 accredited institutions (Private Career Training Institutions Agency, 2012). Large interprovincial and international corporations acquired some local schools in an effort to achieve horizontal and vertical integration in the industry, as well as to export BC curriculum abroad.

The Private Career Training Institutions Agency estimated that in 2006, 30 percent of enrolment in career colleges was international (Private Career Training Institutions Agency, 2008). This risk to British Columbia's reputation as a destination for international students prompted Victoria to introduce its own Educational Quality Assurance trademark in 2009 for qualified public and private institutions that chose to pursue it. In 2011, the definition of career training was broadened to include ESL instruction, where tuition or duration exceeded a certain amount. An increasingly important economic subsector in the province, international language students, was again receiving some regulatory oversight.

Closures

Several changes during the New Era moment could be viewed as tweaking the existing system in that they were individually made for pragmatic reasons. Cumulatively, though, the fact that all were closures could be taken as indications of new policy directions.

In 2001–02, the first year of its mandate, the BC Liberal government announced its intention to dissolve the Centre for Curriculum, Transfer and Technology and the Centre for Education Information Standards and Services. These province-wide agencies mainly served the public college and institute sector but also had some connections with the universities. Some of their functions were simply reallocated to other bodies, but services in support of teaching and learning suffered (Cowin, 2012a). Fisher et al. (2014) describe the government as eliminating or radically transforming most of the system-wide agencies and support structures that had been created over the previous fifteen years.

The Ministry of Advanced Education also announced in February 2002 that the Technical University of BC, which had opened to students just three years earlier, would be closed. The full story of its demise has yet to be told. Trueman (2005) writes,

> Many saw the creation of TechBC and the construction of its landmark urban campus in north Surrey as political monument-building ... How does one evaluate the claim that TechBC was shut down entirely for partisan political reasons? The fact this view is widely held does not make it provable ... It also tends to obscure the many other challenges the fledgling university faced. (pp. 2-3)

The government invited other institutions to submit proposals to inherit the students and assets of the Technical University. Simon Fraser was the successful proponent, leading to the establishment of its Surrey campus.

The Open Learning Agency received extra scrutiny from government. The nature of the government's concerns was not clear, but the agency was disbanded in 2005, with most of its functions redistributed to other institutions.

The Institute of Indigenous Government, a public entity created in 1995, was especially problematic and politically sensitive. It had been hastily launched with inadequate planning (Human Resources Development Canada, 1998), and management issues and very low enrolment led to its closure in 2007. Its assets were transferred to another Aboriginal-governed public institution, the Nicola Valley Institute of Technology.

Analysis: New Era Moment

Social Justice

At best, the BC government paid lip service to social justice concerns during the New Era moment, mentioning access to postsecondary education in some of its public announcements but not really demonstrating that any deeply held desire for greater social justice had actually propelled policy development. Nevertheless, the fact that it even mentioned access indicates the power of this enduring goal in educational discourse in British Columbia.

If we take government pronouncements at face value, the twenty-five thousand seat expansion announced in 2004 was explicitly about increasing access to postsecondary education. However, it is hard to find evidence that fair access for populations with low participation rates was really much of a priority, given the basis on which funding was allocated throughout the province, providing some money to every institution with only little regard to relative enrolment demand and supply. This development contrasts with the careful planning in 1989 for a fifteen thousand seat capacity increase under the Access for All initiative.

The conclusion of the BC auditor general about the distribution of funding was that the enrolment expansion was a roundabout way to address some of the problems arising from an inadequate funding system, enabling the government to direct more money to postsecondary institutions while claiming that it was holding down the per-student funding (Van Iersel, 2006). In other words, the expansion was used for financial and managerial purposes rather than as a tool of social policy. Nevertheless, however muddled the New Era expansion program might have been, it did increase the number of seats available in public postsecondary institutions, and admission requirements in a number of programs became less restrictive.

Similarly, government press releases in 2008 concerning the establishment of five new teaching universities explicitly invoked the goal of access: "British Columbians want to access university degree programs in all regions of the province," stated Advanced Education Minister Murray Coell. "With a new university ... students will be able to access degree programs closer to home" (Ministry of Advanced Education, 2008, April 21). This sentiment may have played well in the local press, but the new university initiative actually made little difference to the availability of degree programs in that university colleges could, and were, already granting bachelor's degrees in any subject and a few master's degrees in applied subjects. Furthermore, public colleges across the province could already grant baccalaureate degrees in applied subjects.

Whatever the rationales and merits of creating a new sector of teaching universities, it is hard to find compelling evidence that social justice for individual students or under-represented groups was a driving force. Perhaps a case could be made in support of the spatial adaptation version of social justice in that more cities beyond the metropolitan areas or on their fringes could now share in the benefits, whatever they might be for teaching institutions, of a university presence.

Like the Macdonald era and the Access for All historical moments, the New Era moment brought about a significant restructuring of the public postsecondary sectors. Unlike in the other moments, much of the public commentary in the legislature and media during the New Era moment regarding the social justice implications of the changes was critical or unsupportive. Rather than seeing developments as increasing the opportunities or life chances of individual citizens, as were the general perceptions of the Macdonald and Access for All moments, a number of commentators in the New Era moment, especially from labour, suspected that the needs of employers and businesses were taking precedence under a neoliberal agenda (Fisher et al., 2014; Meredith, 2012). In at least some quarters, social justice was claimed to be diminishing in non-academic programming.

Human Capital Formation

Human capital considerations were important in the New Era moment. Both approaches to developing human capital, the more general one about a well-educated workforce and the more occupationally specific one, were invoked but in differing postsecondary sectors. In addition, the role of highly qualified personnel in regional economic development was acknowledged.

When the government announced the formation of the Industry Training Authority (Ministry of Advanced Education, 2003, April 30), it explicitly referenced occupational supply and demand, saying that employers' needs for skilled workers were not being met and that demand was projected to increase rapidly for many highly skilled jobs. The examples it provided of industries where demand exceeded the domestic supply of qualified tradespeople, according to the Conference Board of Canada and not its own analyses, were in the building, automotive, and aerospace sectors.

In contrast to the occupational projection approach that has been regularly used mainly with respect to sub-baccalaureate education (and less prominently in baccalaureate education, except for such regulated professions as in health care), references to the generic, or soft, employability skills itemized by the Conference Board of Canada (Bloom and Kitagawa, 1999) have been common in discourse about all sectors of BC public postsecondary education.[11] Applied degrees, both bachelor's and master's, may seem at first to be primarily an occupationally oriented approach to human capital formation, but the lack of any sort of strategy, needs assessment, or planning for their introduction suggests that the policy was driven more by the general approach to human capital formation – to have a better-educated workforce.

The applied degree framework (Ministry of Advanced Education, 2015) reflected a particular understanding of what highly skilled workers might mean in the context of human capital formation. It stated that the priority in applied degree programs was to prepare graduates for employment and that preparation for further studies at a more advanced level was not an essential feature. The vision of applied degrees as largely terminal credentials implies a focus on what some might consider still to be mid-level skills. However, another guiding principle in the framework was to address the need for a highly skilled workforce, especially in light of anticipated labour shortages. It would seem that the definition of a highly skilled workforce was still open to interpretation: terminal baccalaureate education may or may not be seen as high-level training in the context of the current and anticipated knowledge economy.

Nevertheless, the existence of applied degrees indicated the acceptance by government of the argument that innovation and economic growth were dependent on a level of problem solving and creativity that cannot be adequately fostered in students during programs of only two or fewer years in duration. The "essential skills" terminology of the federal government (Employment and Social Development Canada, 2015, October 13) might not have been explicitly referenced in the curricula for applied degrees, but skills such as thinking, working with others, and continuous learning were embedded in understandings of what was needed in such degrees.

Applied degrees also figured in the government's view of the contribution that education could make to regional economic and social development. The applied degree framework noted the contention that learners were more likely to remain in communities where they were trained, thus making the province-wide authorization to grant applied degrees a strategy for reducing labour market recruitment and retention challenges in the hinterland.

Universities have over the years been a component of British Columbia's strategies for attempting to diversify its resource-based economy into knowledge-dependent industries. From the BC government's establishment of Discovery Parks in the early 1980s to serve as incubators for the commercialization of research (City of Burnaby, 2015; Discovery Parks, 2015) through to Ottawa's current innovation strategies (Fisher et al., 2006), the considerable social and cultural capital of universities for attracting research and philanthropic dollars seems to have influenced, for example, the decision to have UBC, not Okanagan University College, bring a university presence to the Okanagan.

When Thompson Rivers University was established, the Ministry of Advanced Education (2005, March 31) claimed that it would bring an estimated $100 million annually to Kamloops and surrounding regions. Some of this benefit would arise from the simple expedient of increasing the payroll at the new university by relocating the Open University from the Open Learning Agency in Vancouver to Kamloops. Other components of this economic growth, however, would presumably come from having some faculty conduct research and from attracting research funding.

Marketization

The new government's first Speech from the Throne in 2001 proclaimed that a new era of marketization had arrived, stating that "British Columbians are well positioned to show the world what we can do when we unleash the power of free enterprise" (British Columbia, 2001, July 24). Although public administration over the past two decades had become more sensitive to market approaches, and BC right-wing political parties ever since Macdonald had presented themselves as champions of free enterprise, the Liberals in 2001 were the first BC government to actually embrace markets enthusiastically (Fisher, House, and Rubenson, 2003). The New Era reforms did not entail the articulation of a new vision for postsecondary education in terms of purposes so much as desire to achieve existing goals in new, and presumably better, ways.

The policy shift in favour of marketization was grounded less in a response to developments in the external environment than in ideological reasons (Fisher et al., 2014). This ideology manifested in postsecondary education primarily through efforts to open it to the private sector

(Dennison and Schuetze, 2004) and the implementation, superficially in some instances and more profoundly in others, of a number of the techniques of new public management.

In the academic sphere, marketization took the form of increased competition, sometimes for students and sometimes simply for institutional legitimacy. Sometimes this competition arose as the result of direct actions by government, but in other cases, it was an indirect consequence of decisions taken to achieve other goals (such as the twenty-five thousand seat expansion in public institutions).

The government's invitation to private and external universities to play a greater role in British Columbia under the Degree Authorization Act was an early and obvious attempt to challenge the public university system and to increase competition for students as a spur to innovation and efficiency in the delivery of academic programming. The introduction of applied degrees in public colleges did not initially appear as quite the same competitive threat to universities, as the new degrees seemed to be a rather different type of credential from the traditional bachelor's degree. However, as actual curriculum emerged in the new program approval process, it became clear that applied degrees in many instances resembled the traditional baccalaureate and just happened to be in disciplines other than arts and science, or in specialized or interdisciplinary niches where no degree had previously been offered in British Columbia. Business degrees, especially, proliferated, and research universities positioned their offerings increasingly as selective admission, elite programs in contrast to the mass approach of their competitors.

The 2004 decision to expand the public system by twenty-five thousand FTE seats over the next six years seems to have been made for reasons that had nothing to do with marketization. However, coming at a time when enrolment demand was beginning to lessen, and representing the main way that the province's grants to public institutions were likely to increase in the short term, the capacity increase had the unintended effect of intensifying student recruitment efforts. To some extent, these efforts brought new students into the system. In addition, however, some of the student recruiting expenditures were little more than institutions poaching each other's prospective students, a net zero gain in the postsecondary participation rate of the province. Institutional marketing departments thrived, and students were invited to travel greater distances to enrol in programs that were supposedly better for them.[12] Whether society as a whole benefitted is an open question, but the thrust ran contrary to the closer-to-home rhetoric of past decades.

Even though student mobility among institutions has remained strong (Student Transitions Project, 2012) because the range of upper-level offerings that smaller institutions can supply is necessarily limited, institutions that once encouraged their students to continue their studies elsewhere increasingly attempted to retain them. Among transfer institutions, an element of competition for students has always been present, but it seems to have intensified over the past decade.

The university colleges had for some time felt that they operated at a competitive disadvantage with universities. In the absence of institutional (as distinct from program) accreditation in Canada to bolster the legitimacy of the degrees they conferred, several had instead sought and achieved membership in the Association of Universities and Colleges of Canada as a proxy for institutional accreditation: Cariboo was admitted in 1996, Okanagan and Fraser Valley in 1997, and finally Malaspina in 2000. Kwantlen had not initially sought membership (Church, 2002). This membership helped to bolster the case that university colleges began to put forward publicly in 2001 that they should become regional universities to level the degree-granting playing field.

Marketization took a different form in non-academic postsecondary education. It consisted of changing the ground rules under which institutions functioned, rather than directly inviting new institutions to operate in the province (as had occurred with the Degree Authorization Act) or new programs to be offered (as had occurred with applied degrees).

The self-regulation of career colleges under the Private Career Training Institutions Agency (PCTIA), essentially guaranteeing students only basic consumer protection for their tuition fees, is the most extreme example of marketization in the New Era. A government member of the legislative assembly explained the rationale for the new policy regarding career colleges: as with any business, a private educational institution relies on its reputation to stay afloat; if its product and reputation were poor, the college would eventually close (Orr, 2003, October 9).

Along with giving business the dominant voice in the Industry Training Authority, the government deregulated eleven compulsory trades in 2003 (accounting for about half of BC apprentices). This opened employment to individuals who were not certified journeymen or apprentices. It was justified as a way to remove barriers for workers who were receiving training that had previously been designated as part of another compulsory trade (Ministry of Advanced Education, 2003, April 30). It also meant that apprenticeship was no longer the only educational path to these occupations. The government asserted that the new Safety Standards Act would be sufficient to protect worker and public safety in the newly deregulated trades (Ministry of Advanced Education, 2003, April 30).

Under the Industry Training Authority, the new public management approach of using principal-agent, contractual arrangements led to the establishment of seven Industry Training Organizations. Government, which had directly overseen apprenticeship until the formation of the Industry Training and Apprenticeship Commission in 1997, was now two steps removed from apprenticeship education: it had delegated functions to the Industry Training Authority, which in turn had delegated them to the Industry Training Organizations.

Historical Moment: Post-neoliberalism

In 2011, Premier Gordon Campbell resigned and was replaced by Christy Clark. The Liberal Party again won the 2013 provincial election, but many members of Clark's cabinet were not those of the New Era under Gordon Campbell.

Changes in postsecondary education from 2011 to 2014, especially in 2014, suggest that the government's adherence to a marketization agenda was weakening, or at least becoming more complex. As with the evolution of thinking about new public management reflected in such concepts as joined-up government, marketization itself has not been repudiated or abandoned. Rather, the steadfast adherence to marketization principles is being complemented by other approaches in specific areas where markets have not achieved the anticipated or desired outcomes, especially in the more vocational postsecondary sectors. Despite the four changes described below that suggest the ideological pendulum may be swinging back toward stances that predate the New Era moment, markets are still embedded in many aspects of the current BC postsecondary environment.

Because the developments analyzed in this section are so recent, the full consequences of the policy changes are not yet known. Furthermore, other significant developments may still be occurring. Nevertheless, even if all the ramifications are not known, the changes from 2011 to 2014 were sufficiently significant to constitute a historical moment.

The first visible indication that not all the New Era reforms were achieving their public policy goals came in 2007, when the government commissioned one of its former assistant deputy ministers of advanced education and former president of the BC Institute of Technology, John Watson, to review the Private Career Training Institutions Act. In addition to a number of minor recommendations, Watson called for private ESL schools to again be regulated (Watson, 2008). He noted that the estimated 150 to 200 language schools were not required to meet any educational or quality standards, and that their approximately 100,000 students (some of whom were in programs of only a few weeks' duration) were unprotected.[13]

The government initially chose not to act on the recommendation to regulate language schools, even though others shared Watson's concern. *BC Business* magazine, for example, had run an article about the "motley, squabbling, government-neglected ESL industry" (Howard, 2006, p. 61), and even the industry-dominated board of the Private Career Training Institutions Agency had itself recommended re-regulation in the Campus 2020 hearings of 2007 (Cowin, 2013b).

Not until November 2009 did the government choose to act, and even then it took a grudging step that had more to do with appearance than substance. The voluntary EQA (Educational Quality Assurance) designation was introduced as a trademark, not as an accreditation mechanism, according to the Ministry of Advanced Education website at that time. Finally, in 2011, an amendment to the Private Career Training Institutions Act broadened the definition of career training to include ESL instruction where tuition or duration exceeded a given amount. Such schools were required to administer a PCTIA-approved, standardized test to students at the beginning and the end of the English-language program. The EQA designation was also strengthened with respect to programs for international students.

Federal changes in June 2014 to the International Student Program required provinces to develop a list of educational institutions that were eligible to host international students on student permits (Ministry of Advanced Education, 2016, January 13). This became the catalyst for Victoria to require all institutions enrolling international students for more than six months to achieve the EQA designation, now described as concerning "government-recognized" quality assurance standards. The number of private and public EQA-designated institutions increased from 125 to 220 over the eighteen-month transition period (Ministry of Advanced Education, 2016, January 13).

Another signal that the government was not entirely satisfied with previous neoliberal reforms came from a review it commissioned, this time in 2013, of the Industry Training Authority. The author of the subsequent report, Jessica McDonald, had been the province's top bureaucrat as deputy to the premier until her resignation in 2009. Among her recommendations were that unions be brought back to the board overseeing apprenticeship and that money be redirected to high-demand occupations, especially in the skilled trades (McDonald, 2014).

It was in 2014 that substantive changes to sub-baccalaureate education emerged. The government announced that it would implement all twenty-nine recommendations from McDonald's review on the Industry Training Authority, starting with the appointment of a new board of directors that included representation from labour, the Aboriginal community, and public postsecondary education (Ministry of Jobs, Tourism and Skills Training, 2014, May 5). The subsidiary Industry Training Organizations were wound down and all their functions transferred back into the Industry Training Authority by November 2014 (Industry Training Authority, 2015). Registrations for the 2014–15 fiscal year consisted of 35,000 adults, 4,500 youth, and 4,000 students in Foundation (pre-apprenticeship) programs (Industry Training Authority, 2015, August). The completion rate, allowing six years to finish an apprenticeship, stood at a dismal 33 percent (Industry Training Authority, 2015, August).

A second change in 2014 was the announcement that the Private Career Training Institutions Agency would be dissolved, and responsibility for regulating private colleges providing more than forty hours of instruction and charging tuition exceeding $1,000 would return to the Ministry of

Advanced Education (Ministry of Energy and Mines, 2014, April 17). The official rationales in the government's news release (Ministry of Advanced Education, 2015, February 11) included raising quality standards and strengthening quality assurance for the sector, as well as reducing regulatory requirements for institutions with a history of good compliance. To obtain a more complete understanding of the pressures at play, though, an investigation conducted by the provincial ombudsperson at much the same time is helpful (K. Carter, 2015).

The ombudsperson's investigative report found that compliance monitoring of the 320 private career colleges had been inconsistent, that the forty-seven thousand students were inadequately informed on such matters as their rights, and that problems were systemic. The report also noted the decline in the number of registered institutions, from 520 in 2006 to 310 in 2013, due to consolidation, voluntary de-registration, closure of institutions, and increased regulatory standards.

A public administrator promptly replaced the board of the Private Career Training Institutions Agency. New legislation was passed in March 2015, with the expectation that it would come into force by regulation in the spring of 2016 (Ministry of Advanced Education, 2015, August 17). This oversight of institutions that produced thirty-eight thousand graduates in 2013–14 would include what the government said were fifty private ESL institutions.[14]

Whereas the above two changes in 2014, concerning private colleges and apprenticeship, were substantive ones that could potentially alter the character of these sectors, the third modification was aspirational, predicated on the future development of a major liquefied natural gas industry in the province, a prospect that currently looks by no means certain. As events unfold, it seems that incentives may be developing for public postsecondary institutions to simply repackage existing activities in an effort to appear responsive to projected labour market needs that they may not even believe. Politics make it difficult at this early stage to know whether a radical change is really occurring.[15]

The likelihood of a new industry emerging is not as important for the purposes of this discussion as the change in government attitude that the new initiative signals. The government was clearly expressing a lack of confidence in the educational market to meet projected labour demands and was instead adopting an interventionist approach.

In April 2014, Victoria announced a strategy, the Skills for Jobs Blueprint, to "re-engineer" secondary and postsecondary education to "profile skilled trades that will soon be in high demand" (Ministry of Jobs, Tourism and Skills Training, 2014, April 29). It consisted of a series of policies, a key one being that postsecondary institutions were to reconfigure their programming over a period of years, so that by 2017–18 a minimum of one-quarter of their budgets would be devoted to training for high-demand occupations. (The policy was silent as to how this might apply to private institutions and indeed about the role in general that the government saw for career colleges and private universities in meeting occupational needs.) Taken at face value, which I think unwise at this point, the Blueprint augured a major restructuring of the public postsecondary system in terms of program mix. It was the first time since the Strand Report (British Columbia Task Force on Employment and Training, 1991) and the Skills Now initiative of 1993 to 1995 of the BC Ministry of Skills, Training and Labour (Dennison, 1995; Fisher et al., 2014) that the distinctive needs and characteristics of sub-baccalaureate education have been a policy focus in British Columbia.

What occupations were in high demand was not initially specified, even though the Ministry of Jobs, Tourism and Skills Training had significantly strengthened its labour market forecasting over the previous few years and was publishing ten-year occupational outlooks on a website titled WorkBC (Ministry of Jobs, Tourism and Skills Training, 2014). Given the focus on apprenticeship training at the government's press conference, and given that the last major attempt to strengthen vocational education in the province had been back in the 1990s (Fisher et al., 2014), university personnel expressed polite concern that academic and liberal education was at risk. In response to the Skills for Jobs Blueprint, the Research Universities' Council of British Columbia (2014, April 29) immediately issued a press release that reframed warnings of growing skills gaps in terms of the employment skills provided in universities.

When government officials did specify what constituted high-demand occupations, they defined them not on the basis of shortfalls in labour supply but in terms of job openings; that is, the high-demand occupations were simply the sixty largest occupations (Usher, 2015, February 4). This suggests that despite all the bold talk of re-engineering postsecondary education, much will continue as usual. In fact, the University of the Fraser Valley found that 85 percent of its programs already fully or partially matched the top sixty in-demand occupations listed in the BC government's labour market forecast (University of the Fraser Valley, 2015). Advanced Education Minister Andrew Wilkinson conceded in 2015 that funding for general education, arts, and science was not going to diminish (Fletcher, 2015, February 10).

The faith-based sector has experienced a few minor developments since 2010. In 2014, due to financial challenges, the Vancouver School of Theology sold a major building, located on land it leases from UBC for 999 years, to UBC (ironically, to serve as the home for UBC's School of Economics). The following year, Regent College began reducing staffing by 30 percent. However, 2015 also saw some expansion in the sector as Trinity Western opened a storefront campus in Richmond to house its leadership and MBA programs.

Langara College and the Vancouver School Board formed a partnership in 2014 to merge their continuing education offerings. Persistent budgetary challenges had reduced the school district's continuing education offerings over a number of years, and it anticipated ongoing difficulties. The new partnership represented another way of achieving operational efficiencies.

Although federal influence in the amount and type of BC postsecondary instruction had largely disappeared, Ottawa retained its dominant role in research funding and continued to make a significant contribution to student financial aid. It still provided modest funding for ESL instruction, routed to public postsecondary institutions through the province. In 2014, though, a little over $20 million of the language funding was withdrawn, with some indication that the federal language funds would move away from postsecondary institutions to non-profit community organizations (Sherlock, 2014, May 31). This shift from public institutions resembled the approach taken under the federal Canadian Jobs Strategy in 1985, but it did not directly or immediately benefit the for-profit sector. Also, the impact was especially severe at just one institution, Vancouver Community College, where almost half the language instruction occurred.

Analysis: Post-neoliberalism Moment

Social Justice

Efforts to promote social justice seem largely absent in the post-neoliberal historical moment. Better protection for international ESL students and for students in private career colleges was a response to their complaints, and it represented a desire to prevent damage to the BC brand internationally rather than to advance the welfare of students.

Although the preface to the Blueprint document recognized that "some British Columbians such as at-risk-youth, Aboriginal people and persons with disabilities face unique challenges in finding their place in the workforce" (British Columbia, 2014, p. 3), the apparent concern for these populations seemed to be subject to the needs of the economy. For example, as the text explained, "every person in British Columbia should be equipped so they can realize career opportunities most in demand by industry" (p. 4). It also described Aboriginal youth as a "huge pool of new talent" (p. 14). Furthermore, some of the funding that was earmarked for the targeted populations was to be drawn from existing federal-provincial agreements in support of these populations. Student needs and futures have been conspicuously absent from the discourse about skills gaps and apprenticeship; the focus has been on the short- to medium-term needs of employers and the economy.

The Skills for Jobs Blueprint nevertheless paid significant attention to Aboriginal people, a marked change from what have often been little more than passing references in previous BC government documents on postsecondary education (as distinct from documents specifically about the primary and secondary education of Aboriginal people). In this respect, the Blueprint is perhaps an example of the compensatory version of social justice – namely, that serious attention is being devoted to a disadvantaged group. Whether it results in a fuller expression of social justice efforts for this population, especially in terms of cultural recognition, remains to be seen.

In a similar vein, the inclusion of an Aboriginal representative on the latest board of the Industry Training Authority might be an example of compensatory or cultural social justice. On the other hand, it might simply be tokenism or an attempt to enhance the probability that the economic development efforts of the dominant society will be effective by including an Aboriginal stakeholder in the strategy-setting body. Once again, only time will tell if a new articulation of social justice is emerging in BC postsecondary education.

Human Capital Formation

Human capital formation dominated the postsecondary policy agenda of the BC Liberals. The Skills for Jobs Blueprint was its major educational policy thrust, a component of what was arguably its top overall goal, the development of a liquefied natural gas industry in the province. The Blueprint's language was strong, talking of re-engineering secondary and postsecondary education, even though the mundane reality may consist partially of repackaging existing activities. Regardless of how the policy ends up being implemented, human capital formation in support of the economy was the rationale behind it.

At the heart of the Blueprint was a policy shift to reallocate education funding toward programs that serve in-demand occupations, matching education with industry needs. The intention to rely on labour market projections figured prominently in the policy document, along with the objective of strengthening the government's ability to produce reliable projections. With concern for high-demand occupations and skill shortages central to the Blueprint, the policy reflected an occupationally specific version of human capital theory rather than an attempt to foster an innovative knowledge-based economy through a better-educated workforce in terms of generic or essential skills.

The Skills for Jobs Blueprint focused strongly on sub-baccalaureate education, especially trades training and apprenticeship. This contrasted with the highly qualified personnel approach (i.e., individuals with a bachelor's degree or higher) that the federal government has viewed as vital for innovation and economic growth (e.g., McKenzie, 2007). It also ran contrary to past Canadian immigration policy in that the Federal Skilled Workers Program had shifted by 2010 from an emphasis on skill shortages in specific occupations to using broader criteria to reflect the ability of a worker to change jobs as the labour market changed (Citizenship and Immigration Canada, 2010).[16]

The Blueprint also espoused a narrower conception of human capital than some of the documentation available through the Research, Technology, and Innovation Division of the BC Ministry of Advanced Education in which the creation of personal and social well-being was considered along with economic development (Klingbeil, 2008). Despite the emphasis in the Blueprint on sub-baccalaureate education, private career colleges – even those that provide technical training for apprentices – did not obviously figure in the intended re-engineering of the postsecondary system to meet the anticipated labour shortages. However, these colleges may have indirectly entered the calculus through related changes to student financial aid.

The 2013 federal reduction in ESL funding in public institutions, coupled with an overall enrolment decline in the Developmental Education category,[17] of which ESL instruction is a component, expressed a concern for neither social justice nor human capital formation. Immigrants who obtain their postsecondary education in other countries but who lack English-language proficiency face substantial barriers to full participation in both economic and social life. The government asserted that other providers of formal and informal education could address the needs arising from the ESL cutbacks, but evidence is lacking at this time to determine if this is occurring.

The 2014 reforms to the governance structure of the Industry Training Authority, an attempt to reshape apprenticeship education, were consistent with a concern for human capital formation, but the evidence is currently inconclusive as to whether human capital considerations were actually the propelling force in this shift in policy direction, as opposed to a desire for efficient and effective public administration. The review of the Authority (McDonald, 2014) that precipitated the changes referred to anticipated labour shortages, but it also called for optimizing the training system to reach the province's full potential to plan and respond to labour needs – an efficiency goal.

Marketization

The main developments with respect to marketization were largely a reversal of previous trends in a few specific areas. The overall neoliberal philosophy was not repudiated, however.

The demise of the Industry Training Organizations, and the return of their functions to the Industry Training Authority, was an abandonment of the new public management techniques of single-purpose organizations and principal-agent relationships. The return of organized labour to the governance of apprenticeship represented an effort to use a more collaborative governance model rather than a private sector approach involving only employers. Another step away from a market-based approach to apprenticeship came in 2015, when the province required companies bidding on large public infrastructure projects to employ a certain number of apprentices (Penner, 2015, September 4).

The re-regulation of English-language training schools and the dissolution of the Private Career Training Institutions Agency were acknowledgments that markets do not always self-regulate as well as a previous government had hoped. One reason for market failure with respect to private career colleges and for-profit degree-granting institutions is that prospective students lack the necessary data on former student experiences and outcomes in private institutions to make informed decisions about where to enrol (Clift, 2016).

Another instance where the government has avoided the discipline of markets concerns the rural public colleges and the northern university, which have chronically failed to meet the enrolment targets set by the BC government. In 2013–14, for example, four of the five northern colleges (each funded to enrol between 1,500 and 3,000 FTE students) achieved between 55 and 90 percent of their targets, and the University of Northern British Columbia (funded for 3,500 FTE students) achieved less than 85 percent of its target (Ministry of Advanced Education, Skills and Training, 2018). Successive governments of all political stripes, including the BC Liberals, nevertheless allowed the situation to continue rather than to impose a more market-oriented discipline on the institutions. This would seem a tacit admission that the government has not seen its social policy goals for postsecondary education as entirely achievable through the techniques of new public management or neoliberalism.

An area where a market orientation has strengthened is in the recruiting of international students from around the globe. Victoria's 2012 strategy to increase international students in British Columbia by 50 percent over four years (Ministry of Advanced Education, 2012) was essentially an economic development strategy, not an effort to internationalize pedagogy and the curriculum.[18]

Developments at Simon Fraser University illustrate the efforts that all BC public postsecondary institutions have been making in recent years: at SFU, the number of international students expanded from 9 percent of undergraduate FTE enrolment in 2008–09 to 17 percent in 2013–14 (Simon Fraser University, 2014). The heavy reliance on revenue from these students is illustrated in the 2012–13 financial statements of Douglas College: $13.6 million in international student tuition fees, compared to $19.4 million from government-subsidized domestic students in credit courses (Douglas College, 2013). (The college's subsequent publicly available financial statements no longer show international tuition fees separately.)

The Educational Quality Assurance designation was originally seen primarily as an element that would help British Columbia compete in the global market for international students. Since then, the EQA has shifted away from branding toward becoming more of an accreditation (but still with some marketing aspects). Rather than specifying a particular set of government standards, the policy language allows institutions to choose any set of standards that the government is willing to recognize. Although some aspects of marketization may have weakened within the province, competitive behaviours of institutions in support of acquiring resources and prestige from elsewhere show no signs of abating.

Conclusion

This chapter begins by identifying four themes that form a backdrop for any history of the contemporary BC postsecondary education system. It then turns to the approach taken in this particular history, summarizing and discussing the findings from the three policy rationales that served as my analytical lenses.

After an overview of the system as it existed in 2015, I finish by using the dual social significance of education – that is, its role as both an emancipating and a stratifying mechanism within society – as a final example of how attention to postsecondary structures and relationships among institutions can illuminate a variety of topics.

Historical Themes

However one might elect to interpret the development of the BC postsecondary system in its entirety, it seems likely that the following four themes would be relevant in some way.

Geographical Access

Spatial distribution and access issues figured prominently in the development of the province's public postsecondary system, unlike in private sector institutions, where they played a much more variable, and overall lesser, role. The challenge of providing postsecondary opportunities to small and remote communities helped to prompt some of the more innovative aspects of the BC system, such as the distinctive character of its community colleges and initiatives in non-metropolitan programming.[1]

The adoption of the American community college model with a strong university transfer component in the early 1960s, a departure from the Canadian norm, was a response to geographical distance as well as to a desire for better social access to education. Given Canada's flat institutional prestige hierarchy relative to the United States (Davies and Hammack, 2005; Skolnik and Jones, 1992), the stage was set for British Columbia to develop a college sector that has enrolled students from probably as representative a cross-section of social classes as any system in North America or Europe. Geographical considerations also figured prominently in the creation of the Open Learning Institute in 1978, the establishment of university colleges and the University of Northern British Columbia in the early 1990s, and in the subsequent transformation of several institutions into teaching universities.

Federal Government

Although operating in something of an intermittent fashion over the decades and necessarily from the educational policy sidelines due to jurisdictional considerations,[2] federal influences on BC postsecondary education have been significant. The explosion since the formation of Canada in 1867 of social, educational, and health services for which provinces are constitutionally responsible, but with no corresponding expansion in their powers of taxation, provided a financial lever through transfer payments to the provinces for the federal government to influence postsecondary education in support of its own goals (Teliszewsky and Stoney, 2007). The use of direct grants and the introduction of federal transfer payments following the Rowell-Sirois Commission (Canada, 1940) not only addressed the imbalance in provincial responsibilities and revenues but also provided a means for Ottawa to sway provincial expenditures through conditions it placed on its funding.

Federal actions were central to the building of most of British Columbia's vocational schools in the 1960s, the transition of universities from a culture of teaching to one of graduate studies and research, the fostering of private institutions by providing student financial assistance, the provision of living allowances and tax breaks for apprentices, the expansion of private career colleges in the 1980s and 1990s through seat purchases and contracts for federal clients, the funding of ESL instruction at colleges, and for indirectly accelerating the shift in the scope and character of continuing education from a social development model to an entrepreneurial one.

Private Sector and Entrepreneurship

Although the BC private postsecondary sector has received little attention in the literature and has fluctuated in size, it is nevertheless a significant component of the postsecondary system. Like the public sector, it has changed and evolved over time, with the trend in public policy since 1980 to increasingly support, if not expand, private postsecondary education. With the exception of short job-entry and English-language programs, the private sector has been more of a complement to the public sector than a competitor.

The sector is complex, providing a range of credentials almost as broad as those of the public sector; only PhD degrees have not been awarded in British Columbia by private institutions. A number of institutions, including all the faith-based and Aboriginal-governed examples, have been not-for-profit. Apprenticeship, straddling the public-private divide with classroom components publicly funded but on-the-job training provided by private employers, has arguably been the most complex and variable of the postsecondary sectors. The religious presence in academic postsecondary education has been more modest in British Columbia than in other parts of Canada and well below the American norm.[3]

The past fifteen years have seen more commercialization within public institutions, strengthening their connections with the private sector. Federal research policy and funding now explicitly promote innovation and commercialization, not only discovery (Fisher et al., 2006). Public institutions have also become more entrepreneurial as they increased the number of cost-recovery programs in continuing education, including post-baccalaureate programs. International students are now seen as an economic stimulus and an entrepreneurial factor.

Loss of a Shared Vision

The Macdonald Report of 1962 forged a consensus among the BC government, the public, and educators about a direction for universities and colleges that lasted into the 1980s. Vocational education and apprenticeship, however, were not an explicit part of this vision, and private institutions were assumed to remain peripheral.

The first controversy regarding system design came in the early 1970s, with the melding of the vocational schools into community colleges. Apprenticeship remained in a separate and sometimes contentious world. By the time of the 1988 report of the Provincial Access Committee, Victoria was again reacting to community pressure rather than developing policy proactively.

The alterations since the mid-1990s came more as incremental decisions than planned development. With the Degree Authorization Act of 2002 and the transformation of six institutions into special-purpose or teaching universities a few years later, educators were left to infer the policy analyses and rationales that lay behind these changes. This situation recalls the words of Dennison (1997), who describes the BC government's 1990s postsecondary policy as erratic, unpredictable, and often unreadable. He observes that generalizing about the intent of government policy during that period is extremely difficult.

The Campus 2020 process (Plant, 2007) attempted to forge a renewed and comprehensive vision for the postsecondary system, but it did not succeed. Advocacy, public relations, and fundraising personnel have increasingly territorialized the resulting vacuum. The way forward is not clear within many institutions, much less among them, and certainly not at the system level. An understanding of how the system is currently evolving – a growing challenge as institutions and government increasingly shield their data from public scrutiny on password-protected websites or on webpages that are not archived when content is updated – and of the issues that were wrestled with along the way, may therefore help in envisioning a future for postsecondary education in British Columbia that is widely shared.

Policy Rationales

Each of the three policy rationales that I examined – social justice, human capital formation, and marketization – proved relevant and informative in interpreting the historical record, albeit to varying extents and in varying ways at various times. The discussion in this section steps back from the details of the rationales to present an integrated overview.

Not only did the rationales provide a concise framework that helped in making sense of a diverse array of actions and developments, but the discipline of examining events through particular lenses fostered interpretations that could otherwise be missed. For example, past interpretations that framed the formation of community colleges in terms of local control are significant and helpful. But they are so compelling that without the marketization lens, it is easy to overlook that the establishment of colleges can also be understood in another (complementary) way – as a laissez faire approach to system development on the part of government.

Not surprisingly, using more than one lens helped make for a more balanced analysis; a single theoretical perspective could have resulted in a skewed picture that, though true, was sufficiently incomplete as to be misleading. Although valuable, using multiple lenses was nevertheless challenging. It required a breadth of knowledge and a grasp of several literatures that took time to develop.

Determining which, and how many, lenses to use, depending on the purpose of a study, is no small task. I selected theory for this study iteratively: first learning some BC history, then reading theories that might be relevant, returning to the history to see which theories had face validity in the BC context, choosing a few theories that were sufficiently diverse so as not to impinge on each other, reading about this smaller set of theories in more depth, clustering the theories into three policy lenses, and finally applying the lenses to the historical record in a systematic manner.

The following high-level findings need to be understood within the parameters of the study:

- The scope was restricted to developments that affected the structure of the system, excluding changes that concerned only what happened within structures.
- The focus was on goals and policy intent, not on the more complex matters of implementation and outcomes.
- When the three analytical lenses were applied to the historical record, certain features became starkly visible, whereas others receded into the background. This methodology enabled the telling of an important story, but it is not the whole story. The use of other lenses would produce other stories.

- The purpose was to find memorable patterns that could serve as a springboard into more specific and nuanced studies.

Each of the three policy rationales proved to be an influential force at various times in the BC postsecondary system over the past half century. The forces fluctuated in importance over time, however. Table 5 shows that at least one of the three rationales, but never more than two, was always prominent in the five historical moments that I examined. Table 5 also suggests that the three rationales provided a complementary, reasonably

TABLE 5
Relevance of policy rationales in each historical moment

Historical moment	Social justice	Human capital formation	Marketization
Macdonald era (early 1960s)	*Prominent* individual and spatial adaptation versions. Some cultural recognition (faith-based)	*Prominent* for vocational education. Backdrop for academic education	Mild for public colleges (laissez faire) and university (competition). Indifferent to existence of for-profit colleges
Continuing education and Canadian Jobs Strategy (early and mid-1980s)	Little attention by province. Federal: some compensatory	*Prominent* in federal policy regarding vocational training	*Prominent.* BC changed continuing education by withdrawing subsidies. Federal strategy to use private sector
Access for All (late 1980s and early 1990s)	*Prominent* in academic education (individual and spatial adaptation). Mild attention to compensatory	Medium: generic skills, not occupational. Regional economic development in Interior university advocacy	Little, except regarding legitimacy of university college degrees
New Era (early to mid-2000s)	Superficial attention by BC government to access for individuals. Perhaps a reversal for non-academic education	*Prominent.* Mainly generic skills. Regional economic development	*Prominent.* Both academic and non-academic education
Post-neoliberal (2010 to present)	Absent	*Prominent.* Victoria emphasized occupational, whereas Ottawa was oriented to generic skills.	Mild reversal in non-academic education

balanced portrait in that the cells identifying prominent rationales are scattered throughout the table rather than clustered together.

With the caveat that Table 5 is several steps removed from the historical realities that it purports to summarize (i.e., it is my summary of my analyses of a selection of historical moments that I defined and identified as significant), a key message from Table 5 is that human capital formation has been central to understanding the development of the contemporary postsecondary system in British Columbia. Social justice considerations were especially significant in the earlier decades, whereas market-oriented rationales strengthened in more recent ones.

Table 5 also suggests two related hypotheses that although speculative nevertheless provide points of departure in the search for social patterns and the development of mid-range theory. Historical generalization is a risky business, and even when seemingly well justified, it at best provides rough rules of thumb (Gottschalk, 1963; Leuridan and Froeyman, 2012). Yet if history is to inform decision making, summary accounts and simplified models are needed, even if they are not perfectly accurate and reliable.

The fluctuating prominence of the policy rationale in each column of Table 5 suggests the hypothesis that although an *institutionalized* policy driver may be neglected for a while, it is likely to eventually reappear. Second, the two reversals in the table suggest the possibility that when a specific policy rationale has been emphasized, the tendency within a given societal paradigm is for it to subsequently weaken and revert to its historical level of significance. (Should such a reversal not occur, this might be evidence of a transition into a new historical period.)

With the foregoing as context, attention will now turn to each of the three policy rationales separately.

Social Justice

Social justice, frequently expressed in terms of access to educational opportunity for individuals, was a strong driver in the 1960s, and it resurfaced powerfully in the late 1980s. In both of these historical moments, significant structural change occurred: public community colleges and two new universities were created in the 1960s, and university colleges were formed two and a half decades later. Efforts to provide compensatory justice did appear later, but more as initiatives within established structures, such as special programs for women seeking to re-enter the workforce or for social assistance recipients. Similarly, cultural recognition efforts occurred more within established institutions, although the 1990s started to see more attention paid to special institutions for the Aboriginal population. The faith-based sector was permitted to exist, although not promoted, in recognition of other cultural subgroups.

The spatial adaptation form of social justice has been an ongoing force in BC public sector institutions since 1960, starting with the dispersal of vocational schools and colleges throughout the province, followed by the conversion of some community colleges into university colleges and the formation of the University of Northern British Columbia in the years around 1990, the makeover of two former university colleges into Thompson Rivers University and UBC Okanagan in the mid-1990s, the introduction of a degree-granting mandate to public colleges in 2002, and finally to the transformation in 2008 of a number of public institutions into teaching universities. Geographical considerations were important components of the rationales for all these changes.

Social justice has been less of a policy driver since 2000, but at least improving the accessibility of postsecondary education still receives nominal recognition. For example, the invitation to private and external universities under the Degree Authorization Act to enter the province and the announcements of new teaching universities were framed as bettering access to degree-level education. The government's annual cap on the tuition fee increases in public institutions, lifted for only a few years in the early 2000s, is another artifact of a desire for equality of educational opportunity.

Social justice rationales, sometimes articulated as efforts to enhance the life chances and the quality of life of citizens throughout the province, have been invoked most strongly with respect to academic and liberal education. They have appeared less frequently in vocational and non-academic discourse. On those occasions when social justice considerations did enter discussions of non-academic education, they typically appeared more as means for enhancing human capital formation than as ends in themselves. For example, although calls to increase the number of apprentices may have resulted in better educational opportunity for individuals and groups – most recently, a concerted effort to make apprenticeship more appealing to Aboriginal people – the precipitating motivation was often a desire to avoid future labour shortages rather than a desire to allow more individuals to enjoy a certain way of life.

When social justice issues were raised in sub-baccalaureate education, they often took the form of compensatory social justice – increasing the participation rate of under-represented groups in certain fields of study, such as immigrants or persons with disabilities. Even here, though, the initiatives had an instrumental flavour rather than being an effort to improve the circumstances of the under-represented groups overall. By and large, such compensatory initiatives were not the most successful aspects of BC postsecondary education, and, as across Canada, the under-represented groups frequently remained under-represented (Andres, 2015).

The variation in the strength of social justice rationales across fields of study reflects societal views and values about non-academic students, especially when considered in the context of the commodified liberal welfare regime in Canada (Esping-Andersen, 1990). Lyons, Randhawa, and Paulson (1991) trace the development of what they call a prejudice against vocational education in Canada, situating Canadian attitudes in a wider North American perception that vocational education prepared second-class citizens and was a form of social policy for people at the margins of society. (This view differed from those of such countries as Germany, with its conservative welfare regime.) More recently, P. Brennan (2014) writes of Canadians viewing the technical and vocational education training system as second class, "for those not bright enough to make it to university, for those who would work with their hands in menial and dirty jobs" (p. 183). Taylor (2016) recounts the hierarchical valuing of fields of study in terms of a distinction between the mental and the manual, of mind versus body.

Human Capital Formation

Human capital formation has been another enduring and important policy rationale, though it too has varied in strength across time and sectors. Like social justice, it has persisted in the background as a central purpose for postsecondary education and has occasionally risen to the foreground for a brief period or in relation to part of the postsecondary system. For example, the Canadian Jobs Strategy affected only portions of public colleges and spurred growth in the private career college sector that by and large had no impact on other postsecondary sectors beyond certain components of public colleges. Human capital considerations have been especially strong with respect to the trades, but enrolment in apprenticeship and government attention to the health of the apprenticeship system have fluctuated considerably (in contrast to the steadier growth trajectory of degree-level education). Despite the recent emphasis given to human capital in the Skills for Jobs Blueprint, the actual impact of this initiative has been modest.

Human capital formation has been a particular focus of the federal government. It was this government that initially made the expansion of vocational education, as well as a variety of short-term training programs for the unemployed and marginalized, a priority that lasted well into the 1980s. Its focus shifted in the 1990s toward highly qualified personnel who could further its research and innovation agenda, a shift that was important within BC postsecondary institutions but did not have as significant implications for the structure of the postsecondary system. The federal presence in this study therefore declined in the later historical moments that I examined.

Compared to the BC government, Ottawa has placed a greater and more consistent emphasis on human capital considerations. Federal policy did continually promote access through student financial aid and compensatory versions of social justice, but its emphasis on human capital was especially important for the structure of the BC system from 1960 to 1990. Whereas Victoria emphasized the occupationally focused version of human capital formation, especially with respect to apprenticeship, Ottawa drew upon both occupational and generic versions. The BC government seemed supportive of the generic version but tended not to use it to propel its educational policies, drawing upon social justice rationales instead and simply accepting gratefully that the resulting developments often had human capital benefits as well.

Production regime theory and the varieties of capitalism literature (Hall and Soskice, 2001) provide an avenue for considering a corollary of the generic versus occupational forecasting interpretations of human capital theory – namely, a society's preference for general versus industry-specific skills. The portability of general skills leaves workers less vulnerable to labour market fluctuations, and therefore fewer social protections are needed to entice workers to invest in them (Estevez-Abe, Iversen, and Soskice, 2001). Gallie (2011) argues that societies with greater social equality foster higher levels of both general and specific skills, especially among lower-skilled workers. The broader implications of the different emphases on general skills across postsecondary sectors, between governments, and over time are germane to the stratification and social justice issues that I discuss below.

Marketization

Marketization was the most variable of the three policy rationales. It was evident in a small way during the 1960s, with the creation of equal status universities, rather than new ones that were subsidiary to UBC, and in the means for establishing regional public colleges. It then appeared strongly in the continuing education and Canadian Jobs Strategy moment of the 1980s, but it affected only specific sectors and subsectors. It burst back on the scene in the early 2000s, this time affecting a broad range of sectors and with a strong ideological dimension that overshadowed pragmatic rationales for making market-oriented reforms. The enthusiasm of government for markets has waned, however, with a few reversals recently made of previous reforms.

Marketization has been a curious blend of visibility and invisibility in BC policy discourse. The long-term, overall trends seem not to have been perceived by the public, even though specific actions, such as those facilitating the operation of private universities or changing the governance of apprenticeship, were certainly noted and were sometimes controversial. With the passage of time, though, debates about specific initiatives subsided, and current students and new postsecondary employees may never realize that the status quo is of relatively recent date, much less that some of the changes were contested.

Marketization, in such forms as competition for research prestige and differential tuition fees across similar programs in different types of public institutions, has become part of the taken-for-granted ethos of postsecondary education in British Columbia. P. Roberts and Peters (2008), and later Giroux (2014), characterized neoliberalism as a worldview in which other ideas about social and cultural life have come to exist. This is now an apt description of marketization in BC postsecondary education. Although the BC version of neoliberalism is a gentle one, and seems to be softening, the power of the ideology is substantial.

In the literature about neoliberalism, globalization, and marketization in postsecondary education (Chan and Fisher, 2008; Levin, 2001; Marginson, 1997b; Metcalfe, 2010; Olssen and Peters, 2005; S.C. Ward, 2012), the tendency has been to present postsecondary institutions as the subjects, either passive or unsuccessfully resistant, of external forces, most commonly originating with economists and right-wing politicians. Managers in postsecondary institutions are then portrayed as eventually coming to accept and expedite the marketization of education. The tone is often one of faculty, and the academy in general, under siege. Although this representation is valuable, it underplays the internal forces in postsecondary institutions that at least facilitate, if not promote, marketization. Slaughter and Rhoades (2004) see the academy as sometimes embracing commercialization, rather than as solely its victim.

I had originally turned to a few concepts drawn from *institutional* theory as alternatives to neoliberal theory for explaining market-oriented and competitive behaviour in sectors other than research universities, sectors where some aspects of academic capitalism (Slaughter and Rhoades, 2004) are less applicable. It became evident, however, that *institutional* concepts such as normative isomorphism – conformity among members of an organization arising from professional standards and a shared formal education (DiMaggio and Powell, 1983) – and the striving for greater legitimacy can be used not only to supplement neoliberal theory but also for identifying some of the mechanisms by which neoliberalism is implemented. For example, normative isomorphism and prestige economies help explain how some postsecondary personnel who are philosophically opposed to neoliberalism nevertheless act in manners consistent with it.

The explanatory power of a central concept in neoinstitutional theory, that of the organizational field (W.R. Scott, 2014), proved significant in the British Columbia postsecondary context. Although not likely to lead to complete explanations, attending to cues within the organizational field about such topics as prestige and legitimacy helps in interpreting how it was that BC postsecondary education came to engage more extensively in such entrepreneurial activities as image advertising, particular strategies for recruiting international students, the provision of infrastructure to help faculty apply for competitive research grants, and the development of new programs based not so much on documented societal need.

BC Postsecondary System in 2015

In this section, I step back from the forces acting on the BC postsecondary system since 1960 and summarize its resulting sectorial composition. This is the foundation for future studies of system interactions.

Public Sector

Research Universities

The University of British Columbia, by far the largest postsecondary institution in the province, has remained somewhat aloof from the other postsecondary institutions in British Columbia, especially as it sought, with considerable success, a stronger presence on the national and international scenes. Unlike other universities and public colleges that have multiple campuses with more integrated administration and student bodies, UBC keeps its distant, smaller campus in the Okanagan distinct from its large Vancouver campus.

Simon Fraser University, a commuter-oriented institution birthed in the 1960s as a radical and innovative campus, and the University of Victoria, which emerged from the genteel Victoria College, are medium-sized. The much newer University of Northern British Columbia in Prince George is small and seeks to respond to the distinctive regional needs of the sparsely populated northern half of the province.

Also small, Royal Roads University in Victoria departs from the traditional North American university model. Oriented toward degree completion for working adults who have some prior postsecondary or relevant job experience (its programs often require the equivalent of a two-year diploma for admission), it operates on something of a continuing education model and makes extensive use of blended and distance education course delivery. Although Thompson Rivers University in the southern Interior is a member of the Research Universities' Council of British Columbia, its comprehensive programming more closely resembles that of BC teaching universities than of the province's research universities.

Teaching Universities

Five of the six small- to medium-sized teaching universities in British Columbia started as community colleges in the 1960s and 1970s. They have retained their open-access philosophy and comprehensive mix of programming – upper-level undergraduate and master's programs were simply added to a base of two-year college programming. The route to university status for four of the institutions (Fraser Valley, Kwantlen, Thompson Rivers, and Vancouver Island) included a stage in the 1990s as baccalaureate university colleges before the province transformed them into universities from 2003 to 2008. The "polytechnic" in Kwantlen's name implies a greater differentiation from the other teaching universities than actually exists.

Capilano and Emily Carr Universities have differing lineages. Capilano went straight from a college, which since 2002 had the same authority as other public colleges to award bachelor's degrees in applied subjects, to a university. Emily Carr is a visual arts school that was designated for many years as a provincial institute. With roots dating back to the 1930s, it was never formally a university college, but the route by which it received degree-granting authority, and eventually university status, paralleled developments in the university college sector.

Colleges

British Columbia currently has eleven public colleges, four of which are located in urban areas (Camosun, Douglas, Langara, and Vancouver), two in small cities (New Caledonia and Okanagan), and five in rural regions (College of the Rockies, North Island, Northern Lights, Northwest, and Selkirk). Their program mix includes adult basic education, one- and two-year applied programs, academic programming of varying duration, and unpredictable amounts of continuing education. The availability of trades training in each college ranges from none to extensive.

The colleges offer a modest number of bachelor programs, partly because it can be difficult for smaller institutions to achieve the enrolment mass across specialized courses to keep unit costs down. The proportion of university transferable courses is highest in the urban and larger colleges. Vancouver Community College is the exception to this generalization but largely because its academic campus, Langara, split off as a separate entity in 1994.

Institutes

Each provincial institute has distinctive characteristics, making generalizations about this sector difficult (beyond noting that over the years, all except one have been located in Vancouver). They have ranged in size from moderately large to very small.

Quantitatively, in terms of enrolment, the BC Institute of Technology dominates the sector. Qualitatively, the Justice Institute was groundbreaking in its approach to public safety training. The Nicola Valley Institute of Technology (not a technical institute despite its origins with a few technical programs) is the only Aboriginal-governed institution to have transitioned into the public sector.

The sector has been unstable, and the number of institutes has shrunk over the decades. One was transformed into a teaching university (Emily Carr), one was disassembled and components given to other institutions (Open Learning), two were merged into the BC Institute of Technology (Pacific Vocational and Pacific Marine Training), one merged into Vancouver Community College (Vancouver Vocational Institute), and one was absorbed by the Nicola Valley Institute of Technology (Institute of Indigenous Government). The result is that there are just three provincial institutes at present: the British Columbia Institute of Technology, the Justice Institute, and the Nicola Valley Institute of Technology.

Private Sector

Career Colleges

Under the new Private Training Act of 2015, the BC government raised the threshold for governmental oversight of career colleges from $1,000 in total tuition fees to $4,000, resulting in yet another discontinuity in statistics about the sector. All institutions above the threshold must be *certified* by the Private Training Institutions Branch of the Ministry of Advanced Education and each program above the minimum threshold *approved*. The standards to become *designated* – that is, to allow the institution to enrol international students and for domestic students to access financial aid from government – are more rigorous than for certification.

In its online institutional directory, the regulator currently lists a little over five hundred campuses, which may range in size from a classroom to a substantial building (Private Training Institutions Branch, 2017). Of these, four hundred were designated, and three-quarters were located in Vancouver and the adjacent Fraser Valley. The number of distinct institutions or corporate entities, including some English-language schools, was approximately three hundred.

The branch's website continues to report enrolment as exceeding fifty-one thousand students, a not very precise or reliable figure that nevertheless seems to have been the best estimate available for the past several years. With new legislation providing for a provincial education number to be assigned to students in private training institutions, decent enrolment data may become available in the near future. (Valuable for British Columbia, this development also takes a step toward filling the national data void about private education – a bigger statistical shortcoming in Canada than in most countries in the Organization for Economic Co-operation and Development.)

English-Language Schools

A private English-language school does not have to be certified by the Private Training Institutions Branch if it offers only language courses and no career programs. However, if it wishes to become designated (a higher standard than certification) in order to enrol international students or to make its students eligible for government loans, the threshold is the presence of an instructional program of at least six months' duration (in contrast to the threshold of forty hours of instruction for career colleges) or (rather than "and" for career colleges) that charges over $4,000 in tuition. Although a portion of the sector is voluntarily regulated, statistical information remains elusive. Thus, I do not know if the sector has changed materially over the past few years.

From the perspectives of labour market supply and social integration policy, the impacts of language schools differ markedly from those of career colleges. Although the operational implications for regulatory purposes may be similar, it would be desirable for policy purposes if statistical data about language schools (and a category for schools that offer both career and language training) were available separately from those for career colleges.

Languages Canada, an industry association that accredits language schools, has sixty member institutions in British Columbia, of which fifty-one are in the private sector. The 2015 enrolment of 49,500 students, down from 67,000 in 2011, included an undisclosed proportion of youth and students in public institutions (Languages Canada, 2017).

Aboriginal-Governed Institutions

Forty Aboriginal-governed institutions belonged to the Indigenous Adult and Higher Learning Association in 2015–16. The Nicola Valley Institute of Technology (NVIT) is the largest of these, enrolling half of the association's three to four thousand students. Most are very small, with fewer than a dozen enrolling more than a hundred students. Except for NVIT, almost all operate without core funding, relying on proposal-driven funding, partnerships, and formal affiliations with other postsecondary institutions.

The Aboriginal community prefers the term "institute" rather than "institution" because of the past institutionalization of Indigenous children in residential schools, but this usage differs from the province's definition of provincial institutes. The Aboriginal-governed institutes are found mainly in small cities and rural locations, with only two operating in Vancouver and one close to Victoria. Approximately 35 percent of students are enrolled in adult basic education or upgrading courses and a further 15 percent in trades programming (Tindall, 2016). Most of the credentials awarded are certificates from programs of one year or less duration.

Faith-Based Institutions

British Columbia has fifteen to twenty faith-based institutions, all Christian, depending on whether inactive, or nearly inactive, institutions are included in the count. The majority of students enrol in institutions associated with evangelical Protestant denominations. The Roman Catholic presence is small, and the only mainline Protestant institution is the Vancouver School of Theology. The institutions fall into four categories:

- Comprehensive curriculum

  Trinity Western University, the largest faith-based institution, is the prime example, but Corpus Christi College and Catholic (formerly Redeemer) Pacific College offer small liberal arts programs at the undergraduate level.

- Graduate theological education and seminaries

  These institutions normally require an undergraduate degree, generally not in theology, for admission. Many operate in partnership or as a consortium, and six are affiliated with the University of British Columbia. Regent College quickly established an international reputation after it opened as North America's first graduate school that provided theological education for the laity rather than to train clergy.

- Undergraduate religious curriculum

  These institutions usually offer one- and two-year programs, plus a few baccalaureate programs, in such subjects as theology, worship, and youth leadership. Bible colleges fall into this category.

- Other and multiple functions

  An example of an institution in this category is one where the emphasis is on faith development and a residential experience rather than on academics.

Private Degree-Granting Institutions

Private institutions sometimes seek and receive approval from the BC Degree Quality Assessment Board for a new degree program but do not immediately, or ever, offer it. This makes the fluctuating number of private baccalaureate and graduate institutions all the more difficult to pin down.

The BC Ministry of Advanced Education listed twenty private and out-of-province degree-granting institutions on its website in mid-2017 (Ministry of Advanced Education, 2017). Even this cataloguing, however, omitted, for example, a graduate-level college of naturopathic medicine that refers to the resulting licensure as a professional designation rather than an academic degree. Likewise, schools of traditional Chinese medicine, which may offer five-year "diplomas" or partner with public institutions, were not listed.

Two of the listed universities have traditional campuses in British Columbia and deliver programs in a range of fields. The faith-based Trinity Western is the largest and has the widest variety of programs. Quest University is a residential, undergraduate liberal arts institution. Four comprehensive, out-of-province universities (Athabasca, Gonzaga, Queen's, and the University of Oregon) provide niche programming on an extension basis that involves a mix of online delivery and temporary classroom space.

Five of the twenty institutions are active at the sub-baccalaureate level but were not advertising any degree programs on their websites in 2017. Their origins were as junior colleges that prepared students for study in other academic institutions. Most of the nine remaining institutions offer programs in specific fields (such as business, psychology, health, and the fine arts), with master's programs well represented.

Enrolment data are not available for the private degree-granting sector, but except for Trinity Western, institutional enrolments are typically measured in units of hundreds, not thousands.

Boundary Spanning

Continuing Education
Continuing education is a quasi-sector, housed in public institutions but behaving like a private entity – the entrepreneurial, less regulated face of public education. It seeks generally to be cost-recovery, but some components may be subsidized by the parent institution, and others may make a profit. It is difficult to document, partly because it fluctuates and is fluid, and partly because there is no central data collection across the BC system. Even within an institution, enrolment data may be elusive when administrative responsibility is mixed: some courses provided centrally through a continuing education unit and some decentrally by faculties or other administrative units.

The definitions, scope, terminology, and organizational structures of continuing education operations are myriad across BC postsecondary institutions. The vast majority of offerings nonetheless fall into just four categories:

- non-credit courses for the general population (sometimes known as community education)
- credit courses for students who have taken the prerequisite courses (sometimes known as extension or part-time studies)
- continuing professional education for specific populations with relevant occupational background
- contract training for individuals selected by a third-party funder.

An indication of the scale of activity can be found in a filing made by BC universities to a national financial association in 2014–15. They collected $93 million that year in tuition fees from non-credit courses (Canadian Association of University Business Officers, 2016). This sum, which excludes revenue from credit courses offered through continuing education, was the same amount as Okanagan College budgeted that year for its entire operation (Okanagan College, 2015).

Apprenticeship
Apprenticeship combines on-the-job learning with smaller amounts of classroom instruction delivered by fourteen public postsecondary institutions and three dozen private career colleges. The system is administered by a separate agency of the BC government, the Industry Training Authority, which also funds institutions to deliver the classroom, or technical training, components.

At the end of 2015, British Columbia had ten thousand sponsors (employers) for thirty-five thousand adult apprentices, of which sixteen thousand were new apprentices who had started within the year – completion rates were then running at 38 percent (Industry Training Authority, 2015, December). Although apprenticeships are offered in close to ninety trades, just five account for a little over half of all apprentices at present (in rank order, they are construction electrician, carpenter, plumber, professional cook, and automotive service technician). During 2014–15, 50 percent of students who completed a Foundation (pre-apprenticeship) Program at a postsecondary institution went on to enter an apprenticeship, often receiving advanced standing (Industry Training Authority, 2015).

Example of Interactive Structural Analysis

This section considers social stratification in and by educational institutions to illustrate how attention to the evolving structure and interactions of postsecondary sectors can inform research and policy development on a variety of topics. Stratification is an important social justice topic that also illuminates the impacts of marketization and institutional differentiation.

John Macdonald (1962) began his report on higher education in British Columbia by highlighting the role of education in "the preservation of those rights and privileges which we believe should be shared by all" (p. 4). The Provincial Access Committee (1988) and the minister of advanced education (Hagen, 1989) expressed similar sentiments about the democratic and community development functions of education during the Access for All historical moment. Despite being a means of improving community well-being and a vehicle for the social mobility of individuals – sometimes described as a ladder to opportunity – educational institutions also have a darker side.

Sociologists have long examined the role of education as a sorting and stratifying mechanism within society, and the ways in which formal schooling can be used to reproduce the privilege of elite groups across generations (e.g., Schudde and Goldrick-Rab, 2015; Shavit, Arum, Gamoran, and Menahem, 2007). Writing about the United States, Brint and Karabel (1989) examined the role of colleges in "managing ambition in a society that generates far higher levels of aspiration for upward mobility than it can possibly satisfy" (p. 213) and ultimately titled their book *The Diverted Dream*.

Marginson (2016a) reaches a bleak conclusion about social justice in postsecondary education: "At the level of overall social aggregates and averages, not only does higher education fail to compensate for prior social inequalities, it helps to confirm, legitimate, and reproduce those inequalities into the next generation" (p. 179). Nevertheless, he argues that this has not always been the case. Analyzing the global impact of the 1960 California Master Plan for higher education, he claims that the plan was unquestionably effective in fostering both access and excellence internationally during its first twenty years, but not since then. The continued success of educational systems in promoting social justice should not be taken for granted.

In the same vein as Marginson (2016c), Usher (2016, May 5) contends that, in the absence of policy interventions, the massification of higher education around the world has been accompanied by a growing hierarchical stratification of institutions. His example of a policy intervention to lessen the risk that postsecondary education would reinforce class distinctions, based on the institutions attended, was the lottery system of admissions for qualified applicants in some programs in the Netherlands (Boyle, 2010; Ministerie van Onderwijs, Cultuur en Wetenschap, 2016).

The Canadian literature has been less quick to identify Canadian postsecondary education as a cause of growing inequality. Rather, it is still assessing the situation and, at most, criticizing governments and institutions for not sufficiently rectifying existing disparities. Diallo, Trottier, and Doray (2009) provide an example of the former type of study. Andres (2015) is an instance of the latter, presenting the appraisal that almost all groups identified in Canada as disadvantaged by the late 1980s remained so well into the twenty-first century.

An important question in British Columbia, as elsewhere, is about the current trend in social stratification: Is mass postsecondary education really becoming less egalitarian and increasingly failing to serve its intended democratic functions? This is a complex question about a fundamental purpose of postsecondary education. No single approach can answer it adequately, yet a number of avenues of investigation would seem to benefit from systems thinking.

One of the many possible approaches begins with structural analysis, to gauge whether the horizontal dimension of the postsecondary system (Gerber and Cheung, 2008) is shifting by examining differential rates of growth across sectors and changes in the composition of the student body in each sector. I have already mentioned that the funding mainly of academic programs in the Access for All moment mildly shifted the sectorial composition, or the horizontal dimension, of the postsecondary system. Over the following two decades, services and courses for vocational education and for the marginalized populations that enrol disproportionately in adult basic education, ESL programs, and some components of continuing education came to represent a smaller proportion of public postsecondary enrolment.

Differences in postsecondary participation patterns across social groups have been examined in Canada largely in terms of the characteristics of students and their families (e.g., Berger, Motte, and Parkin, 2007; Finnie, 2008). Participation in terms of the types of institutions and programs in which various kinds of students enrol has been less conspicuous in the research agenda, as has the socio-economic composition of enrolment in sectors other than public universities and colleges.

After assessing whether the horizontal structure of the system as a whole is changing, researchers could turn to the vertical dimension, comparing institutions or groups of institutions among and within each sector in terms of their status and prestige. From the 1960s through the 1980s, Canadian public policy sought implicitly to establish networks of institutions of approximately equivalent standards, with the result that universities in Canada, unlike those of the United States, were not hierarchically differentiated (Leslie, 1980; Skolnik and Jones, 1992). In 2000, for example, one's alma mater was seen as nowhere near as important in Canada as in the United States, with undergraduate student competition expressed in terms of admission to elite majors (Davies and Hammack, 2005). This egalitarian ethos could be weakening in the BC public system as institutions vie to enhance their prestige, using their program offerings and admissions philosophies, along with an emphasis on research, as some of the means for doing so.

Looking across Canada, Marginson (2016c) claims that the university system is being stretched vertically: that is, the hierarchy is getting steeper (although social mobility remains higher in Canada than in other English-speaking countries). He argues that the most important question is no longer access but rather "access to what?" (p. 11). This question has certainly been posed more than once in recent decades,[4] but the fact that it is still being asked is troubling.

One result of increased vertical differentiation is that students who enter certain postsecondary institutions with some sort of disadvantage, perhaps with less social and cultural capital (Bourdieu, 1977), are more apt to be left behind. Compensatory social justice is put at risk as students, often with family assistance, unconsciously sort themselves into institutions in which they perceive they are likely to fit and comfortably succeed, perhaps doing so without even considering other options (Baker, 2014; Bastedo and Flaster, 2014).

In addition to social justice implications for individuals and groups, any social stratification of enrolment has ramifications for postsecondary institutions and their respective sectors. As the empirical evidence has shown, institutions that start from a position of advantage simply reinforce their advantage (Davies and Zarifa, 2012).

Whether a more hierarchical and differentiated system might be beneficial is open to debate; the discussion takes on a different tenor when framed as the pursuit of excellence (Galinova, 2005; van Zanten, Ball, and Darchy-Koechlin, 2015) rather than as social gatekeeping. Regardless, the horizontal composition of the postsecondary system and its vertical differentiation are important information in understanding educational access and social stratification in particular regions.

Finally, and this is a rarely examined aspect of the effectiveness of the postsecondary system in providing compensatory social justice, student flows within and across sectors could be analyzed in terms of the numbers, destinations, and socio-economic and academic characteristics of mobile students. For example, do students from certain social classes disproportionately transfer out of certain institutions? In at least some jurisdictions, linkages between administrative data and existing surveys of former students could be initial sources of mobility data about patterns of further education and transitions into the labour force (although they typically do not allow for in-depth analysis of socio-economic backgrounds).

Governments and scholars are ill equipped at present to conduct studies of student mobility to determine, for example, the frequency and effectiveness of "second chance" enrolment. The major barrier, of course, is the lack of comparable, robust student data across all postsecondary institutions due to the costs of collecting and presenting them, as well as to politics about disclosing potentially embarrassing information. This is a formidable challenge, and it's likely that little progress will be made in overcoming it, especially with respect to private institutions, unless policymakers and scholars emphasize the importance of viewing postsecondary education as an interacting system rather than as a set of independent sectors.

This study has promoted the notion that comprehensive descriptions and analyses of *every* postsecondary sector – seeing the entire landscape, not only the high-status institutions – are the starting points for gradually identifying the interactions among these sectors. Such interactions within what neoinstitutional theory calls the organizational field are critical for better identifying *all* the roles and impacts of postsecondary institutions.

In considering the structural development of a particular postsecondary system in Canada, I sought to foster systems thinking more generally about postsecondary education. In doing so, I drew upon sources from practitioner as well as scholarly literatures. In British Columbia, the disbanding of several system-wide organizations since 2000 has resulted in less frequent joint meetings of the academics, educators, and government officials who produce documents and formulate policies about postsecondary education. This isolation increases the risk of tunnel vision and of groups talking at cross-purposes. I would like to see the former linkages among these parties revitalized and offer this holistic study as a step in that direction.

Another purpose of this book was to illustrate how using more than one theoretical lens facilitates comprehensive interpretations, a methodology that parallels the fuller pictures that systems approaches provide. I presented and used three policy rationales (social justice, human capital formation, and marketization) and their associated educational goals to interpret the historical record.

Having endured for decades, these policy rationales are now institutionalized (in the sociological sense) and will continue to figure in educational discourse for years to come. Not all commentators define them in the same way, however, and thus I took care to explain what I meant by them. If the rationales are to serve as helpful evaluative criteria in assessing future policy options, rather than confusing or complicating the picture, I would encourage other analysts also to be explicit in defining their understanding and usage of terminology.

Notes

Introduction

1 This is not a structuralist approach as might be seen in anthropology or linguistics.
2 My favourite story about crossing boundaries, one that might even be true, concerns a BC university president who took a vocational trades course at his neighbouring community college. He had purchased a pleasure boat and wanted to know something of marine diesel mechanics before venturing out to explore the remote fjords of the north Pacific.

1 | Setting the Stage

1 This philosophy includes serving all segments of society through an open-access admissions policy that offers equal and fair treatment to all students, provides a comprehensive educational program, and addresses the needs of the local community.
2 See Cowin (2013c) for a summary compendium of the council's research.

2 | Policy Rationales

1 Theories of regional economic growth include basic product theory, demand driven/export theory, supply side theory, clustering and cumulative causation, growth poles, networks, core and periphery models, and innovative environments.

3 | Clear Intentions (1960–79)

1 The four were the BC Institute of Technology, the Emily Carr Institute (now University) of Art, the Pacific Vocational Institute, and the Pacific Marine Training

Institute. The Justice Institute became the first institution in North America to train fire, police, and paramedic personnel in a single organization dedicated to public safety. The Open Learning Institute was created to provide distance education from certificate through baccalaureate levels.

2 One school, in Burnaby, was renamed the Pacific Vocational Institute and was not merged until 1986. It was then absorbed by the adjacent BC Institute of Technology, rather than by a college.

3 The Canadian Apprenticeship Forum (2004) identifies negative perceptions and a low level of support for apprenticeship training as barriers. Sharpe and Gibson (2005) conclude that, nationally, the postsecondary education system has an academic bias.

4 The agreement was updated in 1967 by the federal Adult Occupational Training Act.

5 Technical "training" was distinct from two-year technical "education," a difference that had as much to do with administrative jurisdiction as pedagogy or curricula.

6 The Open Learning Institute merged in 1988 with the public educational television station, the Knowledge Network of the West of 1979, to become the Open Learning Agency.

7 There have been a few minor grants from public sources, such as to UBC's affiliated theological schools in the 1980s, but essentially the faith-based institutions have not received government funding.

8 The BC government granted Notre Dame $310,000 in 1967–68, which rose to $1.8 million in 1975–76. Notre Dame's facilities were then sold to the province in 1977 for a nominal sum so that Selkirk College and the University of Victoria could jointly reopen the campus in 1979 as the David Thompson University Centre. Despite strong local support politically for the centre, the government closed it in 1984 for budgetary reasons (Cowin, 2009).

9 Knott's optimistic vision is remarkable in that UBC had in 1932 endured a 20 percent reduction in provincial government funding as a result of the Great Depression. Victoria had appointed a group of business people to review the province's finances, which had proposed saving money by closing UBC altogether and giving scholarships for students to pursue degrees in universities in other provinces (Waite, 1987).

10 Selkirk in 1966, Capilano and Okanagan in 1968, Malaspina (now Vancouver Island University) and New Caledonia in 1969, Douglas and Cariboo (now Thompson Rivers University) in 1970, Camosun in 1971, and Fraser Valley in 1974. Kwantlen split from Douglas in 1981 and Langara from Vancouver in 1994.

11 Northwest, North Island, Northern Lights, and East Kootenay (now College of the Rockies).

12 The Macdonald Report noted that the minimal admission standard to UBC in 1962 was simply high school graduation. The standard has since risen to also include a marks threshold.

4 | Assumptions Challenged (1980–99)

1 Students typically alternated short, intense sessions of face-to-face instruction with distance education.
2 An eight-month boycott by the Canadian Association of University Teachers was lifted before the university enrolled any students when its board agreed to delegate academic planning to a senate-like body (D. Ward, 1998, March 21).
3 Cariboo is now Thompson Rivers University, and Malaspina became Vancouver Island University.
4 A cautionary note about private institutions data is that branch campuses were sometimes counted as separate institutions and were sometimes excluded, with only the head office counted.
5 In 2016, Trinity Western went to court to challenge the refusal of law societies in three provinces to accredit graduates of its proposed new law school.
6 The lack of consensus at UBC about continuing education was reflected in a 1981 report, *Looking Beyond* (Kulich, Taylor, Tetlow, and University of British Columbia, 1981). In its preface, UBC president Douglas Kenny stated that the university needed a comprehensive, long-range policy on continuing education.
7 The enrolment data were reported as students, but it is unclear whether this represents unduplicated headcounts or course registrations. Given the size of the figure and the technical challenges of producing unduplicated counts, I suspect the measure was course registrations and that students were duplicated.
8 As revealed by annual audited financial statements (University of Northern British Columbia, 2017a; University of Victoria, 2017a) and by institutional accountability plans and reports submitted to the BC government (University of Northern British Columbia, 2017b; University of Victoria, 2017b), their concern proved justified. In 2016–17, the University of Northern British Columbia (UNBC) enrolled 2,632 full-time equivalent (FTE) students, only 76 percent of the target set by the Ministry of Advanced Education. By contrast, the University of Victoria enrolled 16,922, or 105 percent of its target. Operating grants from the BC government at UNBC and the University of Victoria were $51.5 million and $118.2 million respectively, which meant that the grant per FTE student at UNBC was $19,500 compared to $10,500 at the University of Victoria.

9 Poole (1994) finds that, privately, government officials were in full agreement that the new institutions should not become universities but felt that the movement to university status would probably occur anyway due to political pressures, especially in the Okanagan.

5 | Cynicism (2000–15)

1 For example, respondents who answered the 2016 version of the Canadian Graduate and Professional Student Survey were given three positive options (excellent, very good, and good), one neutral option (fair), but just one negative option (poor) in a number of rating questions. This positively skewed scale ensured that not a single respondent would report to the Canadian Association of Graduate Studies that she or he had had a bad or very poor experience at a Canadian university.
2 In 2007, the BC Ministry of Advanced Education's Service Plan listed five government-wide "Great Goals," one of which was to make British Columbia the most literate and best-educated jurisdiction in North America. In 2012, other governmental priorities replaced the Great Goals: jobs and the economy; families first; and open government and citizenship engagement. In 2015, families had disappeared and jobs had top billing, followed by taxpayer accountability principles (Ministry of Advanced Education, 2015).
3 The new name is arguably more accurate in that colleges in most provinces have provided little or no university transfer. That is, they were never community colleges in the same sense as in British Columbia, Alberta, and many American states. A counterargument is that they have all been characterized by an open-access philosophy and that the connotations of "college" and "community college" differ in the United States and Canada.
4 For example, the Trades Training Consortium was formed by public institutions to present a united front in response to Industry Training Authority actions that affected those institutions.
5 Contract training is cost-recovery, or profit-making, instruction wherein a third-party funder, not the institution, specifies both the curricular goals and which students are eligible to enrol (typically clients or employees of the funder).
6 "BCcampus" is the formal name, spelled as one word.
7 For example, some external universities offered instruction in British Columbia in such fields as education and business to cohorts of BC students but awarded degrees from campuses outside the province.
8 These are Capilano, Fraser Valley, Kwantlen Polytechnic, Thompson Rivers, and Vancouver Island Universities.

9 The two degree-granting institutes, the British Columbia Institute of Technology and the Emily Carr Institute of Art and Design, were excluded.
10 Furthermore, as Wylie (2017) argued, almost none of the government's original educational vision for the campus was realized in the subsequent decade.
11 These employability attributes are arguably more traits than skills, but "skills" is the term used by the Conference Board and the federal government.
12 During its early years, UBC Okanagan had a lower GPA threshold for admission than UBC Vancouver, offered numerous scholarships, and created administrative barriers to transferring to the main Vancouver campus, all good examples of the competitive tactics used by institutions as they endeavoured to meet enrolment targets.
13 The BC government ombudsperson reported that in 2011–12, private language schools in British Columbia enrolled 47,300 international students (K. Carter, 2015). Although the 100,000 figure above would probably include some domestic students, good quality enrolment data are lacking for private language schools in the province.
14 In comparison, the nineteen private and out-of-province public institutions with authority to grant degrees in British Columbia enrolled only thirteen thousand students in fifty-five degree programs each year (Ministry of Advanced Education, 2015, August 17).
15 The situation became even more complicated in July 2017 when an NDP–Green Party coalition toppled British Columbia's Liberal government. The leaders of the two coalition parties disagree about liquefied natural gas.
16 Nationally, the share of immigrants with a university degree who had been admitted to Canada under the economic program rose from 31 percent in 1990 to 67 percent in 2011 (Picot, Hou, and Qiu, 2016).
17 The 46,200 domestic headcount students in Developmental Programs in the 2011–12 academic year had steadily diminished to 27,700 in 2016–17 (Ministry of Advanced Education, n.d.).
18 The federal government had struck an advisory panel on international education in October 2011. This eventually led to a federal goal to double international student enrolment in Canada over a ten-year period (Minister of International Trade, 2014).

6 | Conclusion

1 In addition to the actual changes described in this study, several reports explore a range of options for serving the hinterland: for example, Commission on University Programs in Non-Metropolitan Areas (1976), Distance Education Planning Group

and Carney (1977), and the Royal Commission on Post Secondary Education in the Kootenay Region (1974).

2 The federal Constitution Act of 1982's "regulation of trade and commerce" and "unemployment insurance" have been broadly interpreted to refer to economic and labour market development. See Sheffield (1982) for a discussion of how Ottawa viewed its interest in postsecondary education with respect to these fields.

3 The *Digest of Education Statistics, 1990* reports that 23 percent of the 3,340 institutions of higher education in the United States were under either Roman Catholic or Protestant control in 1985–86 (Snyder and Hoffman, 1991). More recent editions of this publication do not provide this level of detail.

4 Andres (1992), for example, asks whether access to a community college is equal to access to a university.

References

Academic Board for Higher Education in British Columbia. (1965). *The role of district and regional colleges in the BC system of higher education.* Vancouver: Author.

Academic Board for Higher Education in British Columbia. (1966). *College standards.* Vancouver: Author.

Adelman, C. (1999). *Answers in the toolbox: Academic intensity, attendance patterns, and bachelor's degree attainment.* Washington, DC: US Department of Education.

Adelman, C. (2008). *The Bologna club: What U.S. higher education can learn from a decade of European reconstruction.* Washington, DC: Institute for Higher Education Policy.

Alberta Advanced Education. (1984). *Participation patterns study. Report of the Committee to Examine Participation Trends of Alberta Post-secondary Students.* Edmonton: Alberta Advanced Education, Planning Secretariat.

Alberta Learning Information Services. (2015). *Certificate, diploma, applied degree, degree... What's the difference?* Edmonton: Government of Alberta. Retrieved from https://alis.alberta.ca/ep/eps/tips/tips.html?EK=179

Alison, G.T. (1971). *Essence of decision: Explaining the Cuban missile crisis.* Boston: Little, Brown.

Allmand, W. (1981). *Report: Parliamentary task force on employment opportunities for the 1980s. Work for tomorrow: Employment opportunities for the 1980s.* Ottawa: House of Commons.

Altbach, P., Gumport, P., & Berdahl, R. (Eds.). (2011). *American higher education in the twenty-first century: Social, political, and economic challenges* (3rd ed.). Baltimore: Johns Hopkins University Press.

Andres, L. (1992). *Paths on life's way: Destinations, determinants, and decisions in the transition from high school.* (Doctoral dissertation, University of British Columbia).

Andres, L. (2015). Taking stock of 50 years of participation in Canadian higher education. In M. Shah, A.K. Bennett, & E. Southgate (Eds.), *Widening higher education participation: A global perspective* (pp. 15–33). Oxford: Elsevier.

Andrews, R. (2011). NPM and the search for efficiency. In T. Christensen & P. Lægreid (Eds.), *The Ashgate research companion to new public management* (pp. 281–94). Farnham, Surrey: Ashgate.

Anisef, P., Okihiro, N., & James, C. (1982). *Losers and winners: The pursuit of equality and social justice in higher education.* Toronto: Butterworths.

Auld, D. (2005). *Selling postsecondary education: The role of private vocational and career colleges.* Toronto: C.D. Howe Institute.

Australia, Department of Education and Training. (2015). *Higher education funding in Australia: A review of reviews from Dawkins to today.* Canberra: Author.

Bahram, B. (2004). *Credit accumulation and transfer and the Bologna Process: An overview.* Oxford, United Kingdom: Higher Education Policy Institute.

Baker, J. (2014). No ivies, oxbridge, or grandes écoles: Constructing distinctions in university choice. *British Journal of Sociology of Education, 35*(6), 914–32. https://doi.org/10.1080/01425692.2013.814530

Ball, S.J. (2012). Performativity, commodification and commitment: An I-spy guide to the neoliberal university. *British Journal of Educational Studies, 60*(1), 17–28. https://doi.org/10.1080/00071005.2011.650940

Bastedo, M.N., & Flaster, A. (2014). Conceptual and methodological problems in research on college undermatch. *Educational Researcher, 43*(2), 93–99. https://doi.org/10.3102/0013189X14523039

Beach, J.M. (2011). *Gateway to opportunity? A history of the community college in the United States.* Sterling, VA: Stylus.

Becker, G.S. (1964). *Human capital: A theoretical and empirical analysis, with special reference to education.* New York: National Bureau of Economic Research.

Beinder, F. (1983). *The community college in British Columbia: The emphasis is on community.* Vancouver: British Columbia Association of Colleges.

Beinder, F. (1986). *College development in British Columbia: Recollections of a layman.* Vancouver: Vancouver Community College.

Bell, D. (1973). *The coming of post-industrial society.* New York: Basic Books.

Bell, D. (2004). *Canada passes the Technical and Vocational Training Act.* Toronto: Ontario Institute for Studies in Education of the University of Toronto. Retrieved from http://schugurensky.faculty.asu.edu/moments/1960TVTAA.html

Bell, L.A. (2007). Theoretical foundations for social justice education. In M. Adams, L.A. Bell, & P. Griffin (Eds.), *Teaching for diversity and social justice* (pp. 1–14). New York: Routledge.

Berger, J., Motte, A., & Parkin, A. (2007). *The price of knowledge: Access and student finance in Canada* (3rd ed.). Montreal: Canada Millennium Scholarship Foundation.

Berghofer, D., & Vladicka, A. (1980). *Access to opportunity 1905–80: The development of post-secondary education in Alberta*. Edmonton: Alberta Advanced Education and Manpower.

Blackmore, J. (2013). Social justice in education. In B. Irby, G. Brown, R. Lara-Alecio, & S. Jackson (Eds.), *The handbook of educational theories* (pp. 1001–09). Charlotte, NC: Information Age.

Blackmore, P. (2016). *Prestige in academic life: Excellence and exclusion*. New York: Routledge.

Blakely, E.J. (1994). *Planning local economic development: Theory and practice* (2nd ed.). Thousand Oaks, CA: Sage.

Bloom, M., & Kitagawa, K. (1999). *Understanding employability skills: Executive summary*. Ottawa: Conference Board of Canada.

Boas, T.C., & Gans-Morse, J. (2009). Neoliberalism: From new liberal philosophy to anti-liberal slogan. *Studies in Comparative International Development, 44*(2), 137–61. https://doi.org/10.1007/s12116-009-9040-5

Bogdanor, V. (Ed.). (2005). *Joined-up government*. Oxford: Oxford University Press for the British Academy. https://doi.org/10.5871/bacad/9780197263334.001.0001

Bohman, J. (2015). Critical theory. In E. Zalta (Ed.), *The Stanford encyclopedia of philosophy, Winter 2015*. Retrieved from https://plato.stanford.edu/archives/win2015/entries/critical-theory

Bok, D. (2013). *Higher education in America*. Princeton: Princeton University Press.

Bond, S. (2002, April 29). *Parliamentary debates (Hansard)*. Victoria, BC: Government of British Columbia.

Bond, S. (2004, May 3). *Parliamentary debates (Hansard)*. Victoria, BC: Government of British Columbia.

Bourdieu, P. (1977). *Outline of a theory of practice*. Cambridge: Cambridge University Press. https://doi.org/10.1017/CBO9780511812507

Bourdieu, P. (1998). The essence of neoliberalism. *Le Monde diplomatique*. Retrieved from http://mondediplo.com/1998/12/08bourdieu

Boyer, E. (1990). *Scholarship reconsidered: Priorities of the professoriate*. San Francisco: Jossey Bass.

Boyle, C. (2010). *Lotteries for education: Origins, experiences, lessons*. Charlottesville, VA: Imprint Academic.

Bradshaw, T. (2013). The post-place community: Contributions to the debate about the definition of community. In M. Brennan, J. Bridger, & T. Alter (Eds.), *Theory, practice and community development* (pp. 11–24). New York: Routledge.

Brennan, J., & Naidoo, R. (2008). Higher education and the achievement (and/or prevention) of equity and social justice. *Higher Education, 56*(3), 287–302. https://doi.org/10.1007/s10734-008-9127-3

Brennan, P. (2014). Raising the quality and image of TVET: Lower-level training or motor for inclusive and sustainable growth? *Prospects: Quarterly Review of Comparative Education, 44*(2), 183–95. https://doi.org/10.1007/s11125-014-9312-3

Brint, S., & Karabel, J. (1989). *The diverted dream: Community colleges and the promise of educational opportunity in America, 1900–1985*. New York: Oxford University Press.

British Columbia. (1983, June 23). *Speech from the throne. Parliamentary debates (Hansard)*. Victoria, BC: Government of British Columbia.

British Columbia. (2001, July 24). *Speech from the throne. Parliamentary debates (Hansard)*. Victoria, BC: Government of British Columbia.

British Columbia. (2014). *B.C.'s skills for jobs blueprint: Re-engineering education and training*. Victoria, BC: Government of British Columbia. Retrieved from https://www.workbc.ca/getmedia/4c54646a-93fa-4566-b148-f43a3f27b240/Booklet_BCsBlueprint_web_140428.pdf.aspx?

British Columbia Council on Admissions and Transfer. (2006). *Recalibrating the BC transfer system – A BCCAT consultation: Final report*. Vancouver: Author.

British Columbia Task Force on Employment and Training. (1991). *Learning & work: The way ahead for British Columbians: Report of the Task Force on Employment & Training*. Victoria, BC: The Task Force and British Columbia Ministry of Advanced Education, Training and Technology.

Brown, A.D. (1998). Narrative, politics and legitimacy in an IT implementation. *Journal of Management Studies, 35*(1), 35–58. https://doi.org/10.1111/1467-6486.00083

Brown, P. (1999). Globalisation and the political economy of high skills. *Journal of Work and Education, 12*(3), 233–51. https://doi.org/10.1080/1363908990120302

Brown, W. (2003). Neo-liberalism and the end of liberal democracy. *Theory and Event, 7*(1). https://doi.org/10.1353/tae.2003.0020

Buchanan, J.M., & Tullock, G. (1962). *The calculus of consent: Logical foundations of constitutional democracy*. Ann Arbor: University of Michigan Press. https://doi.org/10.3998/mpub.7687

Bullen, E.L. (1991). *Access for all: The story of British Columbia's planning for expansion of post-secondary education in the late 1980's*. Unpublished manuscript in the BC Legislative Library prepared for the Ministry of Advanced Education, Training and Technology.

Burbules, N., Lord, B., & Sherman, A.L. (1982). Equity, equal opportunity, and education. *Educational Evaluation and Policy Analysis, 4*(2), 169–87. https://doi.org/10.3102/01623737004002169

Burch, P. (2007). Educational policy and practice from the perspective of institutional theory: Crafting a wider lens. *Educational Researcher, 36*(2), 84–95. https://doi.org/10.3102/0013189X07299792

Butler, E. (2012). *Public choice: A primer.* London: Institute of Economic Affairs.

California State Department of Education. (1960). *A master plan for higher education in California: 1960–1975.* Sacramento: Author.

Cameron, D. (1991). *More than an academic question: Universities, government, and public policy in Canada.* Halifax: Institute for Research on Public Policy.

Cameron, M.A. (1945). *Report of the Commission of Inquiry into Educational Finance.* Victoria, BC: King's Printer.

Canada. (1940). *Report of the Royal Commission on Dominion-Provincial Relations.* Ottawa: King's Printer.

Canada, & Dodge, D. (1981). *Labour market development in the 1980's: A report of the Task Force on Labour Market Development.* Ottawa: Employment and Immigration Canada.

Canadian Apprenticeship Forum. (2004). *Accessing and completing apprenticeship training in Canada: Perceptions of barriers.* Ottawa: Author.

Canadian Association of University Business Officers. (2016). *Financial information of universities and colleges, 2014–2015.* Ottawa: Author.

Carter, C., & Clegg, S. (2011). Institutional theory, new. In G. Ritzer and J. Ryan (Eds.), *The concise encyclopedia of sociology* (pp. 322–23). Malden, MA: Wiley-Blackwell.

Carter, K. (2015). *In the public interest: Protecting students through effective oversight of private career training institutions. Public report no. 51 to the Legislative Assembly of British Columbia.* Victoria, BC: Office of the Ombudsperson.

Center for Community College Student Engagement. (n.d.). *Community college survey of student engagement.* University of Texas at Austin. Retrieved from http://www.ccsse.org

Chan, A., & Fisher, D. (2008). Introduction. In A. Chan & D. Fisher (Eds.), *The exchange university: Corporatization of academic culture* (pp. 1-18). Vancouver: UBC Press.

Chant, S.N.F. (1960). *Report of the Royal Commission on Education.* Victoria, BC: Queen's Printer.

Chaskin, R. (2013). Theories of community. In M. Weil, M. Reisch, & M. Ohmer (Eds.), *The handbook of community practice* (2nd ed., pp. 105–22). Los Angeles: Sage. https://doi.org/10.4135/9781412976640.n5

Christensen, T. (2008). New public management. In S. Clegg & J. Bailey (Eds.), *International encyclopedia of organization studies* (pp. 980–84). Thousand Oaks, CA: Sage. https://doi.org/10.4135/9781412956246.n337

Christensen, T., & Lægreid, P. (2007). Introduction – Theoretical approach and research questions. In T. Christensen & P. Lægreid (Eds.), *Transcending new public management: The transformation of public sector reforms* (pp. 1–16). Burlington, VT: Ashgate.

Christie, B. (1997). Higher education in Nova Scotia: Where past is more than prologue. In G.A. Jones (Ed.), *Higher education in Canada: Different systems, different perspectives* (pp. 221–44). New York: Garland.

Church, R. (2002). *A brief history of the university college mandate issue.* Unpublished manuscript at Malaspina University College (Vancouver Island University), Nanaimo, BC.

Citizenship and Immigration Canada. (2010). *Evaluation of the Federal Skilled Worker Program.* Report No. Ci4-54/2010E-PDF 978-1-100-17226-2. Ottawa: Evaluation Division, Citizenship and Immigration Canada.

City of Burnaby. (2015). *Discovery place – SFU.* Retrieved from https://www.burnaby.ca/Doing-Business/Places-To-Do-Business/Business-Centres/Discovery-Place---SFU.html

Clark, B. (1960). The "cooling out" function in higher education. *American Journal of Sociology, 65*(6), 569–76. https://doi.org/10.1086/222787

Clift, R. (2016). A cautionary tale of marketization of postsecondary education. *Academic Matters*, January, 13–16.

Coalition of BC Businesses. (2001). *The Industry Training and Apprenticeship Commission: What is its future?* Vancouver: Coalition of BC Businesses.

Cohen, A.M., & Kisker, C.B. (2009). *The shaping of American higher education: Emergence and growth of the contemporary systems* (2nd ed.). San Francisco: Jossey Bass.

Commission on University Programs in Non-Metropolitan Areas. (1976). *Report of the Commission on University Programs in Non-Metropolitan Areas.* Vancouver: Author.

Committee of Presidents. (1963). *Post-secondary education in Ontario, 1962–1970: Report of the presidents of the universities of Ontario to the Advisory Committee on University Affairs, May, 1962.* Toronto: University of Toronto Press.

Committee on Higher Education. (1963). *Higher education: Report of the committee appointed by the prime minister under the chairmanship of Lord Robbins, 1961–63.* London: H.M. Stationery Office.

Cowin, B. (2004). Transfer in British Columbia: What does the research tell us? *Research Results*, April. Vancouver: British Columbia Council on Admissions and Transfer.

Cowin, B. (2007). *Overview*. Made in BC: A history of postsecondary education in British Columbia. New Westminster, BC: Douglas College. Retrieved from ERIC database. (ED 501776)

Cowin, B. (2009). *Faith-based institutions*. Made in BC: A history of postsecondary education in British Columbia. New Westminster, BC: Douglas College. Retrieved from ERIC database. (ED505878)

Cowin, B. (2010). *Continuing education in public institutions*. Made in BC: A history of postsecondary education in British Columbia. New Westminster, BC: Douglas College. Retrieved from ERIC database. (ED 512293)

Cowin, B. (2011). *Aboriginal postsecondary education*. Made in BC: A history of postsecondary education in British Columbia. New Westminster, BC: Douglas College. Retrieved from ERIC database. (ED 524626)

Cowin, B. (2012a). *Agencies and organizations*. Made in BC: A history of postsecondary education in British Columbia. New Westminster, BC: Douglas College. Retrieved from ERIC database. (ED 536089)

Cowin, B. (2012b). *Apprenticeship and pre-apprenticeship training*. Made in BC: A history of postsecondary education in British Columbia. New Westminster, BC: Douglas College. Retrieved from ERIC database. (ED 532003)

Cowin, B. (2013a). *Post-baccalaureate programs*. Made in BC: A history of postsecondary education in British Columbia. New Westminster, BC: Douglas College. Retrieved from ERIC database. (ED 540825)

Cowin, B. (2013b). *Private career colleges*. Made in BC: a history of postsecondary education in British Columbia. New Westminster, BC: Douglas College. Retrieved from ERIC database. (ED 545544)

Cowin, B. (2013c). *Student transfer, success and mobility in BC post-secondary institutions: A synthesis of research*. Vancouver: British Columbia Council on Admissions and Transfer.

Craig, D., & Porter, D. (2003). Poverty reduction strategy papers: A new convergence. *World Development, 31*(1), 53–69. https://doi.org/10.1016/S0305-750X(02)00147-X

Craven, A. (2012). Social justice and higher education. *Perspectives: Policy and Practice in Higher Education, 16*(1), 23–28.

Cruikshank, J. (1990). University extension: What happened to the vision? In B.S. Cough (Ed.), *Proceedings of the Annual Conference*. Canadian Association for the Study of Adult Education. Kingston, ON: Faculty of Education, Queen's University.

Culos, G. (2005). *A crucible and a catalyst: Private post-secondary education policy in British Columbia*. (Master's thesis, University of British Columbia).

Damer, E., & Rosengarten, H. (2009). *UBC: The first 100 years*. Vancouver: University of British Columbia.

Davies, S., & Guppy, N. (2010). *The schooled society: An introduction to the sociology of education* (2nd ed.). Don Mills, ON: Oxford University Press.

Davies, S., & Hammack, F.M. (2005). The channeling of student competition in higher education: Comparing Canada and the U.S. *Journal of Higher Education, 76*(1), 89–106. https://doi.org/10.1080/00221546.2005.11772276

Davies, S., & Zarifa, D. (2012). The stratification of universities: Structural inequality in Canada and the United States. *Research in Social Stratification and Mobility, 30*(2), 143–58. https://doi.org/10.1016/j.rssm.2011.05.003

Davis, T., & Harrison, L. (2013). *Advancing social justice: Tools, pedagogies, and strategies to transform your campus.* San Francisco: Jossey Bass.

Dawkins, C.J. (2003). Regional development theory: Conceptual foundations, classic works, and recent developments. *Journal of Planning Literature, 18*(2), 131-72.

Dawkins, J.S., & Australia. (1988). *Higher education: A policy statement.* Canberra: Department of Employment, Education and Training, Australian Government Publication Services.

De la Fuente, A., & Ciccone, A. (2003). *Human capital in a global and knowledge-based economy.* Brussels: European Commission.

Deephouse, D., & Suchman, M. (2008). Legitimacy in organizational institutionalism. In R. Greenwood, C. Oliver, R. Suddaby, & K. Sahlin (Eds.), *The Sage handbook of organizational institutionalism* (pp. 49–77). London: Sage. https://doi.org/10.4135/9781849200387.n2

Degree Quality Assessment Board. (2003–04 to 2006–07). *Annual report.* Victoria, BC: Author and Ministry of Advanced Education.

Deissinger, T., Aff, J., Fuller, A., & Jorgensen, C. (Eds.). (2013). *Hybrid qualifications: Structures and problems in the context of European VET policy.* Bern, Switzerland: Peter Lang. https://doi.org/10.3726/978-3-0351-0585-8

Denison, E. (1962). *The sources of economic growth in the U.S. and the alternatives before us.* Supplementary paper no. 13. New York: Committee for Economic Development.

Dennison, J. (1979a). The community college in comparative and historical perspective: The development of the college concept in British Columbia. *Canadian Journal of Higher Education, 9*(3), 29–40.

Dennison, J. (1979b). *Post secondary education in British Columbia: A perspective for the 1980s.* Unpublished manuscript, Faculty of Education, University of British Columbia.

Dennison, J.D. (1992). *Higher education in British Columbia, 1945–1992: Opportunity and diversity.* Unpublished manuscript in Education Library, University of British Columbia.

Dennison, J.D. (1995). Community college development in Canada since 1985. In J.D. Dennison (Ed.), *Challenge and opportunity: Canada's community colleges at the crossroads* (pp. 13–104). Vancouver: UBC Press.

Dennison, J.D. (1997). Higher education in British Columbia, 1945–1995: Opportunity and diversity. In G.A. Jones (Ed.), *Higher education in Canada: Different systems, different perspectives* (pp. 31–58). New York: Garland.

Dennison, J.D. (2006). From community college to university: A personal commentary on the evolution of an institution. *Canadian Journal of Higher Education, 36*(2), 107–24.

Dennison, J.D., & Gallagher, P. (1986). *Canada's community colleges: A critical analysis.* Vancouver: UBC Press.

Dennison, J.D., & Schuetze, H.G. (2004). Extending access, choice, and the reign of the market: Higher education reforms in British Columbia, 1989–2004. *Canadian Journal of Higher Education, 34*(3), 13–38.

Department of Education. (1971). *Annual report of the public schools of the province of British Columbia, 1970–71.* Victoria, BC: Government of British Columbia.

Department of Education. (1974). *Towards the learning community: Report of the Task Force on the Community College in British Columbia.* Victoria, BC: Department of Education, Government of British Columbia.

Department of Labour. (1967). *Annual report, 1966–67.* Victoria, BC: Government of British Columbia.

Devereaux, M.S. (1984). *One in every five: A survey of adult education in Canada.* Ottawa: Statistics Canada; Department of the Secretary of State, Education Support Sector.

Devine, N. (2004). *Education and public choice: A critical account of the invisible hand in education.* Westport, CT: Praeger.

Diallo, B., Trottier, C., & Doray, P. (2009). *What do we know about the pathways and transitions of Canadian students in post-secondary education? Note 1: Transitions Project, Number 46.* Montreal: Canadian Millennium Scholarship Foundation.

DiMaggio, P.J., & Powell, W.W. (1983). The iron cage revisited: Institutional isomorphism and collective rationality in organizational fields. *American Sociological Review, 48*(2), 147–60. https://doi.org/10.2307/2095101

Discovery Parks. (2015). *History of Discovery Parks.* Retrieved from http://www.discoveryparks.com/about-us/history/

Distance Education Planning Group, & Carney, P. (1977). *Report of the Distance Education Planning Group on a delivery system for distance education in BC.* Victoria, BC: Ministry of Education.

Douglas College. (2013). *Schedule A. Financial statements, years ended March 31, 2013 and March 31, 2012*. New Westminster, BC: Douglas College.

Downs, A. (1967). *Inside bureaucracy*. Boston: Little, Brown. https://doi.org/10.7249/CB156

Drucker, P. (1969). *The age of discontinuity*. London: Heinemann.

Dupre, J., Cameron, D., McKechnie, G., & Rotenberg, T. (1973). *Federation and policy development: The case of adult occupational training in Ontario*. Toronto: University of Toronto Press.

Dwyer, B.M. (1983). *A historical perspective of federal policies for adult occupational training and their impact on post secondary education in British Columbia, 1900–1983*. (Master's paper, University of British Columbia.)

Economic Council of Canada. (1982). *In short supply: Jobs and skills in the 1980s*. Ottawa: Author.

Employment and Social Development Canada. (2015, October 13). *Literacy and essential skills*. Retrieved from https://www.canada.ca/en/employment-social-development/programs/essential-skills.html

Esping-Andersen, G. (1990). *The three worlds of welfare capitalism*. Cambridge: Polity Press.

Estevez-Abe, M., Iversen, T., & Soskice, D. (2001). Social protection and the formation of skills: A reinterpretation of the welfare state. In P.A. Hall & D.W. Soskice (Eds.), *Varieties of capitalism: The institutional foundations of comparative advantage* (pp. 145–83). Oxford: Oxford University Press. https://doi.org/10.1093/0199247757.003.0004

Fallis, G. (2013). *Rethinking higher education: Participation, research, and differentiation*. Kingston, ON: School of Policy Studies, Queen's University.

Finnie, R. (Ed.). (2008). *Who goes? Who stays? What matters? Accessing and persisting in post-secondary education in Canada*. Kingston, ON: School of Policy Studies, Queen's University.

Fisher, D., Rubenson, K., Bernatchez, J., Clift, R., Jones, G., Lee, J., MacIvoer, M., Meredith, J., Shanahan, T., Trottier, C., & University of British Columbia. (2006). *Canadian federal policy and postsecondary education*. Vancouver: Centre for Policy Studies in Higher Education and Training, Faculty of Education, University of British Columbia.

Fisher, D., House, D., & Rubenson, K. (2003). Les politiques publiques et le développement d'un systeme d'education postsecondaire en Colombie-Britannique. *Revue des Sciences de l'Education*, 29(2), 297–318. https://doi.org/10.7202/011034ar

Fisher, D., Rubenson, K., Jones, G., & Shanahan, T. (2009). The political economy of post-secondary education: A comparison of British Columbia, Ontario and

Québec. *Higher Education, 57*(5), 549–66. https://doi.org/10.1007/s10734-008-9160-2

Fisher, D., Rubenson, K., Lee, J., Clift, R., MacIvor, M., & Meredith, J. (2014). The transformation of the PSE system in British Columbia. In D. Fisher, K. Rubenson, T. Shanahan, & C. Trottier (Eds.), *The development of postsecondary education systems in Canada: A comparison between British Columbia, Ontario, and Quebec, 1980–2010* (pp. 35–121). Montreal and Kingston: McGill-Queen's University Press.

Fleming, R. (2010). *Crossing borders and contesting values: Negotiating British Columbia's university sector.* (Doctoral dissertation, Simon Fraser University).

Fleming, R., & Lee, G. (2009). Canada: What's in a title? In N. Garrod & B. Macfarlane (Eds.), *Challenging boundaries: Managing the integration of post-secondary education* (pp. 93–109). New York: Routledge.

Fletcher, T. (2015, February 10). BC views: Post-secondary re-engineering begins. *Penticton Western News.* Retrieved from http://ezproxy.library.ubc.ca/login?url=http://search.proquest.com/docview/1653030082?accountid=14656

Fraser, N. (1997). *Justice interruptus: Critical reflections on the "postsocialist" condition.* New York: Routledge.

Fraser, N., & Honneth, A. (2003). *Redistribution or recognition? A political-philosophical exchange.* New York: Verso. https://doi.org/10.1002/9780470756119.ch54

Freake, R. (2005). *OUC memoirs.* Kelowna, BC: Okanagan University College.

Friedman, M. (1962). *Capitalism and freedom.* Chicago: University of Chicago Press.

Furlong, A., & Cartmel, F. (2009). *Higher education and social justice.* Maidenhead, UK: Society for Research into Higher Education and Open University Press Maidenhead.

Gaber, D. (2002). *Provincial coordination and inter-institutional collaboration in British Columbia's college, university college, and institute system.* (Doctoral dissertation, Oregon State University).

Galinova, E.V. (2005). *The construction of meritocracy within mass higher education.* (Doctoral dissertation, Pennsylvania State University).

Gallagher, C., & Merner, R. (1981). *British Columbia enrolment and degree performance in the Canadian context: A widening gap.* Victoria, BC: University of Victoria.

Gallie, D. (2011). *Production regimes, employee job control and skill development.* LLAKES Research Paper 31, Centre for Learning and Life Chances in Knowledge Economies and Societies. London: Institute of Education, University of London.

Garkovich, L. (2011). An historical view of community development. In J. Robinson & G. Green (Eds.), *Introduction to community development: Theory, practice and service-learning* (pp. 11–34). Thousand Oaks, CA: Sage.

Garrod, N., & Macfarlane, B. (Eds.). (2009). *Challenging boundaries: Managing the integration of post-secondary education*. New York: Routledge.

Garza, H., & Eller, R.D. (1998). The role of rural community colleges in expanding access and economic development. In D. McGrath (Ed.), Creating and benefitting from institutional collaboration, *New Directions for Community Colleges, 103*, 31–41. San Francisco: Wiley. https://doi.org/10.1002/cc.10304

Gerber, T.P., & Cheung, S.Y. (2008). Horizontal stratification in postsecondary education: Forms, explanations, and implications. *Annual Review of Sociology, 34*(1), 299–318. https://doi.org/10.1146/annurev.soc.34.040507.134604

Gereluk, D. (2008). Social justice, education for. In E.F. Provenzo & R.J. Provenzo (Eds.), *Encyclopedia of the social and cultural foundations of education* (pp. 729–32). Thousand Oaks, CA: Sage.

Giddens, A. (1999). *The third way: The renewal of social democracy*. Malden, MA: Polity.

Giles, V. (1983). *The minister's perspective: Personal perceptions and reflections of ministers of education in British Columbia from 1958 to 1979*. (Master's thesis, Simon Fraser University).

Giroux, H.A. (2014). *Neoliberalism's war on higher education*. Toronto: Between the Lines.

Goard, D. (1977). *Report of the Commission on Vocational, Technical and Trades Training in British Columbia*. Burnaby, BC: Province of British Columbia.

Goedegebuure, L., Santiago, P., Fitznor, L., Stensaker, B., & van der Steen, M. (2008). *New Zealand: OECD reviews of tertiary education*. Paris: Organization for Economic Co-operation and Development.

Gonzales, L.D. (2012). Responding to mission creep: Faculty members as cosmopolitan agents. *Higher Education, 64*(3), 337–53. https://doi.org/10.1007/s10734-011-9497-9

Gordon, H. (2014). *The history and growth of career and technical education in America* (4th ed.). Long Grove, IL: Waveland Press.

Gordon, W.L. (1957). *Final report*. Ottawa: Royal Commission on Canada's Economic Prospects.

Gottschalk, L.R. (Ed.). (1963). *Generalization in the writing of history: A report. Committee on Historical Analysis, Social Science Research Council (USA)*. Chicago: University of Chicago Press.

Gray, J. (2008). Neoinstitutional theory. In S. Clegg & J. Bailey (Eds.), *International encyclopedia of organization studies* (pp. 958–60). Thousand Oaks, CA: Sage. https://doi.org/10.4135/9781412956246.n331

Grubb, W.N., & Lazerson, M. (2004). *The education gospel: The economic power of schooling*. Cambridge, MA: Harvard University Press.

Gültekin, S. (2011). New public management: Is it really new? *International Journal of Human Sciences*, 8(2), 343–58.

Haddow, R. (1998). How Ottawa shrivels: Ottawa's declining role in active labour market policy. In L. Pal. (Ed.), *How Ottawa spends, 1998–99: The post-deficit mandate* (pp. 99-126). Toronto: Oxford University Press.

Haddow, R. (2000). How malleable are political-economic institutions? The case of labour-market decision-making in British Columbia. *Canadian Public Administration*, 43(4), 387–411. https://doi.org/10.1111/j.1754-7121.2000.tb01151.x

Hagen, S. (1989). *Access for all: Together. A better BC. Unpublished speaking notes for a press conference, March 20, 1989 by the minister of advanced education and job training*. Legislative Library, Province of British Columbia, Victoria, BC.

Haligan, J. (2011). NPM in Anglo-Saxon countries. In T. Christensen & P. Lægreid (Eds.), *The Ashgate research companion to new public management* (pp. 83–96). Burlington, VT: Ashgate.

Hall, P.A., & Soskice, D.W. (Eds.). (2001). *Varieties of capitalism: The institutional foundations of comparative advantage*. Oxford: Oxford University Press. https://doi.org/10.1093/0199247757.001.0001

Harris, R.S. (1976). *A history of higher education in Canada, 1663–1960*. Toronto: University of Toronto Press.

Hartog, J., & Maassen van den Brink, H. (2007). Prologue. In J. Hartog & H. Maassen van den Brink (Eds.), *Human capital: Advances in theory and evidence* (pp. 1–4). Cambridge: Cambridge University Press. https://doi.org/10.1017/CBO9780511493416.001

Harvey, D. (2007). *A brief history of neoliberalism*. New York: Oxford University Press.

Hayek, F. v. (1944). *The road to serfdom*. Chicago: University of Chicago Press.

Heslop, J. (2004). Alternative paths to SFU: A comparative academic performance study of BC college transfer students and BC direct entry secondary school students admitted to SFU from 1992 to 1999. *Research Results*, October. Vancouver: British Columbia Council on Admissions and Transfer.

Holmberg, D., & Hallonsten, O. (2015). Policy reform and academic drift: Research mission and institutional legitimacy in the development of the Swedish higher education system 1977–2012. *European Journal of Higher Education*, 5(2), 181–96. https://doi.org/10.1080/21568235.2014.997263

Hood, C. (1991). A public management for all seasons? *Public Administration*, 69(1), 3–19. https://doi.org/10.1111/j.1467-9299.1991.tb00779.x

Hood, C., & Peters, G. (2004). The middle aging of new public management: Into the age of paradox? *Journal of Public Administration: Research and Theory*, 14(3), 267–82. https://doi.org/10.1093/jopart/muh019

Howard, R. (2006). Classroom chaos. *BC Business*, 34(6), 52–61.

Human Resources Development Canada. (1998). *Strategic initiatives formative evaluation of the Institute of Indigenous Government – British Columbia*. Catalogue no. SP-AH088-03-98E. Ottawa: Author. Retrieved from http://publications.gc.ca/collections/collection_2013/rhdcc-hrsdc/RH64-101-1999-eng.pdf

Hunter, C.P. (2013). *The Organization for Economic Cooperation and Development's changing (?) discourse on higher education*. (Doctoral dissertation, University of British Columbia).

Hustedde, R., & Ganowicz, J. (2013). The basics: What's essential about theory for community development practice? In M. Brennan, J. Bridger, & T. Alter (Eds.), *Theory, practice and community development* (pp. 163–79). New York: Routledge.

Ife, J. (2002). *Community development* (2nd ed.). Frenchs Forest, New South Wales: Pearson Education Australia.

Indigenous Adult and Higher Learning Association. (2013). *Data collection project 2012/13: Final report*. West Vancouver, BC: Author. Retrieved from http://iahla.ca/wp-content/uploads/Final-2012to13-DCP-Report-v3-Mar-31-2013-Revd-Sept.pdf.

Industry Training Authority. (2012). *Annual service plan report, 2011/12*. Richmond, BC: Author.

Industry Training Authority. (2013). ITA Performance measurement report: Updated to March 31, 2013. Retrieved from http://www.itabc.ca/sites/default/files/docs/about-ita/corporate-reports/%282013MAR31%29%20ITA_Stats_March2013_Final.pdf

Industry Training Authority. (2015). *2014/15-2016/17 Annual service plan report*. Richmond, BC: Author. Retrieved from http://www.itabc.ca/sites/default/files/docs/about-ita/corporate-reports/ITA%202014_15%20Annual%20Report%20Ministry%20Approved.pdf

Industry Training Authority. (2015, August). *ITA performance measurement report, August 2015*. Richmond, BC: Author.

Industry Training Authority. (2015, December). *ITA performance measurement report, December 2015*. Richmond, BC: Author.

Johnston, H. (2005). *Radical campus: Making Simon Fraser University*. Vancouver: Douglas and McIntyre.

Jones, G. (1997). Higher education in Ontario. In G.A. Jones (Ed.), *Higher education in Canada: Different systems, different perspectives* (pp. 137–60). New York: Garland.

Jones, G. (2009). Sectors, institutional types and the challenges of shifting categories: A Canadian commentary. *Higher Education Quarterly, 63*(4), 371–83. https://doi.org/10.1111/j.1468-2273.2009.00439.x

Jones, G.A. (2014). An introduction to higher education in Canada. In K.M. Jashi & S. Paivandi (Eds.), *Higher education across nations* (Vol. 1, pp. 1–33). Delhi: B.R. Publishing.

Jorgenson, D. (2012). *Understanding the knowledge economy.* Presentation at the University of Groningen. Retrieved from https://scholar.harvard.edu/jorgenson/presentations/underdtanding-knowledge-economy

Karlsson, T. (2008). Institutional isomorphism. In S. Clegg & J. Bailey (Eds.), *International encyclopedia of organization studies* (pp. 679–82). Thousand Oaks, CA: Sage. https://doi.org/10.4135/9781412956246.n233

Kerr, C. (1978). Higher education: Paradise lost? *Higher Education, 7*(3), 261–78. https://doi.org/10.1007/BF00139526

Kirst, M., & Stevens, M. (Eds.). (2015). *Remaking college: The changing ecology of higher education.* Stanford, CA: Stanford University Press.

Klingbeil, M. (2008). *Measuring human capital in the knowledge economy.* Victoria, BC: Ministry of Advanced Education, Research, Technology, and Innovation Division.

Knott, W.W.D. (1932). *The junior college in British Columbia.* (Master's thesis, Stanford University).

Knowles, J. (1995). A matter of survival: Emerging entrepreneurship in community colleges in Canada. In J. Dennison (Ed.), *Challenge and opportunity: Canada's community colleges at the crossroads* (pp. 184-207). Vancouver: UBC Press.

Kulich, J., Taylor, R., Tetlow, W., & University of British Columbia. (1981). *Looking beyond.* Vancouver: University of British Columbia.

Lambert-Maberly, A. (2010). Profile of BC college transfer students, 2003/04 to 2007/08. *Research Results*, April. Vancouver: British Columbia Council on Admissions and Transfer.

Languages Canada. (2017). *British Columbia fact sheet, 2016.* Retrieved from https://www.languagescanada.ca/en/british-columbia-chapter

Larner, W. (2000). Neo-liberalism: Policy, ideology, governmentality. *Studies in Political Economy, 63*(1), 5–25. https://doi.org/10.1080/19187033.2000.11675231

Leblanc, F., & Canada. (1987). *Federal policy on post-secondary education: Report of the Standing Senate Committee on National Finance.* Ottawa: Standing Senate Committee on National Finance.

Lemke, T. (2001). "The birth of bio-politics": Michel Foucault's lecture at the Collège de France on neo-liberal governmentality. *Economy and Society, 30*(2), 190–207. https://doi.org/10.1080/03085140120042271

Leslie, P. (1980). *Canadian universities 1980 and beyond: Enrollment, structure, and finance.* Ottawa: Association of Universities and Colleges of Canada.

Leuridan, B., & Froeyman, A. (2012). On lawfulness in history and historiography. *History and Theory, 51*(2), 172–92. https://doi.org/10.1111/j.1468-2303.2012.00620.x

Levin, J.S. (1994). Change and influence in the community colleges of British Columbia. *Canadian Journal of Higher Education, 24*(1), 72–85.

Levin, J.S. (2001). *Globalizing the community college: Strategies for change in the twenty-first century*. New York: Palgrave Macmillan. https://doi.org/10.1057/9780312292836

Levin, J.S. (2003). Organizational paradigm shift and the university colleges of British Columbia. *Higher Education, 46*(4), 447–67. https://doi.org/10.1023/A:1027375308484

Levy, D. (2006). How private higher education's growth challenges the new institutionalism. In H. Meyer & B. Rowan (Eds.), *The new institutionalism in education* (pp. 15–32). Albany: State University of New York Press Albany.

Lilley, S. (2006). *On neoliberalism: An interview with David Harvey*. Retrieved from https://mronline.org/?redirect=1&dir=2006&file=lilley190606

Lincoln, J.R. (1995). [Review of the book *The new institutionalism in organizational research* by W.W. Powell and P. DiMaggio (Eds.)]. *Social Forces, 73*, 1147–48.

Lindahl, M., & Canton, E. (2007). The social returns to education. In J. Hartog & H. Maassen van den Brink (Eds.), *Human capital: Advances in theory and evidence* (pp. 21–37). Cambridge: Cambridge University Press. https://doi.org/10.1017/CBO9780511493416.003

Livingstone, D.W. (2012). Debunking the 'knowledge economy: The limits of human capital theory. In D.W. Livingstone & D. Guile (Eds.), *The knowledge economy and lifelong learning: A critical reader* (pp. 85—116). Dordrecht, Netherlands: Sense. https://doi.org/10.1007/978-94-6091-915-2

Livingstone, D.W., & Guile, D. (Eds.). (2012). *The knowledge economy and lifelong learning: A critical reader*. Dordrecht, Netherlands: Sense. https://doi.org/10.1007/978-94-6091-915-2

Lorenz, C. (2012). If you're so smart, why are you under surveillance? Universities, neoliberalism, and new public management. *Critical Inquiry, 38*(3), 599–629. https://doi.org/10.1086/664553

Lowen, G., & Pollard, W. (2010). The social justice perspective. *Journal of Postsecondary Education and Disability, 23*(1), 5–17.

Lynn, L.E. (2006). *Public management: Old and new*. New York: Routledge.

Lyons, E., Randhawa, B., & Paulson, N. (1991). The development of vocational education in Canada. *Canadian Journal of Education, 16*(2), 137–50. https://doi.org/10.2307/1494967

Macdonald, J.B. (1962). *Higher education in British Columbia and a plan for the future*. Vancouver: University of British Columbia.

Macdonald, J.B. (2000). *Chances and choices: A memoir*. Vancouver: Alumni Association, University of British Columbia.

MacPherson, I. (2012). *Reaching outward and upward: The University of Victoria, 1963-2013*. Montreal and Kingston: McGill-Queen's University Press.

Marginson, S. (1997a). *Educating Australia: Government, economy and citizen since 1960.* Cambridge: Cambridge University Press. https://doi.org/10.1017/CBO 9781139166966

Marginson, S. (1997b). Steering from a distance: Power relations in Australian higher education. *Higher Education, 34*(1), 63–80. https://doi.org/10.1023/A:1003082922199

Marginson, S. (2012). The impossibility of capitalist markets in higher education. *Journal of Education Policy, 28*(3), 1–18.

Marginson, S. (2016a). *The dream is over: The crisis of Clark Kerr's California idea of higher education.* Oakland: University of California Press. https://doi.org/10.1525/luminos.17

Marginson, S. (2016b). High participation systems of higher education. *Journal of Higher Education, 87*(2), 243-71. https://doi.org/10.1080/00221546.2016.11777401

Marginson, S. (2016c). Higher education and growing inopportunity. *Academic Matters, January 2016,* 7–11. Toronto: Ontario Confederation of University Faculty Associations.

Marginson, S., & Considine, M. (2000). *The enterprise university: Power, governance and reinvention in Australia.* Cambridge: Cambridge University Press.

McArthur, A. (1997). *Legitimation of applied knowledge: The creation of a bachelor of technology degree at BCIT.* (Master's thesis, University of British Columbia).

McArthur, J. (2010). Achieving social justice within and through higher education: The challenge for critical pedagogy. *Teaching in Higher Education, 15*(5), 493–504. https://doi.org/10.1080/13562517.2010.491906

McBride, S. (1998). *The political economy of training in Canada.* Paper presented at the Second Annual Conference of the Labour Education and Training Research Network, York University, ON. Retrieved from http://www.yorku.ca/crws/network/members/McBride.pdf

McCaffray, C. (1995). *UNBC, a northern crusade: The how and who of BC's northern university.* Duncan, BC: Author.

McDonald, J. (2014). *The Industry Training Authority and trades training in BC: Recalibrating for high performance.* Independent review prepared for the Ministry of Jobs, Tourism and Skills Training, Government of British Columbia. Retrieved from https://www.workbc.ca/getmedia/729cbe02-d9cb-4c8c-b19c-2c006483e99f/ITA_Review_Final_Report.pdf.aspx

McKenzie, M. (2007). A profile of Canada's highly qualified personnel. Catalogue no. 88–003-XWE. *Innovation Analysis Bulletin, 9*(2). Ottawa: Statistics Canada.

Mella, P. (2012). *Systems thinking: Intelligence in action.* New York: Springer. https://doi.org/10.1007/978-88-470-2565-3

Meredith, J. (2012). *The collapse of apprenticeship and the privatization of vocational training in British Columbia, 1935–2011.* Unpublished presentation at the Centre for Policy Studies in Higher Education and Training, University of British Columbia, March 13.

Metcalfe, A.S. (2010). Revisiting academic capitalism in Canada: No longer the exception. *Journal of Higher Education, 81*(4), 489–514. https://doi.org/10.1080/00221546.2010.11779062

Metcalfe, A.S., & Fenwick, T. (2009). Knowledge for whose society? Knowledge production, higher education, and federal policy in Canada. *Higher Education, 57*(2), 209–25. https://doi.org/10.1007/s10734-008-9142-4

Meyer, J.W., & Rowan, B. (1977). Institutionalized organizations: Formal structure as myth and ceremony. *American Journal of Sociology, 83*(2), 340–63. https://doi.org/10.1086/226550

Meyer, J.W., & Scott, W.R. (1983). Centralization and the legitimacy problems of local government. In J.W. Meyer & W.R. Scott (Eds.), *Organizational environments: Ritual and rationality* (pp. 199–215). Beverly Hills: Sage.

Miller, M.T., & Kissinger, D.B. (2007). Connecting rural community colleges to their communities. In P.L. Eddy & J.P. Murray (Eds.), Rural community colleges, *New Directions for Community Colleges, 137*, 27–34. San Francisco: Wiley. https://doi.org/10.1002/cc.267

Mills, M. (2013). The work of Nancy Fraser and a socially just education system. In B. Irby, G. Brown, R. Lara-Alecio, & S. Jackson (Eds.), *The handbook of educational theories* (pp. 1027–34). Charlotte, NC: Information Age.

Mincer, J. (1958). Investment in human capital and personal income distribution. *Journal of Political Economy, 66*(4), 281–302. https://doi.org/10.1086/258055

Minister of International Trade. (2014). *Canada's international education strategy: Harnessing our knowledge advantage to drive innovation and prosperity.* Catalogue no. FR5–86/2014. Ottawa: Foreign Affairs, Trade and Development Canada.

Ministerie van Onderwijs, Cultuur en Wetenschap. (2016). *How does drawing lots work?* The Hague, Netherlands. Retrieved from http://duo.nl/particulier/international-student/no-more-drawing-lots.jsp

Ministry of Advanced Education. (2002). *Discussion paper: A new model for industry training in British Columbia.* Victoria, BC: Government of British Columbia.

Ministry of Advanced Education. (2003, April 30). *Backgrounder: Industry Training Authority Act* [Press release]. Victoria, BC: Government of British Columbia.

Ministry of Advanced Education. (2004, October 25). *New private training agency improves tuition protection* [Press release]. Victoria, BC: Government of British Columbia.

Ministry of Advanced Education. (2005, March 31). *BC's newest university opens in Kamloops* [Press release]. Victoria, BC: Government of British Columbia.

Ministry of Advanced Education. (2008, April 21). *Premier announces Fraser Valley's first university* [Press release]. Victoria, BC: Government of British Columbia.

Ministry of Advanced Education. (2008, April 29). *Legislation paves way for new universities in BC* [Press release]. Victoria, BC: Government of British Columbia.

Ministry of Advanced Education. (2012). *British Columbia's international education strategy.* Victoria, BC: Government of British Columbia.

Ministry of Advanced Education. (2015). *BC public institutions – Applied degree policy framework.* Victoria, BC: Government of British Columbia.

Ministry of Advanced Education. (2015, August 17). *Factsheet – Private post-secondary institutions in B.C.* [Press release]. Victoria, BC: Government of British Columbia.

Ministry of Advanced Education. (2015, February 11). *Legislation strengthens private career-training sector* [Press release]. Victoria, BC: Government of British Columbia.

Ministry of Advanced Education. (2016, January 13). *Post-secondary institutions raise the quality bar to host international students* [Press release]. Victoria, BC: Government of British Columbia.

Ministry of Advanced Education. (2017). *Search for a post-secondary institution.* Retrieved from https://www2.gov.bc.ca/gov/content/education-training/post-secondary-education/find-a-program-or-institution/find-an-institution

Ministry of Advanced Education. (n.d.). *Post-secondary central data warehouse standard reports: By program area.* Victoria, BC: Government of British Columbia. Retrieved from https://www2.gov.bc.ca/assets/gov/education/post-secondary-education/data-research/standard_reports_program_area_totals.pdf

Ministry of Advanced Education, Skills and Training. (2018). *Full-time equivalent enrolments at BC public post-secondary institutions.* Retrieved from https://catalogue.data.gov.bc.ca/dataset/full-time-equivalent-enrolments-at-b-c-public-post-secondary-institutions/resource/5ccc8108-855c-4802-b60d-cb9da4b96fbf

Ministry of Advanced Education, Training, and Technology, & Centre for Policy Studies in Education (UBC). (1992). *Continuing education in British Columbia's colleges and institutes: A foundation for lifelong learning.* Victoria, BC: The Ministry.

Ministry of Education, Skills and Training. (1996). *Aboriginal post-secondary education and training policy framework.* Victoria, BC: Government of British Columbia.

Ministry of Energy and Mines. (2014, April 17). *Core review strengthens private institutions, libraries and international education* [Press release]. Victoria, BC: Government of British Columbia.

Ministry of Jobs, Tourism and Skills Training. (2014). *British Columbia 2022 labour market outlook.* Victoria, BC: Government of British Columbia.

Ministry of Jobs, Tourism and Skills Training. (2014, April 29). *B.C. launches Skills for Jobs Blueprint to re-engineer education and training* [Press release]. Victoria, BC: Government of British Columbia.

Ministry of Jobs, Tourism and Skills Training. (2014, May 5). *New Industry Training Authority board of directors appointed* [Press release]. Victoria, BC: Government of British Columbia.

Ministry of Labour. (1981). *Annual report, 1980–81.* Victoria, BC: Government of British Columbia.

Ministry of Labour. (1985). *Annual report, 1984–85.* Victoria, BC: Government of British Columbia.

Ministry of Labour. (1991). *Annual report, 1990–91.* Victoria, BC: Government of British Columbia.

Ministry of Labour, Citizens' Services, and Open Government. (1996). *Revitalizing apprenticeship: A strategic framework for British Columbia's apprenticeship training system.* Victoria, BC: Government of British Columbia.

Moe, T. (1997). The positive theory of public bureaucracy. In D.C. Mueller (Ed.), *Perspectives on public choice* (pp. 455–80). Cambridge: Cambridge University Press.

Moran, L. (1993). Genesis of the Open Learning Institute of British Columbia. *Journal of Distance Education, 8*(1), 43–70.

Morphew, C., & Huisman, J. (2002). Using institutional theory to reframe research on academic drift. *Higher Education in Europe, 27*(4), 491–506. https://doi.org/10.1080/0379772022000071977

Mudge, S.L. (2008). What is neo-liberalism? *Socio-economic Review, 6*(4), 703–31. https://doi.org/10.1093/ser/mwn016

Mueller, D. (2004). Public choice: An introduction. In C. Rowley & F. Schneider (Eds.), *The encyclopedia of public choice* (pp. 32–48). Boston: Kluwer Academic.

National Student Clearinghouse Research Center. (2015, Spring). *Snapshot report: Contribution of two-year institutions to four-year completions.* Retrieved from https://nscresearchcenter.org

Nel, E., Hill, T., & Binns, T. (1997). Development from below in the new South Africa: The case of Hertzog, Eastern Cape. *Geographical Journal, 163*(1), 57–64. https://doi.org/10.2307/3059686

Nijkamp, P., & Abreu, M. (2009). Regional development theory. In R. Kitchin & N. Thrift (Eds.), *International encyclopedia of human geography* (pp. 202–07). Amsterdam: Elsevier. https://doi.org/10.1016/B978-008044910-4.00869-5

Niskanen, W.A. (1971). *Bureaucracy and representative government.* Chicago: Aldine, Atherton.

North, C. (2008). What is all this talk about "social justice"? Mapping the terrain of education's latest catchphrase. *Teachers College Record, 110*(6), 1182–1205.

Novak, M. (2000). Defining social justice. *First Things (New York), 108* (December), 11–13. Retrieved from https://www.firstthings.com/ftissues/ft0012/opinion/novak/html

OECD (Organisation for Economic Co-operation and Development). (1989). *Education and the economy in a changing society*. Paris: Author.

OECD (Organisation for Economic Co-operation and Development). (2004). *Innovation in the knowledge economy: Implications for education and learning*. Paris: Author.

OECD (Organisation for Economic Co-operation and Development). (2012). *Better skills, better jobs, better lives: A strategic approach to skills policies*. Paris: OECD Publishing.

OECD (Organisation for Economic Co-operation and Development). (2016). *Education at a glance 2016: OECD indicators*. Paris: OECD Publishing.

Okanagan College. (2015). *Financial statements, March 31, 2015*. Kelowna, BC: Author.

O'Lawrence, H. (2013). *Historical critique of career and technical education in California from 1900–2000 and the status of California community colleges in the 21st century*. Santa Rosa, CA: Informing Science Press.

Olssen, M., Codd, J.A., & O'Neill, A. (2004). *Education policy: Globalization, citizenship and democracy*. Thousand Oaks, CA: Sage.

Olssen, M., & Peters, M.A. (2005). Neoliberalism, higher education and the knowledge economy: From the free market to knowledge capitalism. *Journal of Education Policy, 20*(3), 313–45. https://doi.org/10.1080/02680930500108718

Orr, S. (2003, October 9). *Parliamentary debates (Hansard)*. Victoria, BC: Government of British Columbia.

Pal, L.A. (1988). *State, class, and bureaucracy: Canadian unemployment insurance and public policy*. Montreal and Kingston: McGill-Queen's University Press.

Palmer, V. (2001, September 19). Crucial core services review shrouded in secrecy. *Vancouver Sun*, p. A18.

Panacci, A.G. (2014). Baccalaureate degrees at Ontario colleges: Issues and implications. *College Quarterly, 17*(1), 1.

Parsons, T. (1960). *Structure and process in modern societies*. Glencoe, IL: Free Press.

Pedersen, J., & Dobbin, F. (2006). In search of identity and legitimation: Bridging organizational culture and neoinstitutionalism. *American Behavioral Scientist, 49*(7), 897–907. https://doi.org/10.1177/0002764205284798

Pendleton, S. (2010). Credits to graduation: A comparison of transfer graduates and secondary school graduates at BC research universities. *Research Results*, December. Vancouver: British Columbia Council on Admissions and Transfer.

Penner, D. (2015, September 4). While BC promotes careers in trades, industry groups want more entry points for apprentices. *Vancouver Sun*, p. C1.

Perry, N. (1969). *Report of the Advisory Committee on Inter-university Relations*. Victoria, BC: Department of Education, Government of British Columbia.

Petch, H.E. (1998). *Degree programs at the university colleges: A British Columbia success story.* Victoria, BC: Presidents of the University Colleges of British Columbia.

Peters, M. (n.d.). Neoliberalism. In *The encyclopedia of educational philosophy and theory.* Philosophy of Education Society of Australasia. Retrieved from http://eepat.net/

Picot, G., Hou, F., & Qiu, H. (2016). The human capital model of selection and immigrant economic outcomes. *International Migration (Geneva), 54*(3), 73–88. https://doi.org/10.1111/imig.12235

Plant, G. (2007). *Campus 2020: Thinking ahead: The report. Access and excellence: The Campus 2020 plan for British Columbia's post-secondary education system.* Victoria, BC: Queen's Printer.

Pollitt, C., & Bouckaert, G. (2011). *Public management reform: A comparative analysis – New public management, governance, and the neo-Weberian state* (3rd ed.). Oxford: Oxford University Press.

Poole, D. (1994). *Political/bureaucratic decision-making: The establishment of the first university colleges in British Columbia.* (Doctoral thesis, University of Alberta).

Porter, J. (1971). *The vertical mosaic.* Toronto: University of Toronto Press.

Porter, J. (1979). *The measure of Canadian society: Education, equality and opportunity.* Toronto: Gage.

Powell, W., & Colyvas, J.A. (2008). Microfoundations of institutional theory. In R. Greenwood, C. Oliver, K. Sahlin, & R. Suddaby (Eds.), *The Sage handbook of organizational institutionalism* (pp. 276–98). Thousand Oaks, CA: Sage. https://doi.org/10.4135/9781849200387.n11

Powell, W., & Snellman, K. (2004). The knowledge economy. *Annual Review of Sociology, 30*(1), 199–220. https://doi.org/10.1146/annurev.soc.29.010202.100037

Prince, M., & Rice, J. (1989). The Canadian Jobs Strategy: Supply side social policy. In K. Graham (Ed.), *How Ottawa spends 1989–90: The buck stops where?* (pp. 247–87). Ottawa: Carleton University Press.

Private Career Training Institutions Agency. (2008). *Annual report, 2007–2008.* Burnaby, BC: Author.

Private Career Training Institutions Agency. (n.d.). 2012 enrolment report. Vancouver, BC: Author. Retrieved from https://www.privatetraininginstitutions.gov.bc.ca/sites/www.privatetraininginstitutions.gov.bc.ca/files/files/enrolment_report2011-12.pdf

Private Post-Secondary Education Commission of British Columbia. (1996). *Annual report, 1995/1996.* Burnaby, BC: Author.

Private Post-Secondary Education Commission of British Columbia. (2002). *Annual report, 2001/2002.* Burnaby, BC: Author.

Private Training Institutions Branch. (2017). *Private training institutions directory.* Retrieved from https://www.privatetraininginstitutions.gov.bc.ca/students/pti-directory

Provincial Access Committee. (1988). *Access to advanced education and job training in British Columbia: Report of the Provincial Access Committee.* Victoria, BC: Ministry of Advanced Education and Job Training, Government of British Columbia.

Provincial Apprenticeship Board. (1984). *The future of apprenticeship: A report to the minister of labour, Province of British Columbia.* Victoria, BC: Ministry of Labour.

Pusser, B., & Turner, J. (2004). Student mobility: Changing patterns challenging policy makers. *Change: The Magazine of Higher Learning, 36*(2), 36–43. https://doi.org/10.1080/00091380409604966

Putnam, J.H., & Weir, S.M. (1926). *The survey of the school system.* Victoria, BC: Province of British Columbia.

Reiman, J. (1990). *Justice and modern moral theory.* New Haven: Yale University Press.

Rerup, H. (1993). *40 years history: Vancouver Vocational Institute, 1949–1989.* Vancouver: Unpublished manuscript in the library of Vancouver Community College.

Research Universities' Council of British Columbia. (2014, April 29). *BC research universities look forward to continued work on preparing British Columbians for today's economy* [Press release]. Victoria, BC: Author. Retrieved from http://www.rucbc.ca/news-room?feed=5

Rhoades, G., & Slaughter, S. (2004). Academic capitalism in the new economy: Challenges and choices. *American Academic, June,* 37–59. American Federation of Teachers. Retrieved from https://www.aft.org/pdfs/highered/academic/june04/Rhoades.qxp.pdf

Roberts, N. (1999, July). *Research methodology for new public management.* Draft paper presented at the International Public Management Network, Siena, Italy. Retrieved from http://www.rrojasdatabank.info/roberts.pdf

Roberts, P., & Peters, M. (2008). *Neoliberalism, higher education and research.* Rotterdam: Sense.

Robinson, C. (2000). *Developments in Australia's vocational education and training system.* Leabrook, Australia: National Centre for Vocational Education Research.

Robinson, S.R. (2012). Freedom, aspirations and informed choice in rural higher education: Why they are saying 'no'. *Australian and International Journal of Rural Education, 22*(2), 79–95.

Romer, P. (1990). Endogenous technological change. *Journal of Political Economy, 98*(5, Part 2), S71–S102. https://doi.org/10.1086/261725

Romer, P. (1993). Idea gaps and object gaps in economic development. *Journal of Monetary Economics, 32*(3), 543–73. https://doi.org/10.1016/0304-3932(93)90029-F

Royal Commission of Inquiry on Education in the Province of Quebec. (1965). *Rapport de la commission royale d'enquête sur l'enseignement dans la province de Québec*. Quebec City: Author.

Royal Commission on Higher Education in New Brunswick. (1962). *Report*. Fredericton: Government of New Brunswick.

Royal Commission on Post Secondary Education in the Kootenay Region. (1974). *Report of the Royal Commission on Post Secondary Education in the Kootenay Region*. Victoria, BC: Author.

Rubenson, K., & Gaskell, J. (1987). *Education and the Canadian case*. Vancouver: Centre for Policy Studies in Education, University of British Columbia.

Russell, C. (2013). Human capital theory. In J. Ainsworth (Ed.), *Sociology of education: An a-to-z guide* (Vol. 8, pp. 369–70). Thousand Oaks, CA: Sage.

Savvides, A., & Stengos, T. (2009). *Human capital and economic growth*. Stanford, CA: Stanford University Press.

Schudde, L., & Goldrick-Rab, S. (2015). On second chances and stratification: How sociologists think about community colleges. *Community College Review, 43*(1), 27–45. https://doi.org/10.1177/0091552114553296

Schuetze, H. (2008). Lifelong learning and the learning society: From concept to policy to practice? In L. Doyle, D. Adams, J. Tibbitt, & P. Welsh (Eds.), *Building stronger communities: Connecting research, policy and practice* (pp. 21–34). Leicester, UK: National Institute of Adult Continuing Education.

Schuetze, H.G., & Day, W.L. (2001). *Post-secondary education in BC 1989–1998: The impact of policy and finance on access, participation, and outcomes*. Vancouver: Centre for Policy Studies in Higher Education and Training, University of British Columbia.

Schultz, R., & Stickler, W. (1965). Vertical extension of academic programmes in institutions of higher education. *Educational Record, 1965*(Summer), 231–41.

Schultz, T.W. (1960). Capital formation by education. *Journal of Political Economy, 68*(6), 571–83. https://doi.org/10.1086/258393

Schultz, T.W. (1961). Investment in human capital. *American Economic Review, 51*(1), 1–17.

Scott, J. (2007). Institution. In J. Scott (Ed.), *Sociology: The key concepts* (pp. 90–93). London: Routledge.

Scott, J., & Marshall, G. (2009). *A dictionary of sociology* (3rd rev. ed.). Oxford: Oxford University Press. https://doi.org/10.1093/acref/9780199533008.001.0001

Scott, P. (2009). Structural changes in higher education: The case of the United Kingdom. In D. Palfreyman & T. Tapper (Eds.), *Structuring mass higher education: The role of elite institutions* (pp. 35–55). New York: Routledge.

Scott, W.R. (2001). *Institutions and organizations* (2nd ed.). Thousand Oaks, CA: Sage.

Scott, W.R. (2014). *Institutions and organizations: Ideas, interests and identity* (4th ed.). Thousand Oaks, CA: Sage.

Scruton, R. (2007). *The Palgrave Macmillan dictionary of political thought*. New York: Palgrave Macmillan. https://doi.org/10.1057/9780230625099

Selman, G.R. (1975). *A decade of transition: The extension department of the University of British Columbia, 1960 to 1970*. Occasional papers in continuing education (10). Vancouver: Centre for Continuing Education, University of British Columbia.

Selman, G.R. (1988). *The invisible giant: A history of adult education in British Columbia*. Occasional papers in continuing education (25). Vancouver: Centre for Continuing Education, University of British Columbia.

Selman, M. (2005). An identity for Canadian university education. *Canadian Journal of University Continuing Education, 31*(1), 19–27.

Selznick, P. (1949). *TVA and the grass roots*. Berkeley: University of California Press.

Shapiro, D., Dunbar, A., Wakhungu, P., Yuan, X., & Harrell, A. (2015, July). *Transfer and mobility: A national view of student movement in postsecondary institutions, Fall 2008 cohort* (Signature Report No. 9). Herndon, VA: National Student Clearinghouse Research Center.

Sharpe, A., & Gibson, J. (2005). *The apprenticeship system in Canada: Trends and issues*. Ottawa: Centre for the Study of Living Standards.

Shavit, Y., Arum, R., Gamoran, A., & Menahem, G. (Eds.). (2007). *Stratification in higher education: A comparative study*. New York: Stanford University Press.

Sheffield, E. (1955). Canadian university and college enrollment projected to 1965. In *Proceedings, National Conference of Canadian Universities, 1955*. (pp. 29–46). Ottawa: National Conference of Canadian Universities.

Sheffield, E. (1982). The national scene. In E. Sheffield, D.D. Campbell, J. Holmes, B.B. Kymlicka, & J.H. Whitelaw (Eds.), *Systems of higher education, Canada* (2nd ed., pp. 1–35). New York: International Council for Educational Development.

Sheffield, E., Campbell, D., Holmes, J., Kymlicka, B., & Whitelaw, J. (1982). *Systems of higher education, Canada* (2nd ed.). New York: International Council for Educational Development.

Sherlock, T. (2014, May 31). More than 70 ESL teachers likely to lose jobs: Vancouver Community College. *Vancouver Sun*, p. A6.

Shoho, A., Merchant, B., & Lugg, C. (2011). Social justice: Seeking a common language. In F.W. English (Ed.), *The Sage handbook of educational leadership: Advances in theory, research, and practice* (2nd ed., pp. 35–55). Thousand Oaks, CA: Sage. https://doi.org/10.4135/9781412980036.n4

Simon Fraser University. (2014). *Institutional accountability plan and report, 2014/15–2016/17*. Burnaby, BC: Author.

Singh, M. (2011). The place of social justice in higher education and social change discourses. *Compare: A Journal of Comparative Education, 41*(4), 481–94. https://doi.org/10.1080/03057925.2011.581515

Skolnik, M. (2005). The case for giving greater attention to structure in higher education policy-making. In C. Beach, R. Broadway, & R. McInnis (Eds.), *Higher education in Canada* (pp. 53–76). Kingston, ON: John Deutsch Institute for the Study of Economic Policy, Queen's University.

Skolnik, M. (2012). *College baccalaureate degrees and the diversification of baccalaureate production in Ontario.* Retrieved from University of Toronto research repository https://tspace.library.utoronto.ca/handle/1807/32379

Skolnik, M.L., & Jones, G.A. (1992). A comparative analysis of arrangements for state coordination of higher education in Canada and the United States. *Journal of Higher Education, 11*(2), 151–74.

Slaughter, S., & Rhoades, G. (2004). *Academic capitalism and the new economy: Markets, state, and higher education.* Baltimore: Johns Hopkins University Press.

Smelser, N. (1993). California: A multisegment system. In A. Levine (Ed.), *Higher learning in America, 1980–2000* (pp. 114–30). Baltimore: Johns Hopkins University Press.

Snyder, T.D., & Hoffman, C.M. (1991). *Digest of education statistics, 1990.* Washington: National Center for Education Statistics, US Department of Education.

Soles, A. (n.d.). *Speech* given in Penticton, BC, prior to the school district joining Okanagan College. Unpublished manuscript in possession of author.

Sörlin, S., & Vessuri, H. (Eds.). (2007). *Knowledge society vs. knowledge economy: Knowledge, power, and politics.* New York: Palgrave Macmillan. https://doi.org/10.1057/9780230603516

Steger, M., & Roy, R. (2010). *Neoliberalism: A very short introduction.* Oxford: Oxford University Press. https://doi.org/10.1093/actrade/9780199560516.001.0001

Stewart, G., & Kerr, A. (2010). A backgrounder on apprenticeship training in Canada. *Canadian Apprenticeship Journal, 1*(Winter). Retrieved from http://caf-fca.org/?page=volumes&hl=en_CA

Stewart, W. (1989). *Higher education in postwar Britain.* London: Macmillan. https://doi.org/10.1007/978-1-349-07064-0

Stigler, G. (1971). The theory of economic regulation. *Bell Journal of Economics and Management Science, 2*(1), 3–18. https://doi.org/10.2307/3003160

Stimson, R.J., Stough, R.R., & Roberts, B.H. (2006). *Regional economic development: Analysis and planning strategy* (2nd ed.). Berlin: Springer.

Student Transitions Project. (2012). BC's flexible post-secondary education system supports student mobility. *STP Research Results, Highlights Newsletter,* October.

Victoria, BC: British Columbia Ministry of Advanced Education. Retrieved from https://www2.gov.bc.ca/gov/content/education-training/post-secondary-education/data-research/student-transitions-project

Student Transitions Project. (2015a). BC bachelor's degree completers of 2013/14. *STP Research Results, Highlights Newsletter, October.* Prepared by J. Heslop. Victoria, BC: British Columbia Ministry of Advanced Education. Retrieved from https://www2.gov.bc.ca/assets/gov/education/post-secondary-education/data-research/stp/bach_completers_of_2013-2014_report_v3_2015-10-07.pdf

Student Transitions Project. (2015b). *Student mobility between sectors in the BC public post-secondary system (20120/13).* Unpublished. Prepared by J. Heslop. Victoria, BC: Ministry of Advanced Education.

Sturman, A. (1997). *Social justice in education.* Australian education review, 40. Melbourne: ACER Press.

Suchman, M.C. (1995). Managing legitimacy: Strategic and institutional approaches. *Academy of Management Review, 20,* 571–610.

Suddaby, R. (2010). Challenges for institutional theory. *Journal of Management Inquiry, 19*(1), 14–20. https://doi.org/10.1177/1056492609347564

Sweet, R., & Gallagher, P. (1999). Private training institutions in Canada: New directions for a public resource. *Journal of Educational Administration and Foundations, 13*(2), 54–77.

Szajnowska-Wysocka, A. (2009). Theories of regional and local development - Abridged review. *Bulletin of Geography. Socio-Economic Series, 12*(1), 75–90.

Tan, E. (2014). Human capital theory: A holistic criticism. *Review of Educational Research, 84*(3), 411–45. https://doi.org/10.3102/0034654314532696

Tarique, I. (2013). Human capital theory. In E. Kessler (Ed.), *Encyclopedia of management theory* (pp. 344-47). Thousand Oaks, CA: Sage.

Task Force on Program Review, & Nielsen, E. (1986). *Final report,* 20 volumes. Ottawa: Supply and Services Canada.

Taylor, A. (2016). *Vocational education in Canada: The past, present, and future of policy.* Don Mills, ON: Oxford University Press.

Teliszewsky, A., & Stoney, C. (2007). Addressing the fiscal imbalance through asymmetrical federalism: Dangerous times for the Harper government and for Canada. In G.B. Doern (Ed.), *How Ottawa spends, 2007–2008: The Harper Conservatives – Climate of change* (pp. 25–45). Montreal and Kingston: McGill-Queen's University Press.

Thelin, J. (2010). Horizontal history and higher education. In M. Gasman (Ed.), *The history of US higher education: Methods for understanding the past* (pp. 71–83). New York: Routledge.

Thelin, J.R. (2011). *A history of American higher education* (2nd ed.). Baltimore: Johns Hopkins University Press.

Thompson, A. (2014). *The role of higher education in rural community development.* (Doctoral dissertation, University of Arkansas).

Thompson, L. (1983). BC on TRAC: A new vocational training plan. *Canadian Vocational Journal, 19*(1), 54–58.

Thorensen, D.E., & Lie, A. (2006). What is neoliberalism? Retrieved from personal website at the University of Oslo http://folk.uio.no/daget/What%20is%20Neo-Liberalism%20FINAL.pdf

Tight, M. (2009). *The development of higher education in the United Kingdom since 1945.* Maidenhead, UK: Society for Research into Higher Education & Open University Press.

Tight, M. (2015). Theory development and application in higher education rescarch: The case of academic drift. *Journal of Educational Administration and History, 47*(1), 84–99. https://doi.org/10.1080/00220620.2015.974143

Tindall, D. (2016). *Data collection project, 2015/16.* West Vancouver: Indigenous Adult and Higher Learning Association.

Tolbert, P.S., & Zucker, L.G. (1983). Institutional sources of change in the formal structure of organizations: The diffusion of civil service reform, 1880–1935. *Administrative Science Quarterly, 28*(1), 22–39. https://doi.org/10.2307/2392383

Tolofari, S. (2005). New public management and education. *Policy Futures in Education, 3*(1), 75–89. https://doi.org/10.2304/pfie.2005.3.1.11

Trilokekar, R.D., Shanahan, T., Axelrod, P., & Wellen, R. (2013). Making post-secondary education policy: Toward a conceptual framework. In P. Axelrod, R.D. Trilokekar, T. Shanahan, & R. Wellen (Eds.), *Making policy in turbulent times: Challenges and prospects for higher education* (pp. 33–58). Montreal and Kingston: McGill-Queen's University Press.

Trueman, J. (2005). *Our time will come again: Tracing the story of the Technical University of British Columbia.* Burnaby, BC: Unpublished manuscript in the library of Simon Fraser University.

Tullock, G. (1965). *The politics of bureaucracy.* Washington, DC: Public Affairs Press.

United Nations Educational, Scientific and Cultural Organization. (2012). *International Standard Classification of Education, ISCED 2011.* Montreal: UNESCO Institute for Statistics.

Universities Council of British Columbia. (1976). *Report on Notre Dame University of Nelson.* Vancouver: Author.

University of British Columbia. (2017). *Student enrolment figures: Annual enrolment, 1915–present.* Retrieved from http://archives.library.ubc.ca/general-history/student-enrolment/

University of Northern British Columbia. (2017a). *Consolidated financial statements: Year ended March 31, 2017*. Retrieved from https://www.unbc.ca/sites/default/files/sections/finance/unbcfinancialstatementsmarch312017finalapproved_0.pdf

University of Northern British Columbia. (2017b). *2016/2017 Institutional accountability plan and report*. Retrieved from https://www2.gov.bc.ca/assets/gov/education/post-secondary-education/institution-resources-administration/accountability-framework/iapr/2016-17/unbc_iapr_2016-17.pdf

University of the Fraser Valley. (2015). *Institutional accountability report and plan, 2015–16 to 2017–18*. Abbotsford, BC. Retrieved from https://www.ufv.ca/media/assets/institutional-research/accountabilityreport/UFV-Accountability-Report-2015-16.pdf

University of Victoria. (2017a). *2016-2017 Audited financial statements*. Retrieved from https://www.uvic.ca/vpfo/accounting/assets/docs/financial/uvicfinancialstatements/financial-statements-2016-17.pdf

University of Victoria. (2017b). *2017-18 Institutional accountability plan and report*. Retrieved from https://www2.gov.bc.ca/assets/gov/education/post-secondary-education/institution-resources-administration/accountability-framework/iapr/2016-17/uvic_iapr_2017.pdf

Usher, A. (2015, February 4). The "Skills for Jobs Blueprint." [Web log post]. Toronto: Higher Education Strategy Associates. Retrieved from http://higheredstrategy.com/blog/

Usher, A. (2016, May 5). *Massification causes stratification*. [Web log post]. Toronto: Higher Education Strategy Associates. Retrieved from http://higheredstrategy.com/massification-causes-stratification

van Iersel, A. (2006). *Government's post-secondary expansion – 25,000 seats by 2010*. Victoria, BC: Office of the Auditor General of British Columbia.

van Zanten, A., Ball, S.J., & Darchy-Koechlin, B. (Eds.). (2015). *World yearbook of education 2015: Elites, privilege and excellence: The national and global redefinition of educational advantage*. New York: Routledge.

Vaughan, G. (2006). *The community college story* (3rd ed.). Washington, DC: American Association of Community Colleges.

Vocational Instructors Association of BC. (1991). A betrayal of faith: The transformation of the British Columbia college system. Unpublished occasional paper.

Waite, P.B. (1987). *Lord of Point Grey: Larry MacKenzie of UBC*. Vancouver: UBC Press.

Ward, D. (1998, March 21). 8-month boycott against TechBC ends with deal on academic freedom. *Vancouver Sun*, p. B6.

Ward, S.C. (2012). *Neoliberalism and the global restructuring of knowledge and education*. New York: Routledge.

Watson, J. (2008). *Private career training institutions act review*. Prepared for the Ministry of Advanced Education, Government of British Columbia. Retrieved from http://citeseerx.ist.psu.edu/viewdoc/download?doi=10.1.1.582.2758&rep=rep1&type=pdf

Weick, K.E. (1976). Educational organizations as loosely coupled systems. *Administrative Science Quarterly, 21*(1), 1–19. https://doi.org/10.2307/2391875

Weiermair, K. (1984). *Apprenticeship training in Canada: A theoretical and empirical analysis*. Ottawa: Economic Council of Canada.

Whiteley, R., Aguiar, L., & Marten, T. (2008). The neoliberal transnational university: The case of UBC Okanagan. *Class and Capital, 32*(3), 115–42. https://doi.org/10.1177/030981680809600105

Whittingham, F.J. (1966). *Educational attainment of the Canadian population and labour force, 1960–1965*. Catalogue number 71-505. Ottawa: Dominion Bureau of Statistics.

Witter, S. (n.d.). *Rethinking the public sector role in training: A BC college response*. Unpublished paper. Fraser Valley College, Abbotsford, BC.

Wylie, P. (2017). Memorandum of misunderstanding: Public accountability and the University of British Columbia, Okanagan campus, 2004–17. *BC Studies, 195*, 65–96.

Young, I. (1990). *Justice and the politics of difference*. Princeton: Princeton University Press.

Young, I. (1992). Recent theories of justice. *Social Theory and Practice, 18*(1), 63–79. https://doi.org/10.5840/soctheorpract19921818

Zajda, J., Majhanovich, S., & Rust, V. (2006). Introduction: Education and social justice. *International Review of Education, 52*(1), 9–22.

Zook, G., & United States, President's Commission on Higher Education. (1947). *Higher education for American democracy: A report*. Washington, DC: US Government Printing Office.

Zucker, L.G. (1983). Organizations as institutions. In S.B. Bacharach (Ed.), *Research in the sociology of organizations* (Vol. 2, pp. 1–47). Greenwich, CT: JAI Press.

Index

Aboriginal-governed institutions, 9, 27, 130, 178; enrolment, 71(t), 127(t), 130, 178. *See also* Aboriginal programs and students; Indigenous Adult and Higher Learning Authority; Nicola Valley Institute of Technology

Aboriginal programs and students, 69, 95, 112, 131, 157. *See also* Aboriginal-governed institutions

Academic Board for Higher Education, 88–89

access committee. *See* Provincial Access Committee

Access for All government strategy, 111–12, 115–16, 121, 145. *See also under* historical moments; Provincial Access Committee

accreditation of private institutions, 97, 142, 152–53, 161, 179; designation, 176–77

adult education. *See* continuing education

Adult Occupational Training Act (1967), 81, 104

Advanced Education Council of British Columbia, 98, 123

Alberta, 24, 75, 142; applied degrees, 128, 134; colleges, 66, 74

American postsecondary system. *See* United States

applied degrees, 128, 133–34, 147, 149

apprenticeship, 78–81, 96, 139–41, 181; characteristics, 27, 67, 89, 95, 151; federal role, 78, 84, 86, 163; governance, 20, 68, 97, 141, 160; literature, 14, 129, 188*n*3; Red Seal, 25; registrations, 71(f), 80(f), 127(f), 139, 153, 171, 181. *See also* Industry Training and Apprenticeship Commission; Industry Training Authority; pre-apprenticeship; Skills for Jobs Blueprint

Apprenticeship Act (various years), 79, 81, 97

Apprenticeship and Training Development Act (1977), 69

Apprenticeship Training Agreement (1964), 68, 80, 81

Associated Canadian Theological Schools, 98

audience for book, 5–7. *See also* study parameters

Australia, 14–15, 23, 138, 140

bachelor of technology, 95, 134
Balanced Budget and Ministerial Accountability Act (2001), 132
Basic Training for Skills Development, 104
Beinder, F., 83, 124
Blackhouse, John, 119, 121
Brennan, P., 170
Brint, S., 182
British Columbia Association of Institutes and Universities, 139
British Columbia Council on Admissions and Transfer, 29, 98, 116, 122, 131
British Columbia Department of Labour. *See* British Columbia Ministry of Labour
British Columbia Institute of Technology, 78, 95, 134, 176; establishment, 5, 20, 77, 79
British Columbia Labour Force Development Board, 96
British Columbia Ministry of Labour, 20, 68, 80, 81; career colleges, 69, 96, 97, 100
British Columbia postsecondary system: in 1960, 18–21; distinctive features of community colleges, 26, 28–29, 163; historiography, 6, 12–13, 16, 21–22, 94, 116; inventory, 71(t), 127(t), 174–81; inventory of public institutions, 31–32(t); types of institutions, 25–28
British Columbia School Trustees Association, 74
Budget Transparency and Accountability Act (2000), 132

Bullen, Lester, 114, 119
Burnaby Vocational School, 76–77. *See also* Pacific Vocational Institute

California Master Plan, 14, 15, 83, 182
Cameron report, 72
Camosun College, 175, 188*n*10
Campus 2020 report, 126, 138, 152, 165
Canadian Jobs Strategy, 92, 96, 101, 105, 107, 171. *See also* career colleges; continuing education
Capilano College, 188*n*10. *See also* Capilano University
Capilano University, 128, 138, 175. *See also* Capilano College
career colleges, 27, 69, 82, 84, 100, 181; Canadian Jobs Strategy, 97, 105, 163; number of institutions, 71(t), 97, 127(t), 143, 154, 177; since 2000, 130, 141–43, 150, 176–77. *See also* Private Career Training Institutions Agency
Cariboo College, 94, 188*n*10. *See also* Thompson Rivers University; University College of the Cariboo
Catholic Pacific College. *See* Redeemer Pacific College
Chant commission, 19, 73
Charting a New Course plan, 126
Coast Mountain College. *See* Northwest Community College
Coell, Murray, 145
college, definition, 25–26. *See also* career colleges; community college
College of New Caledonia, 82, 112, 113, 175, 188*n*10
College of the Rockies, 175, 188*n*11

Colleges and Provincial Institutes Act (1977), 66
community, definition, 41-42
community college, 25-26; distinctive features in British Columbia, 28-29, 163; establishment, 21, 66, 74, 76-77, 85, 88; interactions with other sectors, 8-9, 21, 66, 74; minor leases, 103; philosophy, 83, 128, 187n1 (chap. 1). *See also* Canadian Jobs Strategy; continuing education; university college; university transfer; *and individual colleges*
Community College Survey of Student Engagement, 28
compensatory justice, 107, 117-18, 157, 168, 170, 184-85; theory, 36, 40, 43. *See also* social justice
competition. *See* marketization
continuing education, 93, 180-81; BC government policy, 101, 106, 109; characteristics, 23, 27-28, 68-69, 99, 101; contract training, 108, 131, 181, 190n5; enrolment, 68, 103, 104, 131; entrepreneurship, 110, 131, 164; funding for colleges, 92, 93, 102-5; general interest courses, 92, 102, 104; part-time vocational courses, 93, 104, 107; school districts, 21, 74, 103, 156; subcontracting, 92, 105; universities, 102. *See also* Canadian Jobs Strategy
continuing education and Canadian Jobs Strategy. *See under* historical moments
Corpus Christi College, 98, 179
credential types, 25. *See also* applied degrees
Cuban missile crisis, 6

cultural recognition, 36, 41, 169. *See also* social justice

Dahloff, Urban, 115
David Thompson University Centre, 112, 188n8. *See also* Notre Dame University
Dawson Creek, vocational school, 79
Degree Authorization Act (2002), 128, 130, 133-36, 169
Degree Quality Assessment Board, 135, 142, 179
Dennison, J.D., 13, 21
designation. *See* accreditation of private institutions
development, definition, 42
Dominion-Provincial Youth Training Centre, 78
Douglas College, 5, 136, 161, 175, 188n10

East Kootenay Community College. *See* College of the Rockies
educational attainment, 87
Educational Quality Assurance designation, 143, 152, 161
Emily Carr College of Art and Design, 116. *See also* Emily Carr Institute of Art and Design
Emily Carr Institute of Art and Design, 95, 128, 138, 175. *See also* Emily Carr College of Art and Design; Emily Carr University of Art and Design
Emily Carr University of Art and Design, 20, 128, 138, 175. *See also* Emily Carr Institute of Art and Design
England. *See* United Kingdom

English-language training, 156, 159, 177, 191*n*13; regulation, 130, 142, 152, 160
enrolment expansion, 115, 131, 135–36, 144–45, 149
Entry Level Trades Training, 96, 141
Europe, 13, 15, 27

faith-based institutions, 9, 81, 82, 131, 156, 178–79; government policy, 69–70, 84, 169, 188*n*7. *See also* Notre Dame University; Trinity Western University
federal government, 58, 100–2, 104, 153, 163–64, 171; constitutional jurisdiction, 19, 78, 192*n*2; immigration, 158, 159; policy rationales, 46, 58, 86, 108, 171; research, 18, 129, 132–33, 156; vocational education, 20, 65, 80, 81, 86–87, 92. *See also* Canadian Jobs Strategy; English-language training; occupational training program; Technical and Vocational Training Assistance Act (1960)
financial restraint in 1980s, 99, 103, 109
Fisher, D., 13, 21–22
Fisher, Grant, 114
Fleming, R., 123, 136
Foundation Program, 141, 153, 181
Fraser Valley College, 94, 188*n*10. *See also* University College of the Fraser Valley

Gallagher, C., 112
general interest courses. *See* continuing education
Goard report, 68
Grade 13, 19, 72, 74, 112

Hagen, Stanley, 113, 114, 115, 116, 120, 182
Hardwick, Walter, 75
higher education, definition, 23
historical moments: Access for All (late 1980s and early 1990s), 110–17; continuing education and Canadian Jobs Strategy (early and mid-1980s), 99–105; definition, 64; Macdonald era (early 1960s), 71–82; New Era (early to mid-2000s), 132–44; post-neoliberalism (2010 to 2015), 151–56
historical themes, 162–65
Howard, R., 152
human capital formation, 35, 43–49
— generic version, 47, 146, 171
— in historical moments: early 1960s (Macdonald era), 85–87; early and mid-1980s (continuing education and Canadian Jobs Strategy), 107–8; late 1980s and early 1990s (Access for All), 120–21; early to mid-2000s (New Era), 146–48; 2010 to 2015 (post-neoliberal), 158–59
— occupational version, 47, 158, 171
— synthesis, 167(t), 168, 170–72
See also regional economic development

Indigenous Adult and Higher Learning Authority, 130, 178
individual justice, 36, 39–40, 43, 84, 168. *See also* social justice
Industry Training and Apprenticeship Commission, 96, 139, 141. *See also* Industry Training Authority
Industry Training Authority, 129, 139, 153, 159, 190*n*4; actions, 140, 141, 151. *See also* Industry Training and Apprenticeship Commission

Industry Training Organization, 129, 140, 151, 153, 159. *See also* Industry Training Authority
institutes, 27, 66, 91, 176, 178. *See also individual institutes*
Institute of Indigenous Government, 95, 116, 144, 176. *See also* Nicola Valley Institute of Technology
institution, definition, 24, 60
institutional theory, 59–63, 173. *See also* isomorphism; legitimacy; loose coupling; neoinstitutionalism
Interior University Society, 114, 115
International Standard Classification of Education, 23
international students, 142, 153, 157, 176; economic stimulus, 143, 160, 164; enrolment, 143, 161, 191*n*18. *See also* accreditation of private institutions; Educational Quality Assurance designation
isomorphism, 60, 62, 123, 173. *See also* institutional theory

Johnston, H., 85
junior colleges, 26, 72, 74, 113, 180
Justice Institute, 176, 188*n*1

Kamloops: university, 117, 128, 138, 148; vocational school, 79. *See also* Cariboo College
Karabel, J., 182
Kelowna: before 1980, 76, 113; 1980 to 2000, 114, 117, 120; after 2000, 128, 137, 138. *See also* Okanagan College
knowledge economy, 46, 147, 148
Kwantlen College, 5, 94, 188*n*10. *See also* Kwantlen University College

Kwantlen Polytechnic University, 175. *See also* Kwantlen University College
Kwantlen University College, 94, 150, 175. *See also* Kwantlen College; Kwantlen Polytechnic University

Langara College, 20, 136, 156, 175, 188*n*10
Lee, G., 123, 136
legitimacy, 61, 62, 122, 150, 173; career colleges, 135, 141, 142. *See also* institutional theory
literature review. *See each jurisdiction*
loose coupling, 60, 62–63. *See also* institutional theory

Macdonald, John: quotes, 82, 83, 86, 88, 182. *See also* Macdonald report
Macdonald era. *See under* historical moments
Macdonald report, 65, 66, 71–75, 113, 164; government response, 65, 66, 75–77
MacKenzie, Norman (Larry), 72, 73–74
Malaspina College, 94, 188*n*10. *See also* Malaspina University College
Malaspina University College, 94, 150. *See also* Malaspina College; Vancouver Island University
manpower training program. *See* occupational training program
Marginson, S., 182–84
marketization, 50–63, 164
— competition in BC postsecondary system, 9, 88, 110, 122, 149, 150
— in historical moments: early 1960s (Macdonald era), 87–90; early and mid-1980s (continuing education and Canadian Jobs Strategy), 108–10;

228　Index

late 1980s and early 1990s (Access for All), 121–23; early to mid-2000s (New Era), 148–51; 2010 to 2015 (post-neoliberal), 159–61
— synthesis, 167(t), 168, 172–74
See also institutional theory; neo-institutionalism; neoliberalism; new public management; public choice theory
Merner, R., 112

Nanaimo, 20, 78. See also Malaspina College; Vancouver Island University
National Student Clearinghouse. See student mobility: in United States
Nelson, 20, 70, 112. See also Notre Dame University; David Thompson University Centre
neoconservatism, 53, 54
neoinstitutionalism, 60–61, 62, 63, 173, 186. See also institutional theory
neoliberalism, 51–55, 59, 172–73; critiques, 54–55; origins, 52–53, 109. See also marketization
New Brunswick, royal commission, 75
New Era. See under historical moments
new public management, 57–59, 132, 151
Nicola Valley Institute of Technology, 95, 130, 144, 176, 178. See also Institute of Indigenous Government
non-metropolitan programs, 68, 118, 191n1
non-public college. See career colleges
North Island College, 175, 188n11
Northern Lights College, 175, 188n11
Northwest Community College, 128, 175, 188n11

Notre Dame University, 81, 112, 188n8. See also David Thompson University Centre; Notre Dame University College
Notre Dame University College, 20, 70, 82. See also Notre Dame University

occupational training program, 100, 101, 104, 108
Okanagan College, 94, 175, 188n10. See also Okanagan University College
Okanagan University College, 94, 128, 137, 148, 150, 169. See also Okanagan College; University of British Columbia: Okanagan campus
ombudsperson, 154
Ontario, 23, 70, 75, 142; applied degrees, 128, 134
Open Learning Agency, 116, 188n6; closure, 138, 144, 148, 163, 176. See also Open Learning Institute
Open Learning Institute, 68, 106, 188n6. See also Open Learning Agency
organization, definition of specialized usage, 24–25
organizational field, 61, 62, 173, 186. See also neoinstitutionalism

Pacific Marine Training Institute, 176
Pacific Vocational Institute, 78, 176, 188n2. See also Burnaby Vocational School
Parent Commission, Quebec, 75
part-time vocational courses. See continuing education
Petch, Howard, 136
Plant, Geoff, 126, 138. See also Campus 2020 report

policy rationales, 22, 33–35, 125, 165–67. *See also* human capital formation; marketization; social justice
population, 3, 18, 19(f), 49, 111
post-neoliberalism. *See under* historical moments
postsecondary education, definition, 22–23
postsecondary system, definition, 4, 24. *See also* British Columbia postsecondary system
pre-apprenticeship, 20, 80, 81, 141; pre-employment training, 95–96. *See also* Foundation Program
pre-employment programs. *See* pre-apprenticeship
Prince George, 93, 113, 114–15, 119, 121. *See also* College of New Caledonia; Interior University Society; Prince George College; University of Northern British Columbia
Prince George College, 82, 112
private and public returns, 46–47, 108
Private Career Training Institutions Agency, 130, 142, 150, 152, 153–54. *See also* career colleges; Private Post-Secondary Education Commission
private college. *See* career colleges; college; private institutions
private institutions, 3, 5, 71(t), 127(t), 164, 176–80; characteristics, 25, 27, 89; development, 65, 69–70, 81–82, 96–98; interactions with other sectors, 9, 92. *See also* Aboriginal-governed institutions; career colleges; faith-based institutions; private universities
Private Post-Secondary Education Commission, 97, 130, 141. *See also* Private Career Training Institutions Agency
Private Training Act (2015), 176
Private Training Institutions Branch, 176–77. *See also* Private Career Training Institutions Agency
private universities. *See* Degree Authorization Act (2002); Notre Dame University; Trinity Western University
production regime theory, 171
Provincial Access Committee, 111, 114–15, 119, 120, 182
public choice theory, 51, 55–56
public college. *See* community college
public policy rationales. *See* policy rationales
public relations and image, 124, 126, 165
Public Schools Act, 74, 76
Putnam-Weir report, 72

Quebec: Parent Commission, 75; postsecondary system, 24, 75

Redeemer Pacific College, 98, 179
Regent College, 70, 156, 179
regional college. *See* community college
regional economic development, 49–50. *See also* rural communities; spatial adaptation
research universities, 18, 26, 66, 93, 174. *See also individual institutions*
Research Universities' Council of British Columbia, 139, 155, 174
Robbins Committee, 23, 74
Roberts, N., 58
Royal Commission on Canada's Economic Prospects, 85

Royal Commission on Education (1960), 19
Royal Roads University, 93–94, 128, 139, 174
rural communities, 41, 73, 77, 103, 118, 178; characteristics, 42, 86, 95, 112, 134. *See also* regional economic development; spatial adaptation

scholarship of integration, 8
school districts: adult education, 21, 78, 102, 106, 156; establishment of community colleges, 20–21, 66, 74, 76
Scruton, R., 56
Selkirk College, 175, 188*n*10. *See also* David Thompson University Centre
Simon Fraser University, 94, 102, 144, 161, 174; establishment, 5, 76. *See also* Technical University of British Columbia
Skills for Jobs Blueprint, 155, 157–58, 159
Skills Now, 155
Skolnik, M.L., 4
social justice, 34, 35–43, 102, 146, 182
— definition, 36–37
— in education, 39–41
— in historical moments: early 1960s (Macdonald era), 82–85; early and mid-1980s (continuing education and Canadian Jobs Strategy), 106–7; late 1980s and early 1990s (Access for All), 117–19; early to mid-2000s (New Era), 144–46; 2010 to 2015 (post-neoliberal), 157–58
— power and marginalized groups, 38–39
— synthesis, 167(t), 168–70
— units of analysis, 37–38
See also compensatory justice; cultural recognition; individual justice; spatial adaptation
Soles, Andrew, 83
spatial adaptation, 36, 41–43, 118–19, 162–63, 169. *See also* rural communities; social justice
special purpose university. *See* teaching university
Strand report, 155
stratification, social, 182–85
structure, postsecondary, 4, 182–85
structure, social, 38
student mobility: in British Columbia, 10, 11(f), 150; in United States, 13. *See also* university transfer
Student Transitions Project. *See* student mobility
study parameters, 7, 166. *See also* audience for book
sub-baccalaureate education, 23, 146, 155, 158–59, 170; period overviews, 20–21, 129–30, 139–43; specific institutions and sectors, 27, 84, 138, 153, 180
system. *See* postsecondary system, definition
systems perspective, 8–12, 17; in postsecondary literature, 12–15

Task Force on the Community College, 77
teaching university, 26, 128, 136, 138, 145, 175. *See also individual teaching universities*
Technical and Vocational Training Assistance Act (1960), 5, 20, 66, 78–79

Technical University of British Columbia, 92, 93, 94, 143–44. *See also* Simon Fraser University
Terrace, vocational school, 79
Thompson Rivers University, 128, 138, 139, 148, 174, 175. *See also* Cariboo College; University College of the Cariboo
Trades Schools Regulation Act (1936), 82
Trades Training Consortium, 190*n*4
Training Access program, 96
Trinity Junior College, 70, 82. *See also* Trinity Western College
Trinity Western College, 70, 97. *See also* Trinity Junior College; Trinity Western University
Trinity Western University, 98, 135, 156, 179, 180; controversy, 92, 97, 189*n*5. *See also* Trinity Western College
Trueman, J., 144
Truman Commission, 38

United Kingdom, 15, 23, 55, 74
United States, 13–14, 67, 163, 184, 190*n*3, 192*n*3; students, 13, 29, 38. *See also* California Master Plan
Universities Council of British Columbia, 98, 111, 112, 119
University Advisory Council, 119
university aspirations, 123, 136; by cities in the Interior, 112–13, 114, 120, 137–38. *See also* Kamloops; Kelowna; Nelson; Prince George; Victoria College
university college, 91, 95, 98, 116, 123, 128; characteristics, 26, 94, 115; transition into universities, 126, 136–38, 145, 150. *See also individual university colleges*
University College of the Cariboo, 94, 128, 137, 138, 150. *See also* Cariboo College; Thompson Rivers University
University College of the Fraser Valley, 94, 150, 175. *See also* Fraser Valley College; University of the Fraser Valley
University of British Columbia, 21, 79, 174, 179, 189*n*6; before 1960, 18, 20, 70, 73(f), 74; Okanagan campus, 128, 137, 148, 169, 174, 191*n*10
University of Northern British Columbia, 93, 111, 115, 169, 174, 189*n*8. *See also* Interior University Society; Prince George
University of the Fraser Valley, 156, 175. *See also* University College of the Fraser Valley
University of Victoria, 102, 111, 174, 188*n*8, 189*n*8; establishment, 5, 26, 76, 88. *See also* David Thompson University Centre; Victoria College
university transfer, 17, 19, 25, 66, 163; number of students and success rates, 10, 11(f), 26, 29

Vancouver City College. *See* Vancouver Community College
Vancouver Community College, 77, 128, 156, 175, 176, 188*n*10
Vancouver Island University, 175, 188*n*10. *See also* Malaspina University College
Vancouver School Board, 20, 78, 156
Vancouver School of Theology, 98, 156, 178

Vancouver Vocational Institute, 20, 67, 78, 89, 176

Vander Zalm, William (Bill), 103, 107, 113, 122

vertical differentiation of institutions, 163, 184

Victoria College, 18, 26, 74, 76, 174. *See also* University of Victoria

vocational education, 67, 68, 89, 100, 155; federal role, 20, 65, 86, 104, 108, 171; and marginalized communities, 12, 87, 105, 129, 170, 183; in other countries, 14–15, 29; school districts, 21, 78. *See also* Canadian Jobs Strategy; career colleges; continuing education; Technical and Vocational Training Assistance Act (1960); vocational schools

vocational schools, 20, 27, 66–67, 77–79, 169; British Columbia Vocational School, 20, 67, 79; Burnaby Vocational School, 78–79; melding with colleges, 65, 165, 176; Pacific Vocational Institute, 78; Vancouver Vocational Institute, 20, 67, 78, 79, 89

Vocational Training Coordination Act (1942), 80

Widening Gap report, 111–12